STUDIES IN POETRY AND PHILOSOPHY.

By the same Author:

CULTURE AND RELIGION,

IN SOME OF THEIR RELATIONS.

NEW EDITION, WITH PREFACE FROM THIRD EDINBURGH EDITION.

In one volume, 16mo, red cloth, gilt top, paper title, $1.25.

THE following are some of the opinions which the Publishers have received from college officers: —

From President MARK HOPKINS, *of Williams College.*

"It is written with true insight, and in a charming spirit. It is just the thing to aid young men in our colleges, who will read it at the point where they need aid at the present time."

From Professor A. P. PEABODY, *of Harvard University.*

"Permit me to thank you warmly for reprinting a work of such surpassing merit, and so perfectly adapted to the actual state of things in our seminaries of learning. Had the lectures been written for our own University they could not have been better suited to the needs of its students I have seldom seen to so great a degree as in the tone of thought and feeling in this volume the union of profound religious faith and the highest intellectual culture mutually interpenetrating, — culture wreathing faith with its beauty; faith crowning culture with its glory."

From Professor G. P. FISHER, *of Yale College.*

"It is one of the best books I have seen for a long while. It is truly a tract for the times, and I wish that all educated and thinking persons could read it."

From President McCOSH, *of Princeton College.*

"The lectures on Culture and Religion are eminently fitted to interest and to profit educated young men. The Culture stands before us as a statue of pure white marble with a beautiful vein of Piety winding through it."

From President HARRIS, *of Bowdoin College.*

"I have read with great interest Shairp's 'Lectures on Culture and Religion.' The views presented are timely and important, and the republication of the lectures in this country meets an existing want. I hope they will be widely read in our colleges and professional schools."

From J. B. ANGELL, *President Elect of the University of Michigan.*

"The volume is a valuable contribution to the discussion of a question which has not yet received from the religious point of view the exhaustive treatment it deserves. The aim and spirit of Mr. Shairp's book are excellent, and his lectures cannot fail to be both interesting and serviceable to young men. I shall take great pleasure in directing the attention of my students to it."

STUDIES IN POETRY AND PHILOSOPHY.

BY

J. C. SHAIRP,

PRINCIPAL OF THE UNITED COLLEGE OF ST. SALVATOR AND ST. LEONARD, ST ANDREWS

AUTHOR OF "CULTURE AND RELIGION."

PII VATES ET PHŒBO DIGNA LOCUTI.

NEW YORK:
PUBLISHED BY HURD AND HOUGHTON.
Cambridge: Riverside Press.
1872.

[*Reprinted from the Second Edinburgh Edition.*]

RIVERSIDE, CAMBRIDGE:
STEREOTYPED AND PRINTED BY
H. O. HOUGHTON AND COMPANY.

TO

THE RIGHT HONORABLE

SIR JOHN TAYLOR COLERIDGE,

THE NEPHEW OF COLERIDGE,

THE FRIEND OF WORDSWORTH,

THE LIFE-LONG FRIEND OF KEBLE,

AND HIS BIOGRAPHER,

IN WHOSE SERENE AGE AND BEAUTIFUL CHARACTER

ANOTHER GENERATION SEES EMBODIED

THE BEST WISDOM OF HIS POET FRIENDS.

PREFACE TO SECOND EDITION.

THE Essays on Wordsworth, Coleridge, and Keble, were, as stated in the former Preface, intended to be in some sort thank-offerings, — single stones contributed to their memorial cairns. Another name I feel should have followed, or rather have preceded these. Of Walter Scott and his poetry, the first poetry I knew, it was my wish to have said something in another essay, and to have added it to this series, or perhaps put it in the first, which would have been its proper place. But before this was done, his Centenary had come, during which so much was spoken, and well spoken, on the subject, that this does not seem the time for saying more. But if, adopting Wordsworth's lines, we say —

> "Blessings be with them — and eternal praise,
> Who gave us nobler loves, and nobler cares —
> The Poets, who on earth have made us heirs
> Of truth and pure delight by heavenly lays!"

to Walter Scott will fall a large share in that benediction.

These Essays are in no sense criticisms of the poets they deal with, at least as that word is generally understood. To take the measure of these great and good men, and assign them, as the phrase goes, their place in literature, I would not try if, I could, and I could not if I would. Such attempts seem to me to be generally more pretentious than solid. Enough will have been done, if, by pointing to some of the sources of delight I found in them, others may be induced to study them and find the same.

A hope was expressed that all the four Essays, distinct though they are in subject, might yet be found pervaded by a unity of thought and purpose. Of the reviewers who have noticed the Essays — and all whom I have read have done so very kindly — some have perceived no such unity, others have not failed to find it. One reviewer has so well described this thread of connection, that I cannot do better than give his words : —

" His subjects — Wordsworth, Coleridge, Keble, and the Moving Force of the Moral Life — are all, and not slightly, connected. All four subjects may be said to be concerned with the relation of the divine life to that of man : Wordsworth as the prophet of Nature, as the poet who interpreted the relations between the elemental powers of creation and the moral life of man ; Coleridge as the thinker, who tried to find, and partially found, a philosophy of the supersensual life ; Keble as the singer, who applied both these great worlds of thought so far as they fitted into the limitations of his own . . . . ecclesiastical system; and, finally, the subject of Mr. Shairp's last essay — the great moving force which helps man to become what he perceives that he ought to be — is one almost inevitably suggested by the lives of the three men who, from their different points of view, had all been chiefly concerned to discover new links between the life above and the life beneath."

The reviewer in the sequel expresses a doubt whether I have enough insisted on "the affinity of Wordsworth's poetry for the great elemental forces both of nature and of humanity" — "the power which the poet displays of giving a strange elemental vastness to the dominant thread of character in either the human or the natural subject on which he happens to be dwelling, so that his poem yields up not a particular man or a particular place, so much as the same element which, while belonging to either, stretches away into the infinite."

Likely enough I have not dwelt on this with sufficient emphasis, though I certainly have always felt it. But where there is so much room for thought, it is not easy in a short essay to bring out every aspect of the truth with the prominence it deserves. I am therefore grateful to the reviewer for supplying in some measure my deficiency.

The same writer then goes on to object to my defense of Wordsworth against being a merely "subjective" poet, as it is called — one who draws no pictures of human character different from his own. Here again, though at the risk of quoting too largely, I must give the reviewer's own words. "If the terrible word 'subjective' means that poetry so described takes no note of external life and nature, it has, of course, no application to Wordsworth. But if it means that the individual imagination of the poet so overbalances the external features of his object that the point of departure seems in the end to have dwindled into insignificance in comparison with the grandeur of the forces which it has called up before him, we should differ with Mr. Shairp. Wordsworth takes a scene or character, and getting it under the magnifying-glass of his meditative genius, he follows out the most striking train of associations it suggests to him, till he describes, *not* his subject, but what his subject might have been, if these special influences had swept through it as pure and unalloyed as they swept over the heart of the poet who muses thereon."

With much in this account of the matter I should not disagree. To one part of it only I demur. However great the flood of meditative light which Wordsworth pours around the object he describes, the object itself and its external features are not lost or obliterated before it. No doubt when he describes a man, he shows us much more in him and his character than the man was aware of in himself. He paints from the side of the soul rather than that of the body, but the meditative associations called up are universal and catholic, not individual or fanciful ones. And however powerful these are, the external features given remain and agree with the meditations that rise out of them. They answer each to the other. A painter could from Wordsworth's description paint the Cumberland Beggar, Michael, Peter Bell, and each would be a clear individual portrait, differing from the others not only in surroundings, but in every feature, and in the whole expression of countenance. The subjectivity, in short, which I denied to Wordsworth's characters, was that which belongs to so many of Byron's — his Giaour, Corsair, Lara, Alp the Renegade, which are each so many pieces of himself, shadows of his own personality, colored by his own peculiar temperament and destiny. Any painter who tried to render these, vary their outward form and drapery as he might, would still paint but one expression — the same misanthropic scowl would sit on every brow. It was the absence of this kind of subjectivity — this projecting of his own mere individuality into his human characters — that I claimed for Wordsworth. Probably enough, this may have been done too unconditionally ; the limits of his power of representation may not have been carefully enough defined. What I meant was, that within certain limits he truly renders other characters than his own; that his meditations about them do not so far hide their distinctive features but that you would know them if you met them on the highway.

Further to enter into these matters, and to define the limits of Wordsworth's power in this direction — for limits very definite it has — would require more than a Preface. His characters are meditative representations, not dramatic exhibitions of men. For these last no poet ever had less gift.

The four Essays have all been carefully revised, and here and there retouched. In re-reading the Essay on Coleridge, I feel that in what I said but scant justice has been done to his poetry. But to reopen this subject would be to rewrite the essay. That I have made too little of his poetry may have arisen from this, that my chief intention at the time I wrote was to bring out the contents and tendency of Coleridge's philosophic speculations.

The Essay on Keble has received larger additions than any of the others. Indeed, it would have been easy to have added much more, for hardly a year passes but brings to light something which gives new meaning to the character of Keble and "The Christian Year." But if much enlarged, what was meant as an essay would have become a book.

St. Andrew's, *December* 7, 1871.

PREFACE TO THE FIRST EDITION.

THE contents of this volume, written during leisure weeks of recent summers, originally appeared in the "North British Review." They were put together not hastily at first, and have since been revised, in some places retrenched, in more enlarged. This is true of all the papers, except the third, which stands now much as it did at first. Though each of the four Essays has a distinct subject of its own, it is hoped that they will be found to have a unity both of thought and purpose. The first three were written from a desire to acknowledge, as far as possible, a debt of gratitude long owed to three eminent teachers of the last age. The only way in which that acknowledgment could now be rendered, was by trying to hand on some knowledge of the men and of the work they did to a few at least of the younger generation. Each of these three papers has been introduced by a short biography, in the hope that the concrete facts might throw light on the abstract thoughts, and add to them a human interest.

The thought of Wordsworth and Coleridge is

of such worth, that too much cannot be done to commend it to those unacquainted with it. They deserve to be known for this, if for nothing else, that they two were the men of most original genius who have been born into England for a century and more. But original genius has sometimes done questionable work, for which perhaps small thanks are due. Theirs, however, was not only original, it was beneficent genius. To a sense-bound age, rejoicing in a mechanical philosophy, they came speaking from the soul to the soul. In time they awakened a response. Younger men, one by one, turned towards them, and found in their teaching that which at once called out and satisfied their aspirations as no other writings of the time did. Whatever is best, deepest, most spiritual in the thinking and feeling of the last thirty years, is either their product or akin to it. But now again the recoil has come, and we are once more in the midst of a way of thinking which excludes the spiritual. As against this compacted system Wordsworth and Coleridge have certainly no complete system, no spiritual theory of life to furnish, but they supply a body of thought which, though unsystematized, is the best counteractive to be found in English literature, till the full spiritual theory gets born.

There is another aspect in which the mental experience of these men is instructive. This is proclaimed on all hands to be an age of disintegration, when all old things must either be reconstructed or disappear. An uneasy, restless searching after something larger and more satisfying, is no doubt visible on the surface both of books and of society. In this mood of men's minds, is there not something to be learnt from the experience of Wordsworth and Coleridge? Here were two men of amplest power, born into an age fuller of anarchic change than our own. They threw themselves fearlessly on their time, broke with old faiths and institutions, in search of truth set their faces to the wilderness, and after sojourning for a season there, came out on the other side, and found peace. They have been branded for this as mere timid reactionaries. But this I believe to be no true account of them. If they returned in some sense to their first faiths, they did so not in blind conservatism, not as grasping at mere tradition in despair of truth, but as having, after long soul-travail, discovered a meaning in old truths they had not divined before. After wandering many ways of thought, and having learnt in their wanderings to know themselves, they came back and found in Christian truth that which alone met their need. They held it no longer by hearsay from without, but learned it anew from within, apprehending it not in oldness of the letter, but in newness of the spirit. The spiritual principles, which as thinkers they held, found their complement in evangelical religion, and gave to this last increased depth and expansion. This experience of theirs has not lost its import for our own day.

Keble, the subject of the third essay, was not in mental endowments at all the equal of Wordsworth and Coleridge. But he had gifts of his own as singular and as interesting as theirs. The devoutness and saintly purity, embalmed in his poetry, are as rare among men as their genius. Then he represents the most winning, to wit, the poetical and devotional, side of that great movement which has in so many ways changed the religious, the ecclesiastical, and the æsthetical aspects of English life. Many, no doubt, will think this small praise to him. But without entering on this subject, which has many sides, every religious heart must acknowledge not only the devout depth but the catholic sentiment of "The Christian Year."

His strain, overheard among louder-voiced poets, is like that of his favorite red-breast among the other song-birds, and has added to English poetry the note in which it was most wanting.

The last essay is different from the other three. It does not centre round one man and his teaching, but deals with an abstract subject. But the thoughts it contains are, I believe, in harmony with the views set forth in the first three essays, — are indeed, as it were, but a prolongation of these views. In this country the ground principles of morality and religion have generally been carefully kept apart. The moralist and the religious teacher have each warned the other off his own ground, and resented any attempt to combine the two departments as an interference. Both have suffered from this unnatural estrangement. This fourth essay is an attempt to find the common ground on which these two subjects meet. It is certain that, when seen in their close and vital bearing on each other, moral thought will give substance and steadfastness to religion, and religion will give to morality a transcendent sanction and spiritual energy.

This volume is published chiefly in the hope that it may reach some of the thoughtful young. Older persons do not much affect books of this kind. It is otherwise with those in whom thought is just awakening. If what I have written should lead any of these to acquaint themselves with the men here described, and to assimilate their thought, they will, I am sure, be the better for it, and the happier.

ST. ANDREW'S, *March*, 1868.

CONTENTS.

WORDSWORTH.

THE deep stirring of men's minds with which the last century closed, and the present century set in, expressed itself in many ways; in no way more conspicuously than in the prodigality of poetic genius which it poured forth. What gave the impulse to the broader, profounder, more living spirit, which then entered into all regions of thought, who shall determine? To recount the literary commonplaces on the subject, to refer that great movement of mind to the French Revolution, or to the causes of that Revolution, is easy; but such vague talk does not really increase our knowledge. Perhaps it may be for the present enough to say, that the portentous political outbreak in France was itself but one manifestation of the new and changed spirit which, throughout Europe, then penetrated every department of human thought and action. Whatever the causes, the fact is plain, that with the opening of this century there was in all civilized lands a turning up of the subsoil of human nature, a laying bare of the intenser seats of action, thought, and emotion, such as the world had seldom, if ever before, known. That time was, what it has been called, "the new birth of imagination."

The new spirit reached all forms of literature, and changed them. In this country it told more immediately on poetry than on any other kind of literature, and recast it into manifold and more original forms. The breadth and volume of that poetic outburst can only be fully estimated by looking back to the narrow and artificial channels in which English poetry had run since the days of Milton. In the hands of Dryden and Pope, that which was a natural, free-wandering river, became a straight-cut, uniform canal. Or, without figure, poetry was withdrawn from country life, made to live exclusively in town, and affect the fashion. Forced to appear in courtly costume, it dealt with the artificial manners and outside aspects of men, and lost sight of the one human heart, which is the proper haunt and main region of song. Of nature it reproduced only so much as may be seen in the dressed walks and gay parterres of a suburban villa on the Thames. As with the subjects, so with the style. Always there was neatness of language, and correctness, according to a conventional standard; often there was terseness, epigrammatic point, polished vigor; but along with these there was monotony, constraint, tameness of melody. Those who followed, — Collins and Gray, Goldsmith and Thomson, — though with reviving naturalness, and more of melody, could not shake themselves wholly free of the tyrant tradition, and throw themselves unreservedly on nature. Burns, if in one sense an anticipation of the nineteenth century poetry, is really, in reference to his contemporaries, to be regarded as an accident: he grew so entirely outside, and independently, of the literary influences of his time. His poetry was a stream flowing apart, unreached by the main current of literature. Yet, though little affected by contemporary poets, he was powerful with those who came after him. Wordsworth owns that it was from Burns he learnt the power of song founded on humble truth. It was Cowper, however, who first of English poets brought poetry back from the town to the country. His landscape, no doubt, was the tame one of the eastern counties, the fens of England; there was in it nothing of the stern wild joy of the mountains. His sentiment moved among the household sympathies, not the stormy passions. But in Cowper's power of simple narrative and truthful description, in his natural pathos and religious feeling, more truly than elsewhere, may be discerned the dawn of that new poetic era with which this century began.

When we remember that during its first thirty years appeared all the great works of Wordsworth, Scott, Byron, Southey, Coleridge, Shelley, Keats, not to mention many a lesser name, we may be quite sure that posterity will look back to it as one of the most wonderful eras in English literature. What other age in this, I had almost said in any country has been, within the same space of time, so lavish of great poets? In England, at any rate, if the Elizabethan and the succeeding age had each one greater poetic name, no age can show so goodly a poetic company. They who began life while many of those poets were still alive, and who can perhaps recall the looks of some of them, as they still sojourned with us, may not perhaps value to the full the boon which was bestowed on the generation just gone. Only as age after age passes, and calls up no such second company, will men learn to look back to that poetic era with the admiration that is due. To sum up in one sentence the manifold import of all that those poets achieved, I cannot perhaps do better than borrow the discriminative words of Mr. Palgrave in his "Golden Treasury." They "carried to further perfection the later tendencies of the century preceding, in simplicity of narrative, reverence for human passion and character in every sphere, and impassioned love of nature: whilst maintaining on the whole the advances in art made since the Restoration, they renewed the half-forgotten melody and depth of tone which marked the best Elizabethan writers; lastly, to what was thus inherited they added a richness in language and a variety in metre, a force and fire in narrative, a tenderness and bloom in feeling, an insight into the finer passages of the soul, and the inner meanings of the landscape, a larger and a wiser humanity, hitherto hardly attained and perhaps unattainable even by predecessors of not inferior individual genius."

It is worth while to look somewhat more closely at the one of that poetic brotherhood who was the eldest born, the hardiest, the most original innovator of them all. For a survey of Wordsworth and his poetry there would seem to be now the more room, because his popularity, which during his lifetime underwent so remarkable vicissitudes, has, during the interval since his death, receded, and seems now to be at the ebb, with all save the few of genuine poetic instinct.

It would form a strange chapter in literary history to trace the alternate rise and fall in poetic reputations. To go no further back than the contemporaries of Wordsworth, how various have been their fortunes! Some, as Byron, were received, almost on their first appearance, with a burst of applause which posterity is not likely fully to reverberate. Some, as Scott — I speak only of his poetry, — were at first welcomed with nearly equal favor, afterwards for a time retired before a temporary caprice of public taste, but have since resumed what was their earliest, and is likely to be their permanent place. Others, as Campbell, had at once the poetic niche assigned them, which they are likely hereafter to fill; while others, as Shelley and Keats, received little praise of men, till they themselves were beyond reach of it. Wordsworth had a different fortune from any of these. For more than twenty years after his earlier poems appeared, he experienced not simply neglect, but an amount of obloquy such as few poets have ever had to encounter. But sustained by his own profound conviction that his work was true and destined to endure, and by the sympathy of a very few discerning men, he calmly and cheerfully bode his hour. In time the clamor against him spent itself, the reaction set in between the years 1820 and 1830, reached its culmination about the time of his Oxford welcome in 1839, and may be said to have lasted till his death in 1850. Since then, in obedience to that law which gives living poets a stronger hold on the minds of their own generation than any poet, even the greatest, of a past age, Wordsworth may seem to have receded somewhat in the world's estimate. But his influence is, in its nature, too durable to be really affected by these fashions of the hour. It is raised high above the shifting damps and fogs of this lower atmosphere, and shines from the poetic heaven with a benign and undying light. The younger part of the present generation, attracted by newer, but certainly not greater luminaries, may not yet have learned fully to recognize him. But there are many now in middle life, who look back to the time of their boyhood or early youth, when Wordsworth first found them, as a marked era in their existence. They can recall, it may be, the very place and the hour when, as they read this or that poem of his, a new light, as from heaven, dawned suddenly within them. The scales of custom dropped from their eyes, and they beheld all nature with a splendor upon it, as of the world's first morning. The common sights and sounds of earth became other than they were. The heart leapt up to the white streaks of cloud, and looked on the early stars of evening with a young wonder, never felt till then. Man too, and human life, cleared of the highway dust, came home to them more intimately, more engagingly, more solemnly, than before. For their hearts were touched by the poet's creative finger, and new springs of thought, tenderer wells of feeling, broke from beneath the surface. And though time and custom may have done much to dim the eye, and choke the feelings which Wordsworth once unsealed, no time can ever efface the remembrance of that first unvailing, nor destroy the grateful conviction that to him they owe a delicate and inward service, such as no other poet has equally rendered.

Something of this service Wordsworth, I believe, is fitted to render to all men with moderately sensitive hearts, if they would but read attentively a few of his best poems. But to receive the full benefit, to draw out, not random impressions, but the stored wisdom of his capacious and meditative soul, he, above all modern poets, requires no cursory perusal, but a close and consecutive study. It was once common to call him mystical and unintelligible. That language is seldom heard now. But many, especially young persons, or those trained in other schools of thought, or in no school at all, will still feel the need of a guide in the study of his poetry. For what is best in him lies not on the surface, but in the depth. It is so far hidden that it must needs be sought for. Not that his language is obscure: what he has to say is expressed for the most part in words as well ordered, as luminous, as adequate as any words in which thought so subtle and so deep has ever clothed itself. But many of his thoughts are of such a nature, so near, yet so hidden from men's ordinary ways of thinking, that the reader, ere he apprehend them, must needs himself go through somewhat of the same processes of feeling and reflection as the poet himself passed through in creating them. The need of this reflective effort on the part of the reader is inherent in the nature of many of Wordsworth's subjects, and cannot be dispensed with. No doubt the effort is rendered much lighter to us than it was when his poems first appeared; so much of what was then new in Wordsworth has since passed into the atmosphere of literature, and found its way to most educated minds. Still, with all this, there remains a large — perhaps the largest — portion of Wordsworth's peculiar wisdom unabsorbed, nor likely to be soon absorbed, by this excitement-craving, unmeditative age. A thorough and appreciative commentary, which should open avenues to the study of Wordsworth, and render accessible his imaginative heights and his meditative depths, would be a boon to the younger part of this generation. The opening chapter of such a commentary would first set forth the facts and circumstances of the poet's life, would show what manner of man he was, how and by what influences his mind was matured, from what points of view he was led to approach nature and human life, and to undertake the poetic treatment of these. A portion of such a chapter I propose to place now before my readers, — at least so far as to describe the facts of Wordsworth's early life, and the influences among which he lived, up to the time when he settled at Grasmere, and addressed himself to poetry as the serious business of his life.

Wordsworth was sprung from an old North-Humbrian stock, as contrasted with the South-Humbrian race, a circumstance which has stamped itself visibly on his genius. The name of Wordsworth had been long known in the West Riding of Yorkshire, about the course of the Dove and the Don. Of old they had been yeoman, or landed gentry, for both of these they call themselves in old charters, at Penistone, near Doncaster. In this neighborhood they can be traced back as far as the reign of Edward III. From Yorkshire the poet's grandfather is said to have migrated westward, and to have bought the small estate of Sockbridge, near Penrith. His father, John Wordsworth, was an attorney, and having been appointed law-agent to the then Earl of Lonsdale, was set over the western portion of the wide domain of Lowther, and lived in Cockermouth, in a manor-house belonging to that noble family. John Wordsworth married Anne Cookson, daughter of a mercer in Penrith, whose mother, Dorothy, was one of the ancient northern family of Crackenthorpe, a name of note, both in logical and theological lore. These facts may be of little moment in themselves; but they serve to show that in the wisdom of Wordsworth, as in so many another poet, the virtues of an ancient and worthy race were condensed, and bloomed forth into genius. In that old mansion-house at Cockermouth, William was born on the 7th of April, 1770, the second of four sons. There was only one daughter in the family, Dorothy, who came next after the poet. Cockermouth, their birthplace, though beyond the hill country, stands on the Derwent, called by the poet, "fairest of all rivers," and looks back to the Borrowdale mountains, among which that river is born. The voice of that stream, he tells us, flowed along his dreams while he was a child. When five years old, he used to spend the whole summer-day in bathing in a mill-race let off the river, now in the water, now out of it, now scouring the sandy fields, naked as a savage, while the hot, thundery noon was bronzing distant Skiddaw; and then plunging in once more.

His mother, a wise and pious woman, told a friend

that William was the only one of her children about whom she felt anxious, and that he would be "remarkable either for good or evil." According to the Scottish proverb, he would either "mak a spoon or spoil a horn." This was probably from what he himself calls his "stiff, moody, and violent temper." Of this, which made him a wayward and headstrong boy, all that he seems afterwards to have retained was that resoluteness of character which stood him in good stead when he became a man.

Of his mother, who died when he was eight years old, the poet retained a faint but tender recollection. At the age of nine, William, along with his elder brother Richard, left home for school. It would be hard to conceive a school-life more fitted for a future poet than that in which Wordsworth was reared at Hawkshead. This village lies in the vale, and not far from the lake, of Esthwaite, a district of gentler hill-beauty, but in full view, westward and northward, of Kirkstone Pass, Fairfield, and Helvellyn. Hawkshead school, as described in "The Prelude," must have been a strange contrast to the highly-elaborated school-systems of our own day. High pressure was then unknown; nature and freedom had full swing. Bounds and locking-up hours they had none. The boys lived in the cottages of the village dames, in a natural, friendly way, like their own children. Their playgrounds were the fields, the lake, the woods, and the hill-sides, far as their feet could carry them. Their games were crag-climbing for ravens' nests, skating on Esthwaite Lake, setting springes for woodcocks. For this latter purpose they would range the woods late on winter nights, unchallenged. Early on summer mornings, before a chimney was smoking, Wordsworth would make the circuit of the lake. There were boatings on more distant Windermere, and, when their scanty pocket-money allowed, long rides to Furness Abbey and Morecambe Sands.

In Wordsworth's fourteenth year, when he and his brother were at home for the Christmas holidays, their father, who had never recovered heart after the death of his wife, followed her to the grave. The old home at Cockermouth was broken up, and the orphans were but poorly provided for. Their father had but little to leave his children. For large arrears were due to him by the strange, self-willed Earl of Lonsdale, whom De Quincey describes, and these his lordship never chose to make good. But the boys, not the less, returned to school, and William remained there till his eighteenth year, when he left for Cambridge.

From Hawkshead, Wordsworth took several good things with him. In book-learning, there was Latin enough to enable him to read the Roman poets with pleasure in after years; of mathematics, more than enough to start him on equality with the average of Cambridge freshmen; of Greek, I should suppose not much — at least we never hear of it afterwards. It was here that he began that intimacy with the English poets which he afterwards perfected; while for amusement he read the fictions of Fielding and Swift, of Cervantes and Le Sage. But neither at school nor in after life was he a devourer of books.

Of actual verse-making, his earliest attempts date from Hawkshead. A long copy of verses, written on the second centenary of the foundation of the school, was much admired, but he himself afterwards pronounced them but a "tame imitation of Pope." Some lines composed on his leaving school, with a few of which the edition of his works of 1857 opens, are more noticeable, as they, if not afterwards changed, contain a hint of his maturer self. But more important than any juvenile poems, or any skill of verse-making acquired at Hawkshead, were the materials for after thought there laid up, the colors laid deep into the groundwork of his being. In the "Evening Walk," composed partly at school, partly in college vacations, he notices how the boughs and leaves of the oak darken and come out when seen against the sunset. "I recollect distinctly," he says nearly fifty years afterwards, "the very spot where this first struck me. It was on the way between Hawkshead and Ambleside, and gave me extreme pleasure. The moment was important in my poetical history; for I date from it my consciousness of the infinite variety of natural appearances, which had been unnoticed by the poets of any age or country, so far as I was acquainted with them; and I made a resolution to supply in some degree the deficiency. I could not have been at that time above fourteen years of age." Not a bad resolution for fourteen! And he kept it. It would be hardly too much to say that there is not a single image in his whole works which he had not observed with his own eyes. And perhaps no poet since Homer has introduced into poetry, directly from nature, more facts and images which had not before been noted in books.

But more than any book-lore, more than any skill in verse-making, or definite thoughts about poetry, was the free, natural life he led at Hawkshead. It was there that he was smitten to the core with that love of nature which became the prime necessity of his being; not that he was a moody or peculiar boy, nursing his own fancies apart from his companions. So far from that, he was foremost in all schoolboy adventures, — the sturdiest oar, the hardiest cragsman at the harrying of ravens' nests. Weeks and months, he tells us, passed in a round of school tumult. No life could have been every way more unconstrained and natural. But school tumult though there was, it was not in a made playground at cricket or rackets, but in haunts more fitted to form a poet — on the lakes and the hill-sides. Would that some poets, who have since been born, had had such a boyhood, had walked, like Wordsworth, unmolested in the cool fields, not been stimulated at school by the fever of emulation and too early intellectuality, and then hurled prematurely against the life-wrecking problems of existence! Whatever stimulants Wordsworth had came from within, awakened only by the common sights and sounds of nature. All through his school-time, he says that in pauses of the "giddy bliss" he felt —

> "Gleams like the flashing of a shield, the earth
> And common face of nature spake to him
> Rememberable things."

And as time went on, and common school pursuits lost their novelty, these visitations grew deeper and more frequent. At nightfall, when a storm was coming on, he would stand in shelter of a rock, and hear —

> "Notes that are
> The ghostly language of the ancient earth,
> Or make their dim abode in distant winds."

At such times he was aware of a coming down upon him of the "visionary power." On summer mornings he would rise, before another human being was astir, and alone, from some jutting knoll, watch the first gleam of dawn kindle on the lake: —

> "Oft in these moments such a holy calm
> Would overspread my soul, that bodily eyes
> Were utterly forgotten, and what I saw
> Appeared *like something in myself*, a dream,
> A prospect of the mind."

Is not this the germ of what afterwards became the

"Ode on Intimations of Immortality?" or rather, it is of hours like these that that Ode is the glorified remembrance.

In October, 1787, at the age of eighteen, Wordsworth passed from Hawkshead School to St. John's College, Cambridge. College life, so important to those whose minds are mainly shaped by books and academic influences, produced on him but little impression. On men of strong inward bias the University often acts with a repulsive rather than a propelling force. Recoiling from the prescribed drill, they fall back all the more entirely on their native instincts. The stripling of the hills had not been trained for college competitions; he felt that he was not "for that hour, and for that place." The range of scholastic studies seemed to him narrow and timid. The college dons inspired him with no reverence, their inner heart seemed trivial; they were poor representatives of the Bacons, Barrows, Newtons of the old time. As for college honors, he thought them dearly purchased at the price of the evil rivalries and narrow standard of excellence, which they fostered in the eager few who entered the lists. Altogether, he had led too free and independent a life to put on the fetters which college contests and academic etiquette exacted. No doubt he was a self-sufficient, presumptuous youth, so to judge of men and things in so famous a University. Such at least he must have appeared to college authorities; very disappointing too he must have been to friends at home. They had sent him thither, with no little trouble, not to set himself up in opposition to authority, but to work hard, and by working to make his livelihood. And perhaps home friends and college tutors were not altogether wrong in their opinion of him, if we are to judge of men not wholly by after results.

Wordsworth at this time may probably enough have been a headstrong, disagreeably independent lad. Only there were latent in him other qualities of a rarer kind, which in time justified him in taking his own line.

When he arrived in Cambridge, a northern villager, he tells us that there were other poor, simple school-boys from the north, now Cambridge men, ready to welcome him, and introduce him to the ways of the place. So, leaving to others the competitive race, he let himself, in the company of these, drop quietly down the stream of the usual undergraduate jollities: —

> "If a throng were near,
> That way I leaned by nature; for my heart
> Was social, and loved idleness and joy."

It sounds strange to read in the pompous blank verse of "The Prelude," how, while still a freshman, he turned dandy, wore hose of silk, and powdered hair. And again, how in a friend's room in Christ College, once occupied by Milton, he toasted the memory of the abstemious Puritan till the fumes of wine took his brain — the first and last time that the future water-drinker experienced that sensation. During the earlier part of his college course he did just as others did, lounged and sauntered, boated and rode, enjoyed wines and supper-parties, "days of mirth and nights of revelry;" yet kept clear of vicious excess.

When the first novelty of college life was over, he grew dissatisfied with idleness. Sometimes, too, he was haunted by prudent fears about his future maintenance. He withdrew somewhat from promiscuous society, and kept more by himself. Living in quiet, the less he felt of reverence for those elders whom he saw, the more his heart was stirred with high thoughts of those whom he could not see. As he lay in his bedroom in St.

John's, he could look into the ante-chapel of Trinity, and watch the moonlight moving over the countenance of the great statue there —

> "Of Newton, with his prism and silent face,
> The marble index of a mind forever
> Voyaging through strange seas of thought, alone."

He read Chaucer under the hawthorn by Trompington Mill, and made intimate acquaintance with Spenser. Milton he seemed to himself almost to see moving before him, as, clad in scholar's gown, that young poet had once walked those same cloisters in the angelic beauty of his youth.

So his time at Cambridge was not wholly lost. Two advantages at least he gained, noble thoughts about the great men who of old had tenanted that "garden of high intellects," and free intercourse with his fellow-men of the same age and of varied character — a special gain to one whose life, both before and afterwards, was passed so much in retirement.

During the summer vacations he and his sister Dorothy, who had been much separated since childhood, met once more under the roof of their mother's kindred in Penrith. With her he then had the first of those rambles — by the streams of Lowther and Emont — which were afterwards renewed with so happy results. Then, too, he first met Mary Hutchinson, his cousin, and his wife to be: —

> "By her exulting outside look of youth
> And placid tender countenance, first endeared."

It was during his second or third year at Cambridge, when he had somewhat withdrawn from society, and lived more by himself, that he first seriously formed the purpose of being a poet, and dared to hope that he might leave behind him something that would live.

His last long vacation, to reading men often the severest labor of their lives, was devoted to a walking tour on the Continent along with a college friend from Wales. For himself he had long cast college studies and their rewards behind him, but friends at home, it may readily be imagined, could not see such foolhardiness without uneasy forebodings. What was to become of a penniless lad who thus played ducks and drakes with youth's golden opportunities? But he had as yet no misgivings, he was athirst only for nature and freedom. So with his friend Jones, staff in hand, he walked for fourteen weeks through France, Switzerland, and the north of Italy. With four shillings each daily, they paid their way. They landed at Calais, on the eve of the day when the king was to swear to the new constitution. All through France, as they trudged along, they saw a people rising with jubilee to welcome in the dawn of, as they believed, a new era for mankind. Nor were they onlookers only, but sympathizers in the intoxication of the time, joining in village revels and dances with the frantic multitude. But these sights did not detain them, for they were bent rather on seeing nature than man. Over the Alps, along the Italian lakes, they passed with a kind of awful joy. As they hurried down the southern slope of the Alps, Wordsworth tells us that the woods "decaying, never to be decayed," the drizzling crags, the cataracts, and the clouds, appeared to him no longer material things, but spiritual entities, "characters in a dread Apocalypse."

In January, 1789, Wordsworth took a common degree and quitted Cambridge. The crisis of his life lay between this time and his settling down at Grasmere. He had resolved to be a poet, but even poets must be housed, clothed, and fed; and poetry has seldom done this for any of its devotees, least of all such poetry as Wordsworth was minded to write. But it was not the question of bread alone, but a much wider, more complex one, which now pressed on him, — the same which so many a thoughtful youth, on leaving the University, with awakened powers, but no special turn for any of the professions, has had to face, — the question, What next? In such cases the more gifted the querist, the harder becomes the problem.

This mental trial, incident at all times to early manhood, how must it have been aggravated to a youth such as Wordsworth, turned loose on a world just heaving with the first throes of the French Revolution! He had seen it while it still wore its earliest auroral hues, when the people were mad with joy, as at the dawn of a regenerated earth. That he should have staked his whole hope on it, looked for all good things from it, who shall wonder? Coleridge, Southey, almost every high-minded young man of that time, hailed it with fervor. Wordsworth would not have been the man he was, if he could have stood proof against the contagion. On leaving Cambridge he had gone to London. The spring and early summer months he spent there, not mingling in society, for probably he had few acquaintances, but wandering about the streets, noting all sights, observant of men's faces and ways, haunting the open book-stalls. During these months he tells us that he was preserved from the cynicism and contempt for human nature which the deformities of crowded life often breed, by the remembrance of the kind of men he had first lived amongst, in themselves a manly, simple, uncontaminated race, and invested with added interest and dignity by living in the same hereditary fields in which their forefathers had lived time out of mind, and by moving about among the grand accompaniments of mountain storms and sunshine. The good had come first, and the evil, when it did come, did not stamp itself into the groundwork of his imagination. The following summer he visited his travelling companion Jones in Wales, made a walking tour through that country, and beheld at midnight, on Snowdon, that marvelous moonlight vision, which toward the end of "The Prelude" he employs as an emblem of the transmuting power which resides in a high imagination, and which it exerts on the visible universe.

When in London, he had heard Burke speaking from his place in the House of Commons on the great debates called forth by the Revolution, then in full swing: but he had listened unconvinced. In November, 1791, he passed to Paris, and heard there the speeches that were made in the Hall of the National Assembly, while Madame Roland and the Brissotins were in the ascendent. A few days he wandered about Paris, surveyed the scenes rendered famous by recent events, and even picked up a stone as a relic from the site of the demolished Bastile. This rage for historic scenes he however confesses to have been in him more affected than genuine. From Paris he went to Orleans, and sojourned there for some time to learn the language. His chief acquaintance there was Beaupois, according to Wordsworth's description, a rarely gifted soul, pure and elevated in his aims. In youth he had been devoted to the service of ladies, with whom beauty of countenance, grace of figure, and refined bearing made him a great favorite. But now, though by birth one of the old French noblesse, he had severed himself from his order, and given himself with chivalrous devotion to the cause of the poor. One day, as Wordsworth and he were walking near Orleans, they passed a hungry-looking girl leading a half-starved heifer by a cord tied to its horn. The beast was picking a scanty meal from the lane, while the girl, with pallid hands and heartless look, was knitting for her bread. Pointing to her, Beaupois said with vehemence, "It is against that we are fighting." As they two wandered about the old forests around the city, they eagerly discussed, both the great events that were crowding on each other, and also those abstract questions about civil government, and man's natural rights, which the times naturally suggested. Wordsworth owns that he threw himself headlong into those questions without the needful preparation, knowing little of the past history of France and of her institutions, and wholly unversed in political philosophy. He only saw that the best ought to rule, and that they don't. In his boyhood, he says, he had lived among plain people, had never seen the face of a titled man, had therefore no respect for nor belief in such. He therefore now became a patriot and republican, determined that kings and aristocracies should cease, and longed for a government of equal rights and individual worth, whatever that may mean. In the days that were coming, abject poverty was to disappear, equality was to bring in a golden time of happiness and virtue. After some months, spent together in sharing dreams like these, they parted, Wordsworth for Blois, and then for the fierce metropolis; Beaupois to perish ere long —

> "Fighting in supreme command
> Upon the borders of the unhappy Loire."

When, in the autumn of 1792, Wordsworth came from Blois to Paris, the September massacre had taken place but a month before; the king and his family were in prison; the Republic was proclaimed, and Robespierre in power. The young Englishman ranged through the city, passed by the prison where the king lay, visited the Tuileries, lately stormed, and the Place de Carrousel, a month since heaped with dead. As he lay in the garret of a hotel hard by, sleepless, and filled with thoughts of what had just taken place, he seemed to hear a voice that cried aloud to the whole city, "Sleep no more." Years after, those scenes still troubled him in dreams. He had ghastly visions of scaffolds hung with innocent victims, or of crowds ready for butchery, and mad with the levity of despair. In his sleep he seemed to be pleading in vain for the life of friends, or for his own, before a savage tribunal. A page of "The Prelude" is filled with the somewhat vague reflections that came to him as he lay sleepless in his garret. The most definite of these is, that a nation's destiny often hangs on the action of single persons, and that the bonds of one common humanity transcend those of country and race. These vague truisms Lockhart, glad no doubt to make the young republican poet look ridiculous, condenses into this: "He revolved in his mind how the crisis might be averted, and, taking the measure of himself and of the various factions, he came to the conclusion that he, William Wordsworth, was the proper person to rally the nation and conduct the revolution to a happy issue." What authority for this interpretation Lockhart had, except his wish to ridicule Wordsworth, it is not easy to guess. But just at this crisis, when the young poet, whatever line he had taken, was in imminent danger of falling along with his friends, the Brissotins, in the then impending massacres of May, he was forced — by what he then thought a harsh necessity, but afterwards owned to be a gracious providence — to return to England. Lockhart suggests that his friends at home, becoming aware of the peril he was in, prudently recalled him by stopping the supplies.

Returning to England at the close of 1792, he spent some time in London in great unsettlement and mental perplexity. He was horrified with the excesses in which the Revolution had landed, yet not the less he clung to his republican faith, and his hope of the revolutionary cause. When at length Britain interposed, his indignation knew no bounds; this step, he said, was the first great shock his moral nature received. With an evil eye, he watched, off the Isle of Wight, the fleet that was to transport our armies to the Continent, — heard of the disasters of our arms with joy, and of our success with bitterness. When every month brought tidings of fresh enormities in France, and opponents taunted him with these results of equality and popular government, he retorted that these were but the overflow of a reservoir of guilt, which had had been filling up for centuries by the wrong doings of kings and nobles. Soon France entered on a war of conquest, and he was doomed to see his last hopes of liberty betrayed. Still striving to hide the wounds of mortified presumption, he clung, as he tells us, more firmly than ever to his old tenets, while the friends of old institutions goaded him still further by their triumphant scorn. Overwhelmed with shame and despondency at the shipwreck of his golden dreams, he turned to probe the foundations on which all society rests. Not only institutions, customs, law, but even the grounds of moral obligation and distinctions of right and wrong, disappeared. Demanding formal proof, and finding none, he abandoned moral questions in despair. This was the crisis of his malady.

The nether gloom into which he was plunged, and

the steps by which he won his way back to upper air, are set forth in the concluding Books of "The Prelude," and are partly described in the character of the Solitary in "The Excursion." These self-descriptions, though somewhat vague, are yet well worth attention, for the light they throw on Wordsworth's own mental history, and as illustrating by what exceptional methods one of the greatest minds of that time was floated clear of the common wreck in which so many were entangled. His moral being had received such a shock that, both as regards man and nature, he tried to close his heart against the sources of his former strength. The whole past of history, he believed, was one great mistake, and the best hope for the human race was to cut itself off forever from all sympathy with it. Even the highest creations of the old poets lost their charm for him. They seemed to him mere products of passion and prejudice, wanting altogether in the nobility of reason. He tried by narrow syllogisms, he tells us, to unsoul those mysteries of being which have been through all ages the bonds of man's brotherhood. This is rather vague; but perhaps we are not wrong in supposing it to mean that he grew skeptical of those higher faiths which cannot be demonstrably proved. This moral state reacted on his feelings about the visible universe. It became to him less spiritual than it used to be. Turning on it the same microscopic, unimaginative eye which he had turned on the moral world, he learnt, by an evil infection of the time, alien to his own nature, to compare scene with scene, to search for mere novelties of form and color, dead to the moral power and the sentiment that resides in each individual place. He fell for a time under a painful tyranny of the eye, that craves ever new combinations of form, uncounteracted by the reports of the other senses, uninformed by that finer influence that streams from the soul into the eye.

In this sickness of the soul, this "obscuration of the master vision," his sole sister Dorothy came, like his better angel, to his side. Convinced that his office on earth was to be a poet, not to break his heart against the hard problems of politics and philosophy, she led him away from perplexing theories and crowded cities into the open air of heaven. Together they visited, travelling on foot, many of the most interesting districts of their native England, and mingled freely with the country people and the poor. There, amid the freshness of nature, his fevered spirit was cooled down, earth's "first diviner influence" returned, he saw already things again as he had seen them in boyhood. It was not merely that nature acted on his senses and so restored his mind's health. His understanding saw in the processes of earth and sky, going on by steadfast laws, a visible image of right reason. His overwrought feelings were cooled and soothed by the contemplation of objects in which there is no fever of passion, no impatience, no restless vanity. His imagination, dazzled erewhile with the whirl of wild and transitory projects, found here something to rest on that was enduring. This free intercourse with nature in time brought him back to his true self, so that he began to look on life and the frame-work of society with other eyes, and to seek there too for that which is permanent and intrinsically good. At this time, as he and his sister wandered about various out-of-the-way parts of England where they were strangers, he found not delight only, but instruction, in conversing with all whom he met. The lonely roads were open schools to him. There, as he entered into conversation with the poorest, often with the outcast and the forlorn, and heard from them their own histories, he got a new insight into human souls, discerned in them a depth and a worth where none appear to careless eyes. The perception of these things made him loathe the thought of those ambitious projects which had lately deceived him. He ceased to admire strength detached from moral purpose, and learned to prize unnoticed worth, the meek virtues, and lowly charities. Settled judgments of right and wrong returned, but they were essential, not conventional judgments. In his estimate of men he set no store by rank or station, little by those "formalities" which have been misnamed education. For he seemed to himself to see utter hollowness in the talking, so-called intellectual world, and little good got by those who had held most intercourse with it. He now set himself to see whether a life of toil was necessarily one of ignorance; whether goodness was a delicate plant requiring garden culture, and intellectual power a thing confined to those who call themselves educated men. And as he mingled freely with all kinds of people, he found a pith of sense and a solidity of judgment here and there among the unlearned which he had failed to find in the most lettered; from obscure men he heard high truths, words that struck in with his own best thoughts of what was fair and good. And love, true love and pure, he found was no flower reared only in what is called refined society, and requiring leisure and polished manners for its growth. Excessive labor and grinding poverty, he grants, by preoccupying the mind with sensual wants, often crush the finer affections. And it is difficult for these to thrive in the overcrowded alleys of cities, where the human heart is sick, and the eye looks only on deformity. But in all circumstances, save the most abject, sometimes even in these, he had seen the soul triumphing over sense, the heart beating all the truer from living in contact with natural wants, and with the reality of things. In our talk of these matters we mislead each other, and books mislead us still more, — books, which in that day more than now, being written mostly for the wealthy, put things in artificial light; lower the many for the pleasure of the few, magnify external differences and artificial barriers that separate man from man, and neglect the one human heart. In opposition to all this, he himself had found "love in huts where poor men lie," the finest bloom of the affections where the outward man was rude to look upon; under the humblest guise had seen souls that were sanctified by duty, patience, and sorrow: —

> "Of these, said I, shall be my song; of these,
> If future years mature me for the task,
> Will I record the praises, making verse
> Deal boldly with substantial things. My theme
> No other than the very heart of man,
> As found among the best of those who live —
> Not unexalted by religious faith,
> Not uninformed by books, good books, though few —
> In nature's presence: thence may I select
> Sorrow, that is not sorrow, but delight;
> And miserable love, that is not pain
> To think of, for the glory that redounds
> Therefrom to human-kind, and what we are."

Then follows a passage, perhaps the most finely thought, most perfectly expressed, in the whole "Prelude," in which he describes the different kinds of power, the different grades of nobleness, which he had found among the poor. It is too long to quote here, but those who care for these things will find it worth turning to.

His mind being thus restored to tone, and able to look once more on common life with love and imaginative delight, the visible world reassumed the splendor which it had worn for him in childhood, combined with that which only thought could add — a fuller consciousness of the sources whence this beauty comes. His eye now looked on nature with the wonder of the world's childhood, mellowed with the reflectiveness of its mature age.

Such is the pathway by which Wordsworth describes himself as having travelled from darkness up to light, from distrust of all truth and despair, back to clear convictions, and peace and hope. In reading it as set forth in "The Prelude" and "The Excursion," many have complained that his experience was an exceptional one, and contains no help for others. If so, small blame to him. Processes of this kind cannot be transferred bodily from one mind to another, like historical facts or mathematical proofs. It is not possible for minds of the order of Wordsworth's, which live by intuitions, rather than by chains of reasoning, to impart to others, or indeed to do more than hint at those intuitions, which, though the light of all their seeing, are born within them, they know not how. Even those who deal more with processes of reasoning, and who can trace exactly the lines of thought by which they seem to themselves to have been led upward, as Coleridge has in some measure done, although they may communicate to others the intellectual shape which their own spiritual apprehensions have taken, cannot at the same time give that which is the life of these apprehensions. Those who read their arguments may, no doubt, grasp them and find help in them, in so far as their intellectual difficulties are the same as those of the writer. But will this enable them to envisage and make their own the primal truths on which the reasonings repose, and from which alone they draw their power? Is it not of the nature of moral and spiritual truths, that if they once reach a man, they are their own sufficient evidence? Once to feel them is to know them to be true, with a conviction such as no arguments can produce. But who shall enable another thus to feel truths which may be to himself the life of life? Not the reasoner. He at best but convinces the understanding, does not satisfy the spirit. The inspired thinker, poet or other, can do more. He can touch others who are lower sunk than himself, by a kind of spiritual contagion. But even he cannot reach to the bottom, and minister healing to the mind diseased. In the last resort it will not be from the intellects and teachings of others that light will come. That, if it come at all, will come from a region beyond a man's consciousness, and by a process that he cannot analyze. In these deepest, most secret workings of the soul, no one man's experience will exactly fit in with that of any other man.

But here I must pause. For in this account of Wordsworth's hour of darkness and restoration to light, given almost in his own words, I have somewhat outrun the order of dates and places. This restoration, though summed up in the concluding books of "The Prelude," could not have taken place in a few months, but must have been the work of at least several years. Though this inward fermentation working itself to clearness was the most important, the bread-question must, at the same time, have been tolerably urgent. To meet this, he had, as far as appears, simply nothing, except what was allowed him by his friends. Of course neither they nor he could long tolerate such a state of dependence. What, then, was to be done? Three or four courses were open to him — the bar, taking orders, teaching private pupils, and writing for a London newspaper. All passed under his review, but to each and all he was nearly equally averse. It must have been at this time that he felt so keenly those forebodings, afterwards beautifully described in his poem of "Resolution and Independence," when the fate of Chatterton and Burns rose mournfully before him, and he asked himself —

> "How can he expect that others should
> Build for him, sow for him, and at his call
> Love him, who for himself will take no heed at all?"

In this juncture, the newspaper press, an effectual extinguisher to a possible poet, was ready to have absorbed him. He had actually written to a friend in London, who was supporting himself in this way, to find him like employment, when he was delivered from these importunities by a happy occurrence. In the close of the year 1794 and the beginning of 1795, he was engaged in attending at Penrith a friend, Raisley Calvert, who had fallen into a deep consumption. Calvert died early in 1795, and bequeathed to Wordsworth a legacy of £900. He had divined Wordsworth's genius, and believed that he would yet do great things. Seldom in deed has so small a sum produced larger results. It removed at once Wordsworth's anxiety about a profession, rescued him from the newspaper press, set him free to follow his true bent, and give free rein to the poetic power he felt working within him.

One of the first results of the legacy was to restore Wordsworth permanently to the society of his sister. Hitherto, though they met whenever occasion offered, they had not been able to set up house together; but now this was no longer impossible. And surely never sister performed a more delicate service for brother than Dorothy Wordsworth did for the poet. De Quincey has given a full and engaging portrait of that lady, as she appeared some years later than this, but still in her fervid prime, when he first made acquaintance with her brother's family at Grasmere. He describes her as of "warm, even ardent manner," now bursting into strong expression, now checked by decorous self-restraint, of profound sensibility to all things beautiful, with quick sympathy and deep impressibility for all he said or quoted, seemingly inwardly consumed by "a subtle fire of impassioned intellect." And yet withal, so little of a literary lady, so entirely removed from being a blue-stocking, that she was ignorant of many books and subjects which, to most educated persons, were quite commonplace. Such she was when De Quincey first saw her more than ten years after the brother and sister began to live together. We have seen how, when Wordsworth returned from France, depressed with shame, and despondency for his shipwrecked hopes, she turned him from dark and harassing thoughts, and brought him into contact with the healing powers of nature. In many places of his works the poet has borne grateful testimony to all she did for him. At this time, he tells us, it was she who maintained for him a saving intercourse with his true self, opened for him the obstructed passage between head and heart, whence in time came genuine self-knowledge and peace. Again, he says that his imagination was by nature too masculine, austere, even harsh; he loved only the sublime and terrible, was blind to the milder graces of landscape and of character. She it was who softened and humanized him, opened his eyes to the more hidden beauties, his heart to the gentler affections: —

"She gave me eyes, she gave me ears:
And humble cares, and delicate fears;
A heart, the fountain of sweet tears,
And love, and thought, and joy."

If there were no other records of her than those

brief extracts from her journal during the Highland tour, which stand at the head of several of her brother's poems, these alone would prove her possessed of a large portion of his genius. Longer extracts from them occur in the poet's biography and in the edition of the poems of 1857, and often they seem nearly as good as the poems which they introduce. Might not that wonderful journal, even yet, be given entire, or nearly so, to the world?

It was in the autumn of 1795, at Racedown in Dorsetshire, that the brother and sister, on the strength of the nine hundred pounds, set up house together. This was the first home they had of their own, and Wordsworth always looked back to it with a special love. So retired was the place, that the post came only once a week. But the two read Italian together, gardened, and walked on the meadows, and on the tops of the combs. These were their recreations. For serious work, Wordsworth fell first to writing Imitations of Juvenal, in which he assailed fiercely the vices of the time, but these he never published. Then he wrote in the Spenserian stanza the poem of "Guilt and Sorrow," not published till long afterwards, but in which there is more of his real self than in anything he had yet done. Then followed his tragedy, "The Borderers,' which all, even his greatest admirers, feel to be a failure. Besides, there were one or two shorter poems, in his matured manner, such as the "Cumberland Beggar," which was written partly here, partly at Alfoxden. So many trials had Wordsworth to make, "The Evening Walk," the "Descriptive Sketches," "Imitations of Juvenal," "The Borderers," before he found out his true strength and his proper style.

More important, however, than any poetry composed at Racedown was his first meeting there with S. T.

Coleridge. Perhaps no two such men have met anywhere on English ground during this century. Coleridge when at Cambridge had read the "Descriptive Sketches," and finding in them something he had never found in poetry before, longed to know their author. Since leaving Cambridge, though two years and a half younger than Wordsworth, he had gone through half a lifetime of adventure, had served as a private in a cavalry regiment, been an enthusiast for the French Revolution, had tried to emigrate with Southey, and to found a Pantisocracy on the banks of the Susquehanna, been stopped by want of funds, then turned Unitarian preacher, and was now a young poet and philosopher on the loose. Miss Wordsworth describes him as he looked on his first visit to Racedown. For the first three minutes he seemed plain: "Thin and pale, the lower part of the face not good, wide mouth, thick lips, not very good teeth, longish, loose, half-curling, rough, black hair," — a contrast to Wordsworth at this time, with his fine light-brown hair and beautiful teeth. But the moment Coleridge began to speak, you thought no more of these defects. You saw him as his friend afterwards described him —

> "The rapt one of the godlike forehead,
> The heaven-eyed creature."

Or, as he elsewhere more fully portrayed him —

> "A noticeable man with large grey eyes,
> And a pale face that seemed undoubtedly
> As if a blooming face it ought to be;
> Heavy his low-hung lip did oft appear
> Depressed by weight of brooding phantasy;
> Profound his forehead was, though not severe."

During this visit Wordsworth read aloud to Coleridge nearly twelve hundred lines of blank verse, — "superior," says Coleridge, "to anything in our language." This probably included the story of Margaret, or "The Ruined Cottage," which now stands at the opening of "The Excursion," and certainly, in blank verse, Wordsworth never surpassed that. When they parted Coleridge says, "I felt myself a small man beside Wordsworth;" while of Coleridge, Wordsworth, certainly no over-estimater of other men, said, "I have known many men who have done wonderful things, but the only wonderful man I ever knew was Coleridge." Their first intercourse had ripened into friendship, and they longed to see more of each other. As Coleridge was at this time living at the village of Nether Stowey in Somersetshire, the Wordsworths removed in the autumn of 1797 to the country-house of Alfoxden, in the immediate neighborhood. The time he spent at Alfoxden was one of the most delightful seasons of Wordsworth's life. The two young men were of one mind in their poetic tastes and principles, one too in political and social views, and each admired the other more than he did any other living man. In outward circumstances, too, they were alike; both poor in money, but rich in thought and imagination, both in the prime of youth, and boundless in hopeful energy. That summer as they wandered aloft on the airy ridge of Quantock, or dived down its silvan combs, what high talk they must have held! Theirs was the age for boundless, endless, unwearied talk on all things human and divine. Hazlitt has said of Coleridge in his youth, that he seemed as if he would talk on forever, and you wished him to talk on forever. With him, as his youth, so was his age. But most men, as life wears on, having found that all their many and vehement talkings have served no lasting end of the soul, grow more brief and taciturn. Long after, Wordsworth speaks of this as a very pleasant and productive time. The poetic well-head, now fairly unsealed, was flowing freely. Many of the shorter poems were then composed from the scenery that was before his eyes, and from incidents there seen or heard. Among the most characteristic of these were, "We are Seven," "The Mad Mother," "The Last of the Flock," "Simon Lee," "Expostulation and Reply," "The Tables Turned," "Lines to his Sister," beginning "It is the first mild day of March," "Lines in early Spring," beginning "I heard a thousand blended notes," the last containing these words, which give the key-note to Wordsworth's feeling about nature at this time —

"And 'tis my faith that every flower
Enjoys the air it breathes."

If any one will read over the short poems above named, they will let him see further into Wordsworth's mood during this, the fresh germinating spring-time of his genius, than any words about them can.

The occasion of their making a joint literary venture was curious. Coleridge, Wordsworth, and his sister wished to make a short walking tour, for which five pounds were needed, but were not forthcoming. To supply this want they agreed to make a joint poem, and send it to some magazine which would give the required sum. Accordingly, one evening as they trudged along the Quantock Hills, they planned "The Ancient Mariner," founded on a dream which a friend of Coleridge had dreamed. Coleridge supplied most of the incidents, and almost all the lines. Wordsworth contributed the incident of the shooting of the albatross, with a line here and there. "The Ancient Mariner" soon grew, till it was beyond the desired five pounds' worth, so they thought of a joint volume. Coleridge was to take supernatural subjects, or roman-

3

tic, and invest them with a human interest and resemblance of truth. Wordsworth was to take common every-day incidents, and by faithful adherence to nature, and by true but modifying colors of imagination, was to shed over common aspects of earth and facts of life such a charm as light and shade, sunset and moonlight, shed over a familiar landscape. Wordsworth was so much the more industrious of the two, that he had completed enough for a volume when Coleridge had only finished "The Ancient Mariner," and begun "Christabel" and "The Dark Ladie." Cottle, a Bristol bookseller, was summoned from Bristol to arrange for publication, and he has left a gossiping but amusing account of his intercourse with the two poets at this time, and his visit to Alfoxden. He agreed to give Wordsworth £30 for the twenty-two pieces of his which made up the first volume of the "Lyrical Ballads," while for "The Rime of the Ancient Marinere," which was to head the volume, he made a separate bargain with Coleridge. This volume, which appeared in the autumn of 1798, was the first which made Wordsworth known to the world as a poet, for the "Descriptive Sketches" had attracted little or no notice. Of the ballads or shorter poems, which, as we have seen, were mostly composed at Alfoxden, and which reflect the feelings and incidents of his life there, I shall reserve what I have to say for a more general survey. The volume closes with one poem in another style, in which the poet speaks out his inmost feelings, and in his own "grand style." This is the poem on Tintern Abbey, composed during a walking tour on the Wye with his sister, just before leaving Alfoxden for the Continent. Read these lines over once again, however well you may know them. Bear in mind what has been told of the way his childhood and boyhood had passed, living in the eye of nature, the separation that followed from his favorite haunts and ways, the wild fermentation of thought, the moral tempest he had gone through, the return to nature's lonely places, and to common life and peaceful thoughts, with intellect and heart deepened, expanded, humanized, by having long brooded over the ever-recurring questions of man's nature and destiny; bear these things in mind, and as you read, every line of that masterpiece will come out with deeper meaning and in exacter outline. And then the concluding lines, in which the poet turns to his sister, his fellow-traveller, with "the shooting lights in those wild eyes," in which he caught "gleams of past existence" —

> "If solitude, or fear, or pain, or grief,
> Should be thy portion" —

what prophetic pathos do these words assume when we remember how long and mournfully ere life ended those wild eyes were darkened!

Before the volume appeared, Wordsworth and his sister had left Alfoxden, and sailed with Coleridge for Germany. It has been said that the reason for their leaving Somersetshire was their falling under suspicion as hatchers of sedition. A government spy, with a peculiarly long nose, was sent down to watch them. Coleridge tells an absurd story, how, as they lay on the Quantock Hills, conversing about Spinoza, the spy, as he skulked behind a bank, overheard their talk, and thought they were speaking about himself under the nickname of "Spy-nosey." Coleridge was believed to have little harm in him, for he was a crack-brained, talking fellow; but "that Wordsworth is either a smuggler or a traitor, and means mischief. He never speaks to any one, haunts lonely places, walks by moonlight, and is always '*booing* about' by himself." Such was the country talk; and the result of it was, the agent for the owner of Alfoxden refused to re-let the house to so suspicious a character. So the three determined to pack up, and winter on the Continent. At Hamburg, however, they parted company. Their ostensible purpose was to learn German, but Wordsworth and his sister did little at this. He spent the winter of 1798–99, the coldest of the century, in Goslar, and there, by the German charcoal-burners, the poet's mind reverted to Esthwaite and Westmoreland hills, and struck out a number of poems in his finest vein. "She dwelt among the untrodden ways," "Lucy," or "Three years she grew in sun and shower," "Ruth," "The Poet's Epitaph," "Nutting," "The Two April Mornings," "The Fountain," "Matthew," are all products of this winter. So Wordsworth missed German, and gave the world instead immortal poems. Coleridge went alone to Göttingen, learned German, dived for the rest of his life deep into transcendental metaphysics, and the world got no more Ancient Mariners.

In the spring of 1799, Wordsworth and his sister set forth from Goslar on their return to England. As they left that city behind, and felt the spring breeze fan their cheeks, Wordsworth poured forth that joyful strain with which "The Prelude" opens. Arrived in their native land, they passed most of the remainder of the year with their kindred, the Hutchinsons, at Sockburn-on-Tees, occasionally travelling into the neighboring dales and fells of Yorkshire. In September, Wordsworth took Coleridge, who also had returned from abroad, and had seen but few mountains in his life, on a walking tour to show him the hills and lakes of native Westmoreland. "Haweswater," Coleridge writes, "kept my eyes dim with tears, but I received the deepest delight from the divine sisters, Rydal and Grasmere." It was then that Wordsworth saw the small house at the Town End of Grasmere, which he and his sister soon after fixed on as their home.

From Sockburn-on-Tees William and Dorothy Wordsworth set forth a little before the shortest day, and walked on foot over the bleak fells that form the watershed of Yorkshire and Westmoreland. As side by side they paced the long dales, and set their faces to the Hambleton hills, the ground was frozen hard under their feet, and the snow-showers were driving against them. Yet they enjoyed the snow-showers, turned aside to see the frozen waterfalls, and stopped to watch the changing drapery of cloud, sunshine, and snow-drift as it coursed the hills. At night they lodged in cottages or small wayside inns, and there, by the kitchen fire, Wordsworth gave words to the thoughts that had occurred to him during the day. A great part of "Hart-leap Well" was composed during one of these evenings, from a tradition he had heard that day from a native. And of a sunset seen during the same journey, some of the glory still lives in the sonnet ending

> "They are of the sky,
> And from our earthly memory fade away."

The poet and his sister reached Grasmere on the shortest day of the year 1799, and settled in the small two-storied cottage at that part of the village called Town-End. The house had formerly been a public house, with the sign of the Dove and the Olive Bough, but was henceforth to be identified with Wordsworth's poetic prime. The mode of life on which they were entering was one which their friends, no doubt, and most sensible people, called a mad project. With barely a hundred pounds a year between them, they were turning their back on the world, cutting themselves off from professions, chances of getting on, society, and settling themselves down in an out-of-the-way corner, with no employment but verse-making, no neighbors but the homely dalesmen. When a man makes such a choice, he has need to look well what he does, and to be sure that he can go through with it. In the world's eyes nothing but success will justify such a renunciant, and the world will not be too ready to grant that success has been attained. But Wordsworth, besides a prophet-like devotion to the truths he saw, had a prudence, self-denial, and perseverance, rare among the sons of song. To himself may be applied the words he uses in a letter to Sir George Beaumont, when speaking of another subject than poetry: "It is such an animating sight to see a man of genius, regardless of temporary gains, whether of money or praise, fixing his attention solely upon what is interesting and permanent, and finding his happiness in an entire devotion of himself to such pursuits as shall most ennoble human nature. We have not yet seen enough of this in modern times." He himself showed this sight, if any man of his age did. Plain living and high thinking were not only praised in verse, but acted out by him and his sister in that cottage home.

The year 1800 was ushered in by a long storm, which blocked up the roads for months, and kept them much indoors. This put their tempers to the proof, but they stood the test. Spring weather set them free, and brought to their home a much loved sailor brother, John, who was captain of an Indiaman. In their frugal housekeeping the sister, it may be believed, had much to do indoors, but she was always ready, both then and years after, to accompany her brother in his mountain walks. Those who may wish to know more of their abode and way of life, will find an interesting sketch of these given by De Quincey, as he saw them seven years later. There was one small room containing their few books, which was called, by courtesy, the library. But Wordsworth was no reader; the English poets and ancient history were the only two subjects he was really well read in. He tells a friend that he had not spent five shillings on new books in as many years, and of the few old ones which made up his collection he had not read one fifth. As for his study, that was in the open air. "By the side of the brook that runs through Easdale," he says, "I have composed thousands of verses:" —

> "He murmurs near the running brooks
> A music sweeter than their own."

Another favorite resort for composition at this time was the tall fir-wood on the hillside above the old road leading from Grasmere to Rydal. Society they found in the families of the "statesmen" all about. For Grasmere was then, like most of the neighboring dales, portioned out among small but independent peasant lairds, whose forefathers had for ages lived and died on the same farms. With these men Wordsworth and his sister lived on terms of kindliness and equal hospitality. He would receive them to tea in his home, or would go to sup in theirs. If the invitation was to some homestead in a distant vale, the ladies would travel in a cart, the poet walking by its side. Among these men, in their pastoral republic, the life was one of not too laborious industry; the manners were simple, manly, and severe. The statesmen looked after the sheep, grew hay on their own land in the valley, and each could turn out as many sheep to feed on the fell or common (as they call it) during the summer months, as they could provide hay for in the winter. Their chief source of income was the wool from the flock, and this not sold in the fleece, but spun into thread by the wives and daughters. These, with their spinning-wheels, were in high esteem, for they did more to maintain the house than the spade or plough of the husbands. Wordsworth loved this manner of life, not only because he had been familiar with it from childhood, but also because he knew what sterling worth and pure domestic virtues sheltered under these roofs. He lived to see it rudely broken up. Machinery put out the spinning-wheel, and the statesmen's lands passed for the most part into other hands.

The few statesmen's families who survived down to a recent time in and around Grasmere, retained an affectionate and reverent remembrance of the "pawet," as they in their Westmoreland dialect called him, long after he had left them for Rydal Mount. Many stories I have heard them tell of his ways, while living at the Town-End; how, alone, or oftener with his sister, at night-fall, when other people were going to bed, he would be seen setting out to walk to Dunmail Raise, or climbing that outlying ridge of Fairfield which overhangs the forest side of Grasmere, there to be all night long till near the breaking of the day. At such a time it may well have been, when on those heights he was alone with the stars, and the voices of the mountain streams were coming up from far below, that the "Ode on Mortality" first came to him. When in their houses strangers have read aloud, or told in their own words some of his shorter poems descriptive of incident and character, or the two books of "The Excursion" which describe the tenants of the churchyard among the mountains, I have heard old residenters name many of the persons there alluded to, and go on to give more details of their lives.

The first months at Grasmere were so industriously employed, that some time in the year 1800, when a second edition of the first volume of "Lyrical Ballads" was being reprinted, he added to it a new volume containing thirty-seven new pieces. Among these were the poems already mentioned as having been composed during the German winter, as well as some new ones which had been suggested since he settled at Grasmere. Such were the "Idle Shepherd Boys," "Poems on the Naming of Places," "The Brothers," "Michael," all redolent of the Westmoreland fells. These two volumes cannot be said to have failed, for they were reprinted in 1802, and again in 1805; and in 1806, Jeffrey, even when inveighing against a new and better volume of poems, speaks of the "Lyrical Ballads" as "unquestionably popular." I shall not, however, stay to comment on their contents till I have done with narrative. Only a few facts stand out prominently from the happy and industrious tenor of the life at Grasmere. In 1802, that Earl of Lonsdale, who to the last refused to pay to the Wordsworths their due, died, and was succeeded by a better-minded kinsman, who paid to them the original debt of £5,000 due to their father, with £3,500 of interest. This was divided into five shares, of which two went to the poet and his sister. This addition to his income enabled the poet to take to himself a wife, his cousin, and the intimate friend of his sister, Mary Hutchinson, whom he had long known and loved. It is she whom he describes in his exquisite lines —

"A creature not too bright or good
For human nature's daily food;

> A perfect woman, nobly planned,
> To warn, to comfort, and command;
> And yet a spirit still, and bright
> With something of an angel light."

They lived together in as great happiness as is allowed to human beings, till the poet had fulfilled his fourscore years, when she survived him a few years longer.

In the August of 1803, Mrs. Wordsworth having been kept at home by domestic duties, Wordsworth and his sister set out from Keswick with Coleridge on their memorable tour in Scotland. They travelled great part of the way on foot, up Nithsdale, and so on towards the Highlands. Coleridge turned back soon after they had reached Loch Lomond, being either lazy or out of spirits. Everywhere as they trudged along, they saw the old familiar Highland sights, as if none had ever seen them before; and wherever they moved among the mountains, they left footprints of immortal beauty. He expressed what he saw in verse, she in prose, and it is hard to say which is the more poetic. Of all that has been, or yet may be, said or sung about the Highlands, what words can ever equal those entries in her journal? what poems can ever catch the soul of things like the "Address to Kilchurn Castle," "Glen-Almain," "Stepping Westward," and "The Solitary Reaper?" The last of these, perhaps the most perfect of Wordsworth's poems, must have been suggested as they walked somewhere in the region about Loch Voil, between the braes of Balquhidder and Strathire. What was the name of her who suggested it, and where is she now? Who can tell? But whether she be still alive in extremest old age, or, as is far more likely, long since laid in Balquhidder kirkyard or in some other, in that poem she will sing on forever in eternal youth, to delight generations yet to be.

In the beginning of 1805, the first great sorrow fell on Wordsworth's home, in the loss of his brother, Captain Wordsworth. He was leaving England, intending to make one more voyage, and then to return and live with his sister and brother, when, by the carelessness of a pilot, his ship was run on the shambles of the Bill of Portland, and he with the larger part of his crew went down. For long Wordsworth was almost inconsolable, he so loved and honored his brother. His letters at this time, and his poems long after, are darkened with this grief. In one of these letters this striking thought occurs: "Why have we sympathies that make the best of us so afraid of inflicting pain and sorrow, which yet we see dealt about so lavishly by the Supreme Governor? Why should our notions of right towards each other, and to all sentient beings within our influence, differ so widely from what appears to be his notion and rule, if everything were to end here?" Captain Wordsworth had greatly admired his brother's poetry, but saw that it would take time to become popular, and would probably never be lucrative. So he would work for the family at Town-End, he said, and William would do something for the world. "This is the end of his part of the agreement," says the poet; "God grant me life and strength to fulfill mine!"

In 1807, Wordsworth came out with two more volumes of poetry, for the most part produced at Grasmere. He was now in his thirty-seventh year, so that these volumes may be said to close the spring-time of his genius, and to be its consummate flower. Some of his after works may have equaled these, and may even show an increased moral depth and religious tenderness. But there is about the best of the Grasmere poems an ethereal touch of ideality which he perhaps never afterwards reached. Besides the Scottish poems already noticed, there were the earliest installment of sonnets, some of them the best he ever wrote, as that "London seen from Westminster Bridge;" "It is a beauteous evening, calm and free;" "The World is too much with us;" "Toussaint L'Ouverture;" "Milton, thou shouldst be living at this hour!"

These volumes contain also "The Song of Brougham Castle;" "Resolution and Independence;" the poem to the Cuckoo, beginning, "O blithe new-comer;" "Elegiac Stanzas suggested by the picture of Peele Castle;" and last, and chief of all, the "Ode on Intimations of Immortality." The three last named especially have that indescribable, unapproachable ideality, which I have spoken of as the characteristic of his best poems at this time. Indeed, the "Ode on Immortality" marks the highest limit which the tide of poetic inspiration has reached in England within this century, or indeed since the days of Milton.[1]

As Wordsworth's outward as well as his inward history has been traced thus far, it may be well not to take leave of it without here noting the few facts that yet remain. The cottage at the Town-End of Grasmere was his home from the close of 1799 till the spring of 1808. This was the time when his inspiration was at flood-tide. At Town-End, as we have seen, "Michael," "Resolution and Independence," "The Cuckoo," "The Solitary Reaper," and the other memorials of Scotland, "The Song of Brougham Castle," "Stanzas on Peele Castle," and, above all, the immortal "Ode," first saw the light. There too most of

[1] It has lately been suggested that Wordsworth owed the first hint of this great ode to Henry Vaughan's poem called the *Retreat*. But those who have observed how deep down in Wordsworth's nature lay that sense of the mystery and ideality of childhood, and how often it crops out in his works, will be slow to believe that he had to go to any extrinsic source to find it.

"The Prelude" was written, besides many smaller poems. In 1808, as the Town-End cottage had grown too small for his increasing family, he was obliged to move to Allan Bank, — a new house which was hardly finished, on the top of a knoll to the west of Grasmere, overlooking the lake. Here he remained till the spring of 1811; but the house was for some time unfinished, and the chimneys smoked, and to this his biographer has attributed, what he thinks, a comparative dearth of production during these three years. But it should be remembered that it was probably at Allan Bank that the greater part of "The Excursion" was composed, though it was not published till some years later. Coleridge was an inmate of Wordsworth's home during the earlier part of the Allan Bank residence. In the spring of 1811, Wordsworth was obliged to remove thence to the Parsonage of Grasmere, situated between the church and the lake. The poet's stay here was darkened by the loss of two of his little children, a girl and a boy, who were laid side by side in the same grave, hard by in Grasmere churchyard. A small blue stone preserves the following epitaph written by the poet over his boy: —

> "Six months to six years added he remained
> Upon this sinful earth, by sin unstained:
> O blessed Lord! whose mercy then removed
> A Child whom every eye that looked on loved;
> Support us, teach us calmly to resign
> What we possessed, and now is wholly thine!"

This affliction, which at the Parsonage was rendered insupportable by the continual sight of the two graves, made the poet and his family glad to quit the vale of Grasmere for a new home at Rydal Mount, which offered itself in the spring of 1813. This was their last migration, and there the poet and his wife lived till, many years after, they were carried back to join their children in the churchyard of Grasmere.

Rydal Mount saw a good deal of poetry composed, but not much in the poet's finest vein. It witnessed, however, many other good things: an easy competence brought to the poet's door in the shape of a distributorship of stamps, — the steady growth of his reputation from comparative obscurity till he took his acknowledged place beside the chief kings of English song. — thirty-seven years of contented and beneficent life, rounded by a peaceful close. Besides the two children lost in 1812, the poet's family consisted of a daughter and two sons. The daughter, "Dora," afterwards Mrs. Quillinan, died before her father; the two sons still survive. These facts are not irrelevant, but essential ones to the understanding of Wordsworth. Few poets have been by nature so fitted for domestic happiness, and fewer still have been blessed with so abundant a share of it. The strength and purity of his home affections, so deep and undisturbed, entered into all that he thought and sang. Herein may be said to have lain the heart of "central peace" that sustained the whole fabric of his life and poetry.

The account I have given of the growth of Wordsworth's mind from childhood to maturity has been extracted mainly from "The Prelude," and is meant to throw light on the aim and spirit of his poetry. If a discriminating mental history of the poet could be given, followed by an edition of his works, in which the several poems were arranged, not in the present arbitrary manner, but chronologically according to the date of their composition, this would form the best of all commentaries. There were three epochs in Wordsworth's poetry, though these shade so insensibly the one into the other, that any attempt exactly to define them must be somewhat arbitrary. What I have already called the spring-time of his genius would reach from his first settling at Racedown, or at any rate his going to Alfoxden in 1797, till his leaving Grasmere Town-End in 1808. The second epoch, or full midsummer of his poetry, would include his time at Allan Bank and his first years at Rydal Mount, as far as 1818 or 1820. This was the time when "The Excursion," "Laodamia," "Dion," and the "Duddon Sonnets" were composed. The third epoch, or the sober autumn, reaching from about 1820 till he ceased from the work of composition, is the time of the ecclesiastical and other sonnets, of "Yarrow Revisited," and the Scottish poems of 1833; and lastly, of the memorials of his Italian tour in 1837.

But to return to the poems of the first epoch. It was the two volumes of 1807, those which, as we have seen, contained the very prime ore of his genius, that called forth Jeffrey's well-known vituperation. The unfairness of that review lay in this, that the weak parts of the book were brought out in strong relief, while the best were thrown as far as possible into the background. Over "the unfortunate Alice Fell," as it has been called, the critic makes himself merry, and by extracting a number of homely matter-of fact lines and stanzas, which occur here and there in the other poems, contrived to make Wordsworth's name a by-word for many a day for bathos and puerility. But his verdict on the very best — those which all the world has since acknowledged — prove that to the Edinburgh lawgiver on matters of taste, poetic originality was as a picture to a blind man's eye. "Yarrow Unvisited" he calls "a very tedious, affected performance." After quoting from and describing "Resolution and Independence," he thus concludes: "We defy the bitterest enemy of

Mr. Wordsworth to produce anything at all parallel to this from any collection of English poetry, or even from the specimens of his friend Mr. Southey." In the same strain he quotes from the "Ode to the Cuckoo," in which he thinks that the author, striving after force and originality, produces nothing but absurdity. Lastly, the "Ode on Immortality" is "the most illegible and unintelligible part of the publication." The only parts of the two volumes quoted with approbation are the Brougham song and three sonnets. These facts I have mentioned, not from a wish to disinter long since buried strifes, but because allusion to them is necessary to bring out the true force of Wordsworth both as a man and a poet. The result of this review was to stop the sale of his poems for a number of years. But whoever else might be snuffed out by a severe review, Wordsworth could not be so silenced. To a friend who wrote condoling with him on the severity of the criticism — and it must be remembered that in those days the verdict of the "Edinburgh" was all but omnipotent — he replied: "Trouble not yourself upon their present reception; of what moment is that compared with what I trust is their destiny! — to console the afflicted; to add sunshine to daylight, by making the happy happier; to teach the young and gracious of every age to see, to think, and feel, and, therefore, to become more actively and securely virtuous; this is their office, which I trust they will faithfully perform, long after we (that is, all that is mortal of us) are mouldering in our graves." Again: "I doubt not that you will share with me an invincible confidence that my writings (and among them these little poems) will coöperate with the benign tendencies in human nature and society, wherever found; and that they will, in their degree, be efficacious in making men wiser, better, and happier." This language is not vanity, but the calm confidence of a man who feels the rock under his feet, knows that he is in harmony with the everlasting truth of things. In the issue between the critic and the poet, the world, long neutral, or rather adverse to the latter, at length sided with him, and will continue permanently to do so. Before his death he saw posthumous fame secured to him; but it is instructive to note what a change thirty years had made in his feeling regarding it. In 1837, he thus writes to another correspondent: "I am standing on the brink of that vast ocean I must sail so soon; I must speedily lose sight of the shore; and I could not once have conceived how little I now am troubled by the thought of how long or how short a time they who remain on that shore may have sight of me."

What is there in these poems which there is not in any other? What is their peculiar virtue? To seize and set forth in words the heart of anything with which we have been long familiar is not easy; nevertheless something of this kind must, however imperfectly, be attempted. In the opening of "The Prelude," Wordsworth tells us that when he first seriously thought of being a poet, he looked into himself to see how he was fitted for the work, and seemed to find there "that first great gift, the vital soul." In this self-estimate he did not err. The vital soul, it is a great gift, which, if ever it dwelt in man, dwelt in Wordsworth. Not the intellect merely, nor the heart, nor the imagination, nor the conscience, nor any of these alone, but all of them condensed into one, and moving all together. In virtue of this vital soul, whatever he did see he saw to the very core. He did not fumble with the outside or the accidents of the thing, but his eye went at once to the quick, — rested on the essential life of it. He saw what was there, but had escaped all other eyes. He did not import into the outward world transient fancies or feelings of his own, "the pathetic fallacy," as it has been named; but he saw it, as it exists in itself, or perhaps rather as it exists in its permanent moral relations to the human spirit.

Again, this soul within him did not work with effort; no painful groping or grasping. It was as vital in its respectivity as in its active energy. It could lie long in a "wise passiveness," drawing the things of earth and sky and of human life into itself, as the calm, clear lake does the imagery of the surrounding hills and overhanging sky.

"Think not, 'mid all this mighty sum
Of things forever speaking,
That nothing in itself will come,
But we must still be seeking."

Those early spring poems at Alfoxden, from which these lines are taken, specially express what I mean, — the wonderful interchange that went on between him and all the things about him, they flowing into him, he flowing out into them. His soul attracted them to itself, as a mountain-top draws the clouds, and at their touch woke up to feel its kinship with the mysterious life that is in all nature, and in each separate object of nature. This is the cardinal work of the imagination, to possess itself of the life of whatever thing it deals with. In the extent to which he did this, and the truthfulness with which he did it, lies Wordsworth's supreme power.

Hence one may observe that all genuine imagination is essentially truthful, and the purer it is, the more truthful. The reports it brings in, so far from being mere fancies, are the finest, most hidden truths. In Wordsworth, the higher his inspiration rises, the more penetrating is his truthfulness. What may be the relation between the truths which imagination reveals, and those which are the result of scientific discovery, who shall determine? — it would be a fine inquiry for one who can to work at; but every one must feel that —

> "The moon doth with delight
> Look round her when the heavens are bare,"

gives the essence of a clear moonlight sky more truthfully in its relation to the human spirit, than any mere meteorologist can do. What words, poetic or scientific, will ever render the mountain stillness like these few plain ones? —

> "The sleep that is among the lonely hills;"

or the impression made by a solitary western peak, like —

> "There is an eminence of these our hills,
> The last that parleys with the setting sun."

It is this rendering of the inner truth of things which Mr. Arnold has happily called "the interpretative power of poetry." This must be that which Wordsworth himself means when, in his preface, he says that "poetry is the breath and finer spirit of all knowledge; it is the impassioned expression which is in the countenance of all science." And it is "the vital soul" in the poet which penetrates into this, and reads it off for other men. This, too, is what is meant when we find it said in "The Prelude" that imagination, in its highest use, is but another name for "absolute power, clearest insight, reason in her most exalted mood;" and that this imagination, exercised on outward nature and on human life, is the parent of love, or feeling intellect. This language will, no doubt, to some sound mystical. But it is the language of one who possessed that which he spoke of in larger mass, and of finer quality, than any Englishman since Shakespeare and Milton. It is the presence of this power in Wordsworth which is the source of that indescribable charm which many have felt in his poetry, and have found in none other before or since. They were brought by it for a moment soul to soul with truth, caught, as they read, a glimpse into the life of things such as no other poet of these days has given them. This clearness of vision, rare at all times, becomes much rarer as the ages go on. The naming era, when men could still give names to things, is long past, and with disuse the faculty has died out. Under heaps of words, which we receive without effort, dead metaphors, fossils of extinct poetic acts, the moulding power of imagination lies buried. And not only language has got stiff and hardened, but society has become complicated in a thousand ways; phrases, custom, conventionality, doubts, disputes, lie many layers thick above every new-born soul. The revolutionary age into which Wordsworth was born may have made some rents in these, and let the basement of truth be here and there seen through. And yet, even with this help, what power must have dwelt in that quiet eye to put all these obstructions aside, and see things anew for itself, as if no one had ever looked on them before!

This power manifests itself in Wordsworth especially in two directions, as it is turned on nature, and as it is turned on man. Let us, for the sake of clearness, examine them separately, though, in reality, they often blend. Between Wordsworth's imagination, however, as it works in the one direction and in the other, there is this difference. In dealing with nature, it has no limit: it is as wide as the world; as much at home when gazing on the little celandine, as when moving with the vast elemental forces of earth and heaven. In human life and character his range is narrower, whether these limitations came from within, or were self-imposed. His sympathies embrace by no means all human things, but within the range which they do embrace, his eye is no less penetrating and true. About nature, it has become so much the fashion to rave, there has been so much counterfeit enthusiasm, that it is a subject one almost dreads speaking of. But whatever it may be to most men, there can be no doubt that free nature, mountain solitudes, were as essential to Wordsworth's heart, as the air to his lungs. About this, nothing he has said goes beyond the simple truth. Of his manner of dealing with it in his poetry, the following things may be noted : —

First, When he would place some particular landscape before the reader, he does not heap up an exhaustive enumeration of details. Only one or two of the most essential features faithfully given, and then from these he passes at once to the sentiment, the genius of the place, that which gives it individuality, and makes it this and no other place. Numerous instances of the way in which he seizes the inner spirit of a place and utters it, will occur to every reader. To give one out of many: after sketching briefly the outward appearance of the four fraternal yew-trees of Borrowdale, who else could have condensed the total impressions into such lines as these, so intensely imaginative, so profoundly true ! —

"Beneath whose sable roof
Of boughs, as if for festal purpose, decked
With unrejoicing berries — ghostly shapes
May meet at noontide; Fear and trembling Hope,
Silence and Foresight; Death the Skeleton,
And Time the Shadow; there to celebrate,

As in a natural temple, scattered o'er
With altars undisturbed of mossy stone,
United worship; or in mute repose
To lie and listen to the mountain flood,
Murmuring from Glaramara's inmost caves."

When in this passage, or in that wonderful poem, "What, are you stepping westward?" and many more, we find the poet spiritualizing so powerfully the familiar appearances and common facts of earth, adding, as he himself says, —

"The gleam,
The light that never was, on sea or land,
The consecration, and the poet's dream,"

one is tempted to ask, Is this true, is the light real, or only fantastic? Now in this, I conceive, lies Wordsworth's transcendent power, that the ideal light he sheds is a true light, and the more ideal it is, the more true. Poets, all but the greatest, are apt to adorn things with fantastic or individual hues, to suffuse them with their own temporary emotions, which Mr. Ruskin has called the "pathetic fallacy." The ideal light which Wordsworth sheds does not so, but brings out only more vividly the real heart of nature,[1] the in-

[1] This expression has been objected to as vague or meaningless. It is certainly a condensed form of words, but it aims at expressing a real though subtle truth. If asked to explain it, I should do so in this way: Each scene in nature has in it a power of awakening in every beholder of sensibility, an impression peculiar to itself, such as no other scene can exactly call up. This may be called the "heart" or "character" of that scene. It is quite analogous to, if somewhat vaguer than, the particular impression produced upon us by the presence of each individual man. Now the aggregate of the impressions produced by many scenes in nature, or rather the power in nature on a large scale of producing such impressions on us, is what, for want of another name, I have called the "heart" of nature. The test of what is the real heart or character of any scene is to be ascertained by the experience of what the largest number of men of the truest poetic sensibility feel in the presence of that scene. What it is in nature which produces these impressions on human imaginations I do not undertake to say. But that one cannot explain the cause or mode of operation, is no reason why one should not notice and name the fact.

most feeling, which is really there, and is recognized by Wordsworth's eye in virtue of the kinship between nature and his soul. If it be asked How is this? I can but reply, that there is a wonderful and mysterious adaptation between the external world and the human soul, the one answering to the other in ways not yet explained by any philosopher.

Secondly, It is perhaps but turning to another side of the same quality to note what a base of natural, rather than philosophical idealism lay at the bottom of the eye which Wordsworth turned on nature. Whereas to most men the material world is a heavy, gross, dead mass, earth a ball of black mud, painted here and there with some color, Wordsworth felt it to be a living, breathing power, not dead, but full of strange life; his eye almost saw into it, as if it were transparent. So strongly did this feeling possess him, that in childhood he was a complete idealist. Speaking of himself at that age, he says, "I was often unable to think of external things as having external existence, and I communed with all I saw as something, not apart from, but inherent in my own immaterial nature. Many times while going to school have I grasped at a wall or tree to recall myself from the abyss of idealism to the reality. At that time I was afraid of such processes. In later periods of life I have deplored, as we have all reason to do, a subjugation of an opposite character, and have rejoiced over these remembrances." Here is idealism, far beyond that of Berkeley or any other philosopher, engendered not by subtle arguments of metaphysics, but born from within by sheer force of soul, before which the solid mass of earth is fused and unsubstantialized. Out of moods like these, or rather the remembrance of them, are projected some of his most ideal lights, such as form the charm of his finest poems, like the lines to the Cuckoo, and the "Ode on Immortality." Hence came the —

> "Obstinate questionings,
> Of sense and outward things,
> Fallings from us, vanishings,"

which he looked back to with thankful joy in mature manhood. With these abstract and visionary feelings there blended more tender human remembrances of that early time, making together a beautiful light of morning about his after days, and touching even the common things of life with an affecting, tender solemnity.

Thirdly, With this spiritualizing power of soul Wordsworth combined another faculty, which might seem the most opposed to it, — wonderful keenness and faithfulness of eye for the minutest facts of the outward world. Seldom in his library, much in the open air, at all hours, in all seasons, from childhood to old age, his watchful observant eye had stored his mind with all the varied and ever-changing aspects of nature. His imagination was a treasure-house whence he drew forth things new and old, the old as fresh as if new. No modern poet has recorded so large and so varied a number of natural facts and appearances, which had never before been set down in books. And these he brings forth, not as if he had noted and carefully photographed them, to be reproduced whenever an occasion offered, but as familiar knowledge that had come to him unawares, and recurred with the naturalness of an instinct. Many no doubt had seen before, but who before him had so described the hare? —

> "The grass is bright with raindrops; on the moors
> The hare is running races in her mirth;
> And with her feet she from the plashy earth

Raises a mist, that, glittering in the sun,
Runs with her all the way, wherever she doth run."

Or again, who else would have noted the effect of a leaping trout, or of a croaking raven, in bringing out the solitariness of a mountain tarn? —

"There sometimes doth a leaping fish
Send through the tarn a lonely cheer;
The crags repeat the raven's croak
In symphony austere."

Or again, in the calm bright evening after a stormy day —

"Loud is the Vale! the voice is up
With which she speaks when storms are gone,
A mighty unison of streams!
Of all her voices, one!

"Loud is the Vale! this inland depth
In peace is roaring like the sea;
Yon star upon the mountain-top
Is listening quietly."

Who but Wordsworth would have set off the uproar of the vale by the stillness of the star on the mountain head? Here, in passing, I may note the strange power there is in his simple prepositions. The star is *upon* the mountain-top; the silence is *in* the starry sky; the sleep is *among* the hills; "the gentleness of heaven *is on* the sea," not "broods o'er," as the later editions have it. This double gift of soul and eye, highest ideality and most literal realism combined, have made him of all modern poets nature's most unerring interpreter.[1]

Fourthly, Hence it comes that all the moods and outgoings of nature are alike open to him; every kind

[1] No one, that I know, has yet laid his finger on a single mistake made by Wordsworth with regard to any appearance of nature, or fact in natural history, though keen observers have done this in the case of both Walter Scott and Burns.

of country renders up to him its secret. He is alike true, whether in describing the boundless flats of Salisbury Plain, combs and dells of western Somersetshire, fells and lakes of native Cumberland, Yorkshire moors and dales, wilder glens of our own Highlands, or the pastoral quiet of the Border hills. Who save him could have gathered up the whole feeling of Yarrow into that consummate stanza, "Meek loveliness," etc., etc.?

If there is preëminence in any one department, it is in the interpretation of his own mountains. This is so altogether adequate and profound, that it has often seemed as if those dumb old solitudes had, after slumbering since the beginning of time, at last waked to consciousness in him, and uttered their inmost heart through his voice. No other mountains have ever had their soul so perfectly expressed. Philosophers have dreamed that nature and the human soul are the two limbs of a double-clefted tree, springing from and united in one root; that nature is unconscious soul, and the soul is nature become conscious of itself. Some such view as this, if it were true, might account for the marvelous sympathy there is between Wordsworth's poetry and the spirit that is in his own mountains, and for his power of rendering their mute being into his solemn melodies.

But it is now time to look at that other side of things in which his vitality of imagination is seen. His meditative eye penetrates not less deep when turned on the heart and character of man, than when it contemplates the face of nature. It has, however, been already noted, that while in the latter department his range is limitless, in the former it is not only restricted, but restricted within very marked and definite bounds. For man as he is found in cities, or as he appears in the complex conditions of advanced civilization, Wordsworth cares little ; he turns his back on the streets, the drawing-rooms, the mart, and the 'change, but lovingly enters the cottage and the farm, and walks with the shepherd on his hills, or the vagrant on lonely roads. The choice of his characters from humble and rustic life was caused partly by the original make of his nature, partly from his early training, which made him more at home with these than with artificial man, partly also from that republican fervor which he imbibed in his opening manhood. He believed that in country people what is permanent in human nature, the essential feelings and passions of mankind, exist in greater simplicity and strength. Their manners, he thought, spring more directly from such feeling, and more faithfully express them. Their lives and occupations too are " with grandeur circumfused." Thus they are invested with a glory, beyond others, from the background of wild and beautiful nature against which they are seen. These are the reasons he gives for selecting his subjects from humble life, and within this range he, for the most part, confines himself. There is still another limitation. Even in these characters he is not so much at home in dealing with their trivial outside appearance, or little laughable peculiarities of manner or costume. He has small caring for these things, and when he sets to describe them he often fails, as in the " Idiot Boy " perhaps, and in " Goody Blake." A few touches of real humor would have wonderfully relieved these personages, but this Wordsworth has not to give. He cannot, as Burns often does, exhibit his humble characters dramatically, does not laugh and sing, much less drink, with his peasants ; he is not quite one of themselves, sharing their thoughts, and having no other and higher thoughts. What he sets himself to portray is their serious feelings, the deep things of their souls, that in which the peasant and the peer are one, and in which, as Wordsworth thinks, the advantage may often lie with the former. He has, as Coleridge has said, "deep sympathy with man as man; but it is the sympathy of a contemplator, rather than a fellow-sufferer or co-mate; but of a contemplator from whose view no difference of rank conceals the sameness of nature; no injuries of time and weather, of toil, or even of ignorance, wholly disguise the human face divine." In fact it is the moral and spiritual part of man which he most sees and feels, and other things are interesting chiefly as they affect this. His thoughts dwell in —

> "The depth, and not the tumult of the soul,"

not on the surface manners, nor on the effervescent and transitory emotions, but on those which are steadfast and forever. It is in virtue of his deep insight into these, that common incidents assume for him an importance and interest which to less reflective men has seemed exaggerated or sometimes even ludicrous. The reflections, however, which they awake in him are not only true and deep, but they are such as add new dignity or tenderness to human life. A frail old man thanked him fervently for cutting through for him at a blow an old root, which he had long been haggling at in vain. The tears in the old man's eyes drew out from Wordsworth this reflection —

> "I've heard of hearts unkind, kind deeds
>   With coldness still returning;
> Alas! the gratitude of men
>   Hath oftener left me mourning."

In setting forth such characters as The Brothers, Michael, the Cumberland Beggar, etc., etc. (though in the last of these there is somewhat too much moralizing), he gives them not only as common acquaintances see them, or as they appear to themselves; this he does, but something more. He lets us see them in their relations to those unseen laws of the moral world, of which they themselves may be unaware, but which they suggest to the inspired insight of the poet. And in this way the emotions called forth by the sight of suffering do not end in mere emotion, but strike into a more enduring, that is, a moral ground, and so are idealized and relieved. This moral vision has a wonderful power to elevate, often to solemnize, things, the lowliest and most familiar. It has been said that Burns has caused many an eye to look on the poorest thatched cottage of the Scottish peasantry with a feeling which, but for Burns, the beholder had never known. The same may be said of Wordsworth, with a difference. He has revealed, in the homeliest aspects of humble life, a beauty and worth not recognized before, or long forgotten. He has opened for men new sources of interest in their kind, not only in shepherds and peasants, but in tattered beggars, and gypsies, and wayworn tramps.

Much stuff has been talked and written about Wordsworth being a merely subjective poet. Critics had good need to be sure they were right before they characterize great poets by such vague, abstract words; for they quickly get into the minds of the reading public, and stick there, and do much mischief. True it is that Wordsworth has read his own soul, not that which was accidental or peculiar in him, but that which he had in common with all high and imaginative men. But is this all? has he done nothing more? If ever man caught the soul of things, not himself, and expressed it, Wordsworth did. That he has done it in nature almost limitlessly we have seen. In man he has done it not less truly, though more restrictedly. Taking the restrictions at their utmost, what contemporary poet (I do not speak of Scott in his novels) has left to his country such a gallery of new and individual portraits as a permanent possession? The deeper side of character no doubt it is, — the heart of men, not their clothes, — but it is character in which there is nothing of himself, nothing which all men might not or do not share. The affliction of Margaret, the Mad Mother, Gypsies, Laodamia, the Highland Reaper, the Waggoner, Peter Bell, Matthew, Michael, the Cumberland Beggar, all the tenants of the Churchyard among the Mountains — what are these? What, but so many separate, individual, outstanding portraits, into which all of himself that enters is only the eye that can see and read their souls on their deeper side. For it is not their outward contour, nor their complexion, nor dress, he busies himself with. He painted, as Titian and Leonardo did their great portraits, with the deeper soul predominating in the countenance. If he seized this, he cared little for the rest. Let us discard, then, that foolish talk about Wordsworth as a merely subjective poet, who could give nothing but his own feelings, or copies of his own countenance.

There are many other aspects in which this vital power of imagination in Wordsworth might be viewed. Only one more of these I must note, and then pass on. He pushed the domain of poetry into a whole field of subjects hitherto unapproached by the poets. In him, perhaps more than any other contemporary writer either of prose or verse, we see the highest spirit of this century, in its contrast with that of the preceding, summed up and condensed. What most strikes one, in recurring to the poetry of the Pope and Addison period, is its external character, and the limited range of subjects which it dealt with. In the writings of that time, the play of the intellect is little leavened by sentiment, little of individual character is suffered to transpire. The heart, it would seem, was either dormant, or kept under strict surveillance, and not allowed to interfere with the working of the understanding. Literature appeared like a well-bred, elderly gentleman in ruffles and peruke, of polished but somewhat chilling manners, which meet all warmth of feeling with the frost of etiquette. And just as in such society conversation is restricted to certain subjects, of these touches but the surface, and does even that in set phrases, so it was with the literature of the golden days of Queen Anne and the first two Georges. From this very limitation in the range both of subjects and treatment, there arose in the hands of the masters a perfection of style within these limits; just as in the finitude of Grecian architecture, perfection is more easily attained than in Gothic with its infinite aims. In the writers who followed, so-called classicism degenerated into conventionality in subject, in treatment, and in language. In Cowper, as has been said, we see the beginning of the recoil. But it was by Wordsworth that the revolt was most openly proclaimed and most fully carried out. The changed spirit was no doubt in the time, and would have made its way independently of any single man. But no one power could have helped it forward more effectually than the capacious and inward-seeing soul of Wordsworth. Whereas the poetry of the former age had dealt mainly with the outside of things, or if it sometimes went further, did so with such a stereotyped manner and diction as to make it look like external work, Wordsworth everywhere went straight to the inside of things. We have seen already how, whether in his own self-revelations, or in his descriptions of the visible creation, or in his delineations of men, he passed always from the surface to the centre, from the outside looks to the inward character. This one characteristic set him in entire opposition to the art of last century. Out of it arose the entire revolution he made in subjects, treatment, and diction. Seeing in many things which had hitherto been deemed unfit subjects for poetry, a deeper truth and beauty than in those which had hitherto been most handled by the poets, he reclaimed from the wilderness vast tracts that had been lying waste, and brought them within the poetic domain. In this way he has done a wider service to poetry than any other poet of his time, but since him no one has arisen of spirit strong and large enough to make full proof of the liberty he bequeathed.

The same freedom, and by dint of the same powers, he won for future poets with regard to the language of poetry. He was the first who both in theory and practice entirely shook off the trammels of the so-called poetic diction which had tyrannized over English poetry for more than a century. This diction of course exactly represented the half-courtly, half-classical mode of thinking and feeling. As Wordsworth rebelled against this conventionality of spirit, so against the outward expression of it. The whole of the stock phrases and used-up metaphors he discarded, and returned to living language of natural feeling, as it is used by men, instead of the dead form of it which had got stereotyped in books. And just as in his subjects he had taken in from the waste much virgin soil, so in his diction he appropriated for poetic use a large amount of words, idioms, metaphors, till then by the poets disallowed. In doing so, he may here and there have made a mistake, the homely trenching on the ludicrous, as in the lines about the washing-tub and some others, long current in the ribaldry of critics. But, bating a few almost necessary failures, he did more than any other by his usage and example to reanimate the effete language of poetry, and restore to it healthfulness, strength, and feeling. His shorter poems, both the earlier and the later, are for the most part very models of natural, powerful, and yet sensitive English; the language being like a garment woven out of and transparent with the thought. Of the diction of his longer blank verse poems, which is far from being so faultless, I shall have something to say in the sequel.

As to the theory which he propounds in his famous Preface, that the language of poetry ought nowise to differ from that of prose, this is only his protest against the old poetic phraseology, too sweepingly laid down. His own practice is the best commentary on, and antidote to, his theory, where he has urged it to an extrème. Coleridge and De Quincey have both criticised the "Preface" severely, so that in their hands it would seem to contain either a paradox or a truism. Into this subject I cannot now enter. This only may be said on the Wordsworthian side, as against these critics, that while the language of prose receives new life and strength by adopting the idioms and phrases used in the present conversation of educated men, that of poetry may go further, and borrow with advantage the language from cottage firesides. Who has ever listened to a peasant father or mother describing the last illness of one of their own children, or speaking of those who were gone, without having heard from their lips words which, for natural and expressive feeling, were the very essence of poetry! Poets may well adopt these, for, if they trust to their own resources, they can invent nothing equal to them.

These reflections on the main characteristics of Wordsworth arose out of a survey of the poems written during his first Grasmere period. But they have passed beyond the bounds for which they were originally intended, and may apply in large measure to his poems of the second period, written at Allan Bank in Grasmere, and during his first years at Rydal Mount. These were "The Excursion," "The White Doe of Rylstone," "The Duddon Sonnets," and some smaller poems. In these there is perhaps less of that ethereal light, that spiritualizing power shed over nature, which forms the peculiar charm of the best of his earlier poems. But if there is less penetrating interpretation of nature, there is a deepened moral wisdom, a larger entering into the heart of universal man. I spoke above of the limitations of his earlier poetry in this latter region. These in his later poems are perhaps less apparent, partly from the expansion of the philosophic mind by years of meditation, and by kindly though limited intercourse with men; partly from a gradual lessening of the exclusive bias towards humble life, as his Republican fervor abated.

To discuss "The Excursion," as its importance demands, would require a long separate treatise. It was a theme worthy of a great philosophic poem, which Wordsworth proposed to himself. A being, like the Solitary, by domestic bereavement, and by ardent hopes of the first French Revolution, too rudely disappointed, driven into skepticism and despondency — how can such an one win his way back to sympathy with man, and to faith in God? The outward circumstances of such a subject may vary, but itself is of perennial import. French Revolutions may not repeat themselves with every generation, but unbelieving cynicism is an evil of continual recurrence, — an evil which is not checked by, but would rather seem increasingly to attend on, our much vaunted march of mind. As to the poet's way of dealing with the problem, there is ground for the disappointment which many have felt, that the truths of revelation, though everywhere acknowledged, are nowhere brought prominently forward. It is the religion which the poet has extracted from nature and man's moral instincts on which he mainly dwells; yet it is such a religion, so pure and so elevated, as these sources, but for the light they draw from the revelation close at hand, never could have supplied. In the crisis of the poem, when the poet has to apply his medicine to the mind diseased, and when the Solitary is importunate for an answer, the poet turns aside, and recommends communion with nature, and free intercourse with men, in a way which to many has seemed like a disavowal of the power of Christian faith. This seems, however, too severe a judgment. Wordsworth knew clearly that there are many cases in which, as the passages to the heart have been closed by false reasonings and morbid views, the way to it is not to be found by any direct arguments, however true. What is wanted is some antidote which shall bring back the feelings to a healthful tone, remove obstructions from within, and so, through restored health of heart, put the understanding in a condition which is open to the power of truth. Awaken healthful sensibilities in the heart, and a right state of intellect will be sure to follow. This is Wordsworth's moral pathology. And the restorative discipline he recommends is that which in his own mental trial he had found effectual. This I believe to be the true account; and yet one cannot help thinking there was not only room, but even a call for a fuller acknowledgment of the Christian verities. The defect probably arose from the poet's carrying his own experience, and his peculiar views about the sanative power of nature, further than they hold true, at least for the majority of men. While such is the advice given to the Solitary, the course practically taken is to lead him to the churchyard among the mountains at Grasmere, there to hear from the lips of the pastor how they lived and died, the lowly tenants of the surrounding graves, in order that hearing he may learn —

> "To prize the breath we share with human kind;
> And look upon the dust of man with awe."

To many who little care for the philosophy, "The Excursion" will always be dear for the pictures of mountain scenes, and the pathetic records of rural life which it contains. The two books of the "Churchyard among the Mountains," are beyond all the others sustained in interest, and perfect in style. In themselves they form a noble poem, full of deep insight into the heart, of attractive portraits of character, and of tender and elevating views of human life and destiny. No one with a heart to feel can read them carefully without being the better for it. Of all the lives there portrayed, perhaps there is none which goes so straight to the heart as the affecting story of Ellen: —

> "As, on a sunny bank, a tender lamb
> Lurks in safe shelter from the winds of March,
> Screened by its parent, so that little mound
> Lies guarded by its neighbor; the small heap
> Speaks for itself; an Infant there doth rest;
> The sheltering hillock is the Mother's grave.
> If mild discourse, and manners that conferred
> A natural dignity on humblest rank;
> If gladsome spirits, and benignant looks,
> That for a face not beautiful did more
> Than beauty for the fairest face can do;
> And if religious tenderness of heart,

Grieving for sin, and penitential tears
Shed when the clouds had gathered and disstained
The spotless ether of a maiden life;
If these may make a hallowed spot of earth
More holy in the sight of God or man;
Then, on that mound, a sanctity shall brood
Till the stars sicken at the day of doom."

Then follows the character of the cottage girl, her love, betrayal, the broken vow; her shame and sorrow, relief by the birth of her child, the necessity to leave her own and nurse a neighbor's; her own child's sickness, and her cruelly enforced absence from it; its death, her long vigils by its grave, a weeping Magdalene — ended by her own decline: —

"Meek saint! through patience glorified on earth!
In whom, as by her lonely hearth she sate
The ghastly face of cold decay put on
A sun-like beauty, and appeared divine!
. . . . . . She said,
'He who afflicts me knows what I can bear;
And, when I fail, and can endure no more,
Will mercifully take me to Himself'
So through the cloud of death her spirit passed
Into that pure and unknown world of love
Where injury cannot come."

They say that Wordsworth wants passion. For feeling, not on the surface but in the depth, pathos pure and profound, what of modern verse can equal this story and that of Margaret? The very roll of these lines above quoted is oracular. There is in them the echo of a soul the most capacious, tender, and profound, that has spoken through modern poetry.

The mention of these lines suggests one word in passing, on Wordsworth's blank verse. In "The Excursion," and more still in "The Prelude," it often greatly needs condensation, may even be said to be tediously prolix. When speaking of homely matters, there is circumlocution at times amounting to awkwardness ; and when philosophizing there is, unlike the smaller poems, too profuse a use of long-winded Latin words, to the neglect of the mother Saxon. Yet, even in these passages, there is hardly a page without some atoning lines in the true Wordsworthian mould. Even in those disquisitions of "The Excursion" which seem most prosy, as the paragraphs on a system of National Education, there are seldom wanting some of those glances of deeper vision, by which old neglected truths are flashed with new power on the consciousness, or new relations of truth, which had hitherto lain hidden, are for the first time revealed. Of such apothegms of moral wisdom, how large a number could be gleaned from that poem alone! But it is in the passages where Wordsworth's inspiration kindles that the full power of his blank verse is to be seen. Wordsworth's blank verse, so prolix in ordinary narrative, so grand in its loftier passages, brings forcibly to mind what I once heard Hartley Coleridge say of his whole poetry. When employed to do a hackney's work along the common highway, he stumbles and blunders at almost every step; it is only when he strikes a higher strain and "soars steadily into the region" that you discover him to be a veritable Pegasus. His blank verse is seen at its best in such passages of "The Excursion" as these: The Wanderer's account of his own feelings when, a boy, he watched the sunrise over Athole, and indeed the whole description of his boyhood ; the story of Margaret, already spoken of; the description of the Langdale Pikes; the Solitary's history of himself; the Wanderer's advice to him at the close of Despondency Corrected; and I may add, almost the whole of the two books of the Churchyard. On the characters who form the chief speakers in the poem, the Pedlar or Wanderer, the Solitary, and the Pastor, I cannot now dwell. Those who wish to see from what materials Wordsworth framed them, will find some interesting memoranda from his own lips, contained in the biography by his nephew, and now incorporated in the edition of his Poems of 1857. It seems strange to look back to the outcry that was long made against the employment of a pedlar as the chief figure of the poem. That this should now seem to most quite natural, or at least noways offensive, may serve to mark the change in literary feeling which Wordsworth himself did so much to introduce.

"The Excursion" was published in 1814, and the following year brought to light another long poem, "The White Doe of Rylstone." A great part of it, however, had been composed as early as 1807, while Wordsworth was on a visit to his wife's family at Sockburn-upon-Tees. Whether he then visited Bolton Abbey and its neighborhood for the first time does not appear. This poem, pronounced by the great critic of the day to be "the very worst poem he ever saw imprinted in a quarto volume," has a very bewitching and unique charm of its own. The scene is laid in the days of Queen Elizabeth, and begins and ends with Bolton Priory, and the story of a white doe which haunts it. This doe had been the favorite of Emily Norton, sole daughter of Richard Norton of Rylstone Hall, who, with his eight sons, had marched forth in the army of the Catholic Lords engaged in the insurrection known as the Rising of the North. Emily and a ninth son, Francis, were of the Protestant faith, and disapproved of the enterprise. But he, without taking part in the expedition, follows his father, to be of what use he can; sees him and his eight brothers led to execution, and is himself accidentally slain, and buried in Bolton Priory. The sister's lot is to remain behind, to hear of the utter extinction of her house, and by force of passive fortitude, —

"To abide
The shock, and finally secure
O'er pain and grief a triumph pure."

The white doe, which had been her companion in happier days, comes to her side and seems to enter into her sorrow, attends her when on moonlight nights she visits Bolton Abbey, and her brothers' grave, and long years after she is gone continues to haunt the hallowed place and couch by that same grave. "Everything attempted by the principal personages fails in its material effects, succeeds in its moral and spiritual." This is Wordsworth's own account of it. Certainly the active and warlike parts of the poem are needlessly tame and unexciting, forming a marked contrast with the way Scott would have handled the same subjects. That Wordsworth could, if he had chosen, have improved these parts of his poem, there can be no doubt, for the song of "Brougham Castle," and several of the warlike sonnets prove that he could, when so minded, strike a Tyrtæan strain. But if, in "The White Doe," he fails where Scott would have succeeded, he does what neither Scott nor any one else could equally have done. It is, in truth, a poem not of action at all, but entirely of sentiment, and sentiment as deep as life. Gazing on Bolton's ruined abbey, as it stands on its green holm, looked down on by majestic woods and quiet uplands, and lulled by the murmuring Wharf, his whole heart is filled by the impressive and hallowed scene. And all the feelings awakened within him he gathers up and concentrates in this legendary creature, making her at every turn, whether passing into shadow under broken arch, or throwing a gleam into gloomy vault, or crouching in the moonlight on the last Norton's green grave, bring out some new lineament, call up some fair imagination. She is the most perfectly ideal embodiment of the finer spirit of the place that it could have entered into poet's heart to conceive.

Of "Peter Bell" and "The Wagoner," both composed long before, but published after "The White Doe," I have not now space to say one word. At the time when he was preparing his eldest son for college, Wordsworth studied carefully several of the Latin poets, which led to his attempting two or three poems on classical subjects. One of these, "Laodamia," will always stand out prominent even among his happiest productions. Throwing himself naturally into the situation, he informs the old Achaian legend with a fine moral dignity peculiarly his own: —

> "Elysian beauty, melancholy grace,
> Brought from a pensive, though a happy place."

At the same time there is a visible change from the simple homespun Saxon diction of the lyrical ballads to a more full-mouth amplitude which suited well such a subject as "Laodamia," but which grew upon him more and more till it became verbosity.

And now but a word on the third period of Wordsworth's poetry. This began, one may say, about the year 1820, and lasted till the close of his poetic life. It was the time when he wrote the "Ecclesiastical Sonnets," which, though containing here and there some gems, — such as that on "Old Abbeys" —

> "Once ye were holy, ye are holy still;
> Your spirit freely let me drink, and live;"

are not, on the whole, equal to many of his earlier ones. Sonnet writing begun at Grasmere, had long been a favorite relaxation with him in the midst of larger works. The sonnets are like small off-lets from the main stream of his poetry, into which whatever thoughts from time to time arose might overflow. This form is well fitted for the detached musings of a meditative poet. As each new thought awakes, a new form for it has not to be sought, the mould is here ready, and all the poet has to do is to cast the liquid metal into it. Wordsworth's sonnets are so numerous and so important that they form quite a literature, which, if justice were done them, would demand an extended notice for themselves. The rest of the poems of this epoch are memorials of four separate tours: two on the Continent in 1830 and 1837, two in Scotland in 1831 and 1833. Taken as a whole, none of these tours produced anything equal to his earliest one in Scotland. But the former of the two continental tours produced one poem almost equal to any of his prime, that on the Eclipse in 1820. The description there of Milan Cathedral, with its white hosts of angels, and its starry zone, —

> "All steeped in that portentous light,
> All suffering dim eclipse,"

is in his finest later style.

But that among all these later poems which most wins regard is the beautiful and affecting thread of allusion to Walter Scott that runs through them. Open-minded appreciation of contemporary poets was not one of Wordsworth's strong points. A very marked one-sidedness, not hard to explain, arose out of at once his weakness and his strength. Disparaging remarks about Scott's poetry were reported from his conversation, and these seem to have been present to Lockhart's thought as he penned his last notice of

Wordsworth. He might have recalled at the same time the many kind and beautiful lines in which he who never said in verse what he did not truly feel, has embodied his feelings about Scott. Wordsworth had cordially welcomed "The Lay of the Last Minstrel," and always continued to like it best of Scott's poems. He and the "Shirra" first met in the latter's house in Lasswade, just after Wordsworth and his sister had left Yarrow unvisited —

"For when we're there, although 'tis fair,
'Twill be another Yarrow."

In 1814, as he descended from Traquair accompanied by the Ettrick Shepherd, he exclaimed —

"And is this — Yarrow? — *This* the stream
Of which my fancy cherished,
So faithfully a waking dream?
An image that hath perished!"

In September 1831, Wordsworth and his daughter Dora set out on a visit to Abbotsford, to see Scott once more before the latter left Tweedside for Italy in hopes of repairing there his broken health. It was a brief visit, as Scott was on the very eve of his departure, but, ere they parted, they snatched one more look at Yarrow, — the last both for Scott and Wordsworth: —

"Once more, by Newark's Castle-gate
Long left without a warder,
I stood, looked, listened, and with thee,
Great Minstrel of the Border."

And though the hand of sickness lay heavy upon Scott, they did their best —

"To make a day of happy hours,
Their happy days recalling."

But throughout the "Yarrow Revisited," written in remembrance of that day, there is visible the pressure of an actual grief, little in harmony with the pensive ideal light that is upon the two former Yarrows. "On our return in the afternoon," says Wordsworth, "we had to cross Tweed (by the old ford) directly opposite Abbotsford. The wheels of our carriage grated upon the pebbles in the bed of the stream that there flows somewhat rapidly. A rich, but sad light, of rather a purple than a golden hue, was spread over the Eildon Hills at that moment, and thinking it probable that it might be the last time Sir Walter would cross the stream, I was not a little moved, and expressed some of my feelings in the sonnet beginning —

"'A trouble not of clouds, or weeping rain.'"

This is the noble sonnet in which he says —

"The might
Of the whole world's good wishes with him goes;
Blessings and prayers in nobler retinue
Than sceptred king or laureled conqueror knows,
Follow this wondrous Potentate."

"At noon, on Thursday," Wordsworth continues, "we left Abbotsford, and on the morning of that day Sir Walter and I had a serious conversation *tête-à-tête*, when he spoke with gratitude of the happy life which, upon the whole, he had led. He had written in my daughter's album before he came into the breakfast-room that morning, a few stanzas addressed to her; and while putting the book into her hand, in his own study, standing by his desk, he said to her in my presence, 'I should not have done anything of this kind, but for your father's sake — they are probably the last verses I shall ever write.'" And they were the very last. I remember one most affecting stanza of these lines, which I heard long ago from one who had seen them in the album, — that same album which contained autograph and unpublished lines written by Coleridge, Southey, and other poets of the time, for Wordsworth's daughter. When I wrote this two years ago, the lines had never been made public; and therefore I felt that I had no right to give the stanza which I remembered. Since then, Bishop Wordsworth has quoted it in a published letter, and the seal of secrecy is thus removed. The allusion is to Scott's early friendship with Wordsworth: —

" 'Tis well the gifted eye which saw
The first faint sparks of genius burn,
Should mark its latest flash with awe,
Low glimmering from its funeral urn."

They who wish to see all the four stanzas will find them, along with an interesting note, in the " Selections from the Works of Scott," lately edited by Mr. Mortimer Collins, in Moxon's " Miniature Poets."

During the same journey, Wordsworth seems to have revisited, besides Yarrow, other places in Scotland, which he had seen and sung in his earlier day. Among these he again passed through the Trosachs, bright with their autumnal glory. The record of this visit is that sonnet, so full of the calm, yet not mournful meditation which that season brings everywhere, and especially in such a place, deepened, perhaps, by his feeling for the Border Minstrel from whom he had just parted: —

" There's not a nook within this solemn Pass,
But were an apt confessional for one
Taught by his summer spent, his autumn gone,
That life is but a tale of morning grass
Withered at eve. From scenes of art which chase
That thought away, turn, and with watchful eyes
Feed it 'mid Nature's old felicities,
Rocks, rivers, and smooth lakes more clear than glass
Untouched, unbreathed upon."

Compare this with the stave which Wordsworth chanted on the same ground long before, when —

"Stepping westward seemed to be
A kind of heavenly destiny:
I liked the greeting; 'twas a sound
Of something without place or bound,
And seemed to give me spiritual right
To travel through that region bright.
The voice was soft, and she who spake
Was walking by her native lake;
The salutation had to me
The very sound of courtesy:
Its power was felt, and while my eye
Was fixed upon the glowing sky,
The echo of the voice enwrought
A human sweetness with the thought
Of travelling through the world that lay
Before me in my endless way."

Between the sonnet and these lines, the one in his best early, the other in his best latest style, you have the whole difference between the vernal hopefulness, the ethereal ideality of his prime, and the sober coloring, the more chastened feeling which thirty years had brought.

Once again, in 1833, Wordsworth visited Scotland, but by that time Scott was lying in the ruined aisle at Dryburgh, within sound of his own Tweed. Two years after this, in the autumn of 1835, on hearing of the death of the Ettrick Shepherd, he poured forth that fine lament over his brother poets who had followed each other so fast "from sunshine to the sunless land." In it he alludes once again to his two visits to Yarrow, the one with the shepherd-poet for his guide, the other with Sir Walter.

Once more, the last time, when on a tour in Italy in 1837, amid the "Musings near Aquapendente," his heart reverts to Scott. Seeing the broom in flower on an Italian hill-side, his thoughts turned homeward to think how it would be budding on Fairfield and Helvellyn. Then the thought strikes him, what use of coming so far to see these new scenes, if his thoughts kept wandering back to the old ones?

"The skirt of Greenside fell,
And by Glenridding-screes, and low Glencoign,
Places forsaken now, though loving still
The Muses, as they loved them in the days
Of the old minstrels and the border bards."

One there was, he says, who would have sympathized with him —

"Not the less
Had his sunk eye kindled at those dear words
That spake of bards and minstrels; and his spirit
Had flown with mine to old Helvellyn's brow,
Where once together, in his day of strength,
We stood rejoicing, as if earth were free
From sorrow like the sky above our heads."

He alludes to the day, then thirty years gone, when Sir Walter, Sir Humphry Davy, and Wordsworth had ascended Helvellyn together. Then he goes on: —

"Years followed years, and when, upon the eve
Of his last going from Tweedside, thought turned,
Or by another's sympathy was led
To this bright land, Hope was for him no friend,
Knowledge no help; Imagination shaped
No promise. Still, in more than ear-deep seats,
Survives for me, and cannot but survive
The tone of voice which wedded borrowed words
To sadness not their own, when, with faint smile
Forced by intent to take from speech its edge,
He said, 'When I am there, although 'tis fair,
Twill be another Yarrow.' . . .

"Peace to his spirit! why should Poesy
Yield to the lure of vain regret, and hover
In gloom on wings with confidence outspread
To move in sunshine! Utter thanks, my soul!
Tempered with awe, and sweetened by compassion
For them who in the shades of sorrow dwell,
That I — so near the term to human life
Appointed by man's common heritage —
Am free to rove where Nature's loveliest looks,
Art's noblest relics, history's rich bequests,

> Failed to reanimate and but feebly cheered
> The whole world's Darling."

This poem, and the one suggested by Hogg's death, burst out from the somewhat tamer reflections of his later days as the last gleams of his old fervor. Henceforth he wrote little more poetry, but he continued almost to the end to keep retouching his former poems. Careful as he had always been in the work of composition, he went over them again and again in his later years, changing them here and there, but seldom for the better. What seemed asperities were smoothed away, but for the most part the original ruggedness is poorly exchanged for the more faultless, but tamer, afterthought. It would be an interesting, and for those who make a study of these things a profitable, task, to bring together, by comparing one edition with another, the successive changes which many well-known lines were in this way made to endure. One or two specimens only must now suffice. In "The Solitary Reaper," instead of the strong vernacular line —

> "I listened, till I had my fill,"

of the original edition, we now have the faultless, but tame —

> "I listened, motionless and still."

Again, in the poem describing Mary Hutchinson, —

> "And yet a spirit still, and bright
> With something of an angel light,"

there is one change to "angelic light," and in another edition I think I have seen "celestial light." Again, in that consummate sonnet, beginning —

> "It is a beauteous evening, calm and free,"

some one had suggested that *beauteous* is an *album* word, and so the first line was tortured into —

> "A fairer face of heaven could not be;"

and again into something like this —

> "From fret and stir the clouds are free,"

as I remember once seeing it printed. Happily the original line is now restored. But in the same sonnet the first form of the line —

> "The gentleness of heaven is on the sea,"

with its transparent simplicity, has been finally superseded by the more commonplace —

> "The gentleness of heaven broods o'er the sea."

During those silent years, the aged poet might be seen in green old age (and who that has seen that venerable figure will forget it?), either as he moved about the roads in the neighborhood of Rydal Mount, or drove towards Grasmere or Ambleside in his small, rustic-looking phaeton, or as he appeared on Sundays, in the corner of the family pew near the pulpit. in the small church of Rydal. There, Sunday by Sunday, he was seated, his head inclining forwards, and the long silver white hair like a crown of glory on either side of the broad majestic brow.

Towards the close of 1847, the household at Rydal Mount was darkened by a great grief, the death of the poet's daughter Dora, Mrs. Quillinan. "Our sorrow, I feel, is for life," he wrote, "but God's will be done!" And it was for life. At the age of seventy-seven such a loss was not to be got over. Still, with firm step, though saddened heart, he might be seen going about. As late as the autumn of 1849, as a stranger came down the road from the back of Rydal Mount, he met Wordsworth walking slowly back towards his house from the highway, to which he had just conducted some visitors. His head leant to one side, somewhat as it does in his picture, and in his hand he carried a branch with withered leaves. He who passed him happened to have on a plaid, wrapt round him in Scottish shepherd's fashion. This attracted his notice, and as the stranger looked round, thinking it might be the last sight he should ever have of him, the poet had turned round, and was looking back too. There was one long look, but no word, and both passed on.

> "Matthew is in his grave, yet now,
> Methinks, I see him stand,
> As at that moment, with a bough
> Of wilding in his hand."

In the March of next year he was still able to walk to Grasmere and to Ambleside, the last two walks he took. The last day he was out of doors, he sat down on the stone seat of a cottage porch, where he had been calling, and watched the setting sun. It was a cold, bright evening, and he got a chill which resulted in pleurisy. He survived the attack, but sank from after weakness. On the 7th of April, his eightieth birthday, he was prayed for in Rydal chapel, morning and evening. On Saturday, the 20th, when asked by his son whether he would receive the communion, he replied, "That is just what I want." When his wife wished to let him know that there was no hope of recovery, she said to him, "William, you are going to Dora." He made no answer at the time, but next day, as one of his nieces drew aside his curtain, he awoke from a quiet sleep, and said, "Is that Dora?" He breathed his last, almost imperceptibly, on Tuesday the 23d of April, exactly at noon, the same day as that on which Shakespeare was born and died.

A few days after, he was laid in that corner of Grasmere churchyard where his children had been laid before him, and to which his wife and sister have since been gathered. A plain blue stone, with no other word on it than "William Wordsworth," marks the spot. On one side of it are the eight yew-trees planted there long before, under his direction, and carefully tended by himself. On the other, the Rotha, through a clear, calm, deep pool, creeps quietly by. Fairfield, Helm-crag, and Silver-How look down upon his grave. Westminster contains no resting-place so fit for him.

And now, looking back on those fourscore years, may it not be said that if any life in modern times has been well-rounded and complete, Wordsworth's was? From first to last it was one noble purpose, faithfully kept, thoroughly fulfilled. The world has rarely seen so strong and capacious a soul devote itself to one, and that a lofty end, with such singleness and concentration of aim. No doubt there was a great original mind to begin with, one that saw more things, and deeper, than any other poet of his time. But what would this have achieved, had it not been backed by that moral strength, that ironness of resolve? It was this that enabled him to turn aside from professions that he was little suited for, and with something less than a hundred a year face the future. In time, doubtless, other helps were added, and long before the end he had obtained a competence. But this is only another instance of the maxim, "Providence helps those who help themselves." That life at Town-End had encountered and overcome the difficulty before the help came. Again, the same moral fortitude appears in the firmness with which he kept his purpose, and the industry with which he wrought it out. Undiscouraged by neglect, undeterred by obloquy and ridicule, in the face of obstacles that would have daunted almost any other man, he held on his way unmoved, and wrought out the gift that was in him till the work was complete. Few poets have ever so fully expressed the thing that was given them to utter. And the result has been that he has bequeathed to the world a body of high thought and noble feeling which will continue to make all who apprehend it think more deeply and feel more wisely to the end of time.

The question has often been asked how far Wordsworth was a religious poet; that he was a religious man no one doubts. In his earlier poems especially, as in "Tintern Abbey," and others, men have pointed to passages, and said, These are in their tendency Pantheistic. The supposition that Wordsworth ever maintained a Pantheistic philosophy, ever held a deliberate theory of the Divine Being as impersonal, is contradicted both by many an express declaration of his own and by what is known of his life.

But it is none the less true that, though he never held the Pantheistic doctrine, the presence of nature, when he was in the heydey of imagination, stirred in him what is called the Pantheistic feeling in its highest and purest form. The subject is a deep one, and to do it justice would require not a few sentences, but a volume. The truth seems to be that the outward world, which to commonplace minds is no more than a piece of dead mechanism, is in reality full of a vast all-pervading life, which is very mysterious. Not to be grasped by the formulas of science, this life is apprehended mainly by the imagination, and by those men most deeply in whom imagination is most ample and profound. Possessing this faculty, larger in measure, and more genuine in quality, than any man since Shakespeare, Wordsworth felt with proportionate intensity the life which fills all nature. In her presence he felt in some measure, as only the first fathers of the Aryan race in the world's infancy felt, the —

"Something far more deeply interfused,
Whose dwelling is the light of setting suns,
And the round ocean, and the living air,
And the blue sky, and in the mind of man:
A motion and a feeling that impels
All thinking things, all objects of all thought,
And rolls through all things."

Comparative mythology is only now deciphering traces of the primeval intuitions of a something Divine in nature, traces which lie far down in the lowest layers of the world's early religions. And those who study those things have found in no other modern poet so many thoughts yielding glimpses into that morning feeling for nature which seems to have vanished with the world's childhood. As life went on with Wordsworth, the visionary gleam grew dimmer, and the moral faith grew stronger, so that his later poems contain less of that mystical feeling about nature which is the peculiar charm of the earlier ones, but more recognition of those truths by which conscience lives, and which Christianity reveals. That he has not clearly bridged over the chasm, has not fully harmonized the earlier with the later feeling, must be admitted. But for this defect, this limitation of insight, who is he that has a right to blame him? — only that man who having felt as broadly and profoundly the infinite life I allude to, has reconciled it with higher religious truth, and taught men so to do. But where is such reconciliation to be found? only here and there in some verses of the Psalms, or in the Prophecies of Isaiah; or still more in brief passages of the Gospels do these two sides of truth seem to meet in harmony.

In Wordsworth's treatment of human nature the same question meets us in another form. In "The Prelude," and other poems of the first epoch, it cannot be denied that the self-restorative power of the soul seems to be asserted, and the sufficingness of nature to console the wounded spirit is implied in a way which Wordsworth, if distinctly questioned, would, perhaps at any time, certainly in his later years, have disavowed. That he was himself conscious of this defect may be gathered from the change he made in the reflections with which the story of Margaret, in "The Excursion," closes. This story was written among the last years of last century, at Racedown or Alfoxden. Through all the early editions of his poems it stood thus: —

"The old man, noting this, resumed, and said,
'My friend! enough to sorrow you have given,
The purposes of wisdom ask no more;
Be wise and cheerful, and no longer read
The forms of things with an unworthy eye.'"

In the one-volume edition of his works, which appeared in 1845, we for the first time read the following addition, inserted after the third line of the above: —

"Nor more would she have craved as due to One
Who, in her worst distress, had ofttimes felt
The unbounded might of prayer; and learned with soul
Fixed on the Cross, that consolation springs,
From sources deeper far than deepest pain,
For the meek Sufferer. Why then should we read
The forms of things with an unworthy eye?"

A little further on, the "Wanderer" proceeds to say that once as he passed that way the ruined cottage conveyed to his heart —

"So still an image of tranquillity,
So calm and still, and looked so beautiful
Amid the uneasy thoughts which filled my mind,
That what we feel of sorrow and despair
From ruin and from change, and all the grief
The passing shows of Being leave behind,
Appeared an idle dream that could not live
Where meditation was."

Instead of the last line and a half, the later editions have the following: —

"Appeared an idle dream that could maintain
Nowhere dominion o'er the enlightened spirit,
Whose meditative sympathies repose
Upon the breast of faith."

To say that as years increased Wordsworth's faith in the vital Christian truth grew more confirmed and deep, and that in himself were fulfilled his own words —

"Peace settles where the intellect is meek,
The faith Heaven strengthens where He moulds the creed,"

is only to say that he was growingly a good man. This growth many a line of his later poems, besides incidental notices in his letters, and other memoranda of his nephew's biography, clearly attests. No doubt the wish will at times arise that the unequaled power of spiritualizing nature, and of originating tender and solemn views of human life, had, for the sake of other men, been oftener and more unreservedly turned on the great truths of Christian faith. When such a regret does arise, it is but fair that it should be tempered by remembering, as he himself urges, that "his works, as well as those of other poets, should not be considered as developing all the influences which his own heart recognized, but rather those which he felt able as an artist to display to advantage." At another time he assured a correspondent that he had been averse to frequent mention of the mysteries of Christian faith, not because he did not duly feel them, but because he felt them too deeply to venture on a free handling of them. Above all, if he has not, any more than the greatest of former poets, done all that our hearts desire, let us be thankful for the work he has done.

What that work is, the great religious poet of the time, himself a disciple of the elder bard, hinted, in the words with which he dedicated to Wordsworth his

Oxford lectures on poetry: "Ut animos ad sanctiora erigeret;" "to raise our minds to holier things."

Perhaps I cannot better sum up the whole matter than by adopting, if I may, the words of a correspondent. He observes, 1st, That while Wordsworth spiritualizes the outward world more than any other poet has done, his feeling for it is essentially manly. Nature, he always insists, gives gladness to the glad, comfort and support to the sorrowful. 2d, There is the wondrous depth of his feeling for the domestic affections, and more especially for the constancy of them. 3d, He must be considered a leader in that greatest movement of modern times — care for our humbler brethren; his part being, not to help them in their sufferings, but to make us reverence them for what they are, what they have in common with us, or in greater measure than ourselves. These are the tendencies breathed from every line he wrote. He took the commonest sights of earth, and the homeliest household affections, and made you feel that these, which men commonly take to be the lowest things, are indeed the highest.

If he seldom ventures within the inner sanctuary, he everywhere leads to its outer court, lifting our thoughts into a region "neighboring to heaven, and that no foreign land." If he was not universal in the sense in which Shakespeare was, and Goethe aimed to be, it was because he was smitten with too deep an enthusiasm for those truths by which he was possessed. His eye was too intense, too prophetic to admit of his looking at life dramatically. In fact, no poet of modern times has had in him so much of the prophet. In the world of nature, to be a revealer of things hidden, the sanctifier of things common, the interpreter of new and unsuspected relations, the opener of another sense in men; in the moral world, to be the teacher of truths hitherto neglected or unobserved, the awakener of men's hearts to the solemnities that encompass them, deepening our reverence for the essential soul, apart from accident and circumstance, making us feel more truly, more tenderly, more profoundly, lifting the thoughts upward through the shows of time to that which is permanent and eternal, and bringing down on the transitory things of eye and ear some shadow of the eternal, till we —

> "Feel through all this fleshly dress
> Bright shoots of everlastingness" —

this is the office which he will not cease to fulfill, as long as the English language lasts. What earth's far-off lonely mountains do for the plains and the cities, that Wordsworth has done and will do for literature, and through literature for society; sending down great rivers of higher truth, fresh purifying winds of feeling, to those who least dream from what quarter they come. The more thoughtful of each generation will draw nearer and observe him more closely, will ascend his imaginative heights, and sit under the shadow of his profound meditations, and, in proportion as they do so, will become more noble and pure in heart.

COLERIDGE.

MORE than enough has perhaps been said in disparagement of the eighteenth century. It is not therefore to speak more evil of that much abused time, but merely to note an obvious fact, if I say that its main tendency was towards the outward and the finite. Just freed from the last ties of feudalism, escaped too from long religious conflicts which had resulted in war and revolution, the feelings of the British people took a new direction; the nation's energies were wholly turned to the pacific working out of its material and industrial resources. Let us leave those deep, interminable questions, which, as experience has shown, lead only to confusion, and let us stick to plain, obvious facts, which cannot mislead, and which yield such comfortable results. This was the genius and temper of the generation that followed the Revolution of 1688. Nor was there wanting a man to give definite shape and expression to this tendency of the national mind. Locke, a shrewd and practical man, who knew the world, furnished his countrymen with a way of thinking singularly in keeping with their then temper; a philosophy which, discarding abstruse ideas, fashioned thought mainly out of the senses; an ethical system founded on the selfish instincts of pleasure and pain; and a political theory which, instead of the theocratic dreams of the Puritans or the divine right of High-

Churchmen, or the historic traditions of feudalism, grounded government on the more prosaic but not less unreal phantasy of an original contract. This whole philosophy, however inconsistent with what is noblest in British history, was so congenial a growth of the British soil, that no other has ever struck so deep a root, or spread so wide, and with such endearing influence. This way of thinking, introduced by Locke for the purpose of moderating the pretensions of human thought, came to be believed in by his followers as its highest achievement. The half century after Locke was no doubt full of mental activity in certain directions. It saw Physical Science attain its highest triumph in the Newtonian discoveries; History studied after a certain manner by votaries more numerous than ever before; and the new science of Political Economy created. But while these fields were thronged with busy inquirers, and though Natural Theology was much argued and discussed, yet from the spiritual side of all questions, from the deep things of the soul, from men's living relations to the eternal world, educated thought seemed to turn instinctively away. The guilds of the learned, as by tacit consent, either eschewed these subjects altogether, or, if they were constrained to enter on them, they had laid down for themselves certain conventional limits, beyond which they did not venture. On the other side of these lay mystery, enthusiasm, fanaticism — spectres abhorred of the wise and prudent. It is a striking proof of how entirely the mechanical philosophy had saturated the age, that Wesley, the leader of the great spiritual counter-movement of last century, the preacher of divine realities to a generation fast bound in sense, yet in the opening of his sermon on Faith indorses the sensational theory, and declares that to man in his natural condition sense is the only inlet of knowledge.

The same spirit which pervaded the philosophy and theology of that era is apparent not less in its poetry and literature. Limitation of range, with a certain perfectness of form, contentment with the surface view of things, absence of high imagination, repression of the deeper feelings, man looked at mainly on his conventional side, careful descriptions of manners, but no open vision, — these are the prevailing characteristics. Doubtless the higher truth was not even then left without some witnesses. Butler and Berkeley in speculation, Burns and Cowper in poetry, Burke in political philosophy, — these were either the criers in the wilderness against the idols of their times, or the prophets of the new truth that was being born. Men's thoughts cannot deal earnestly with many things at once; and each age has its own work assigned it; and the work of the eighteenth century was mainly one of utilitarian understanding, of criticising and questioning things hitherto believed, of active but narrow intelligence divorced from imagination, from deep feeling, from reverence, from spiritual insight. And when this one-sided work was done, the result was isolation, individualism, self-will; the universal in thought lost sight of, the universal in ethics denied; everywhere, in speculation as in practice, the private will dominant, the Universal Will forgotten. To exult over the ignorant past, to glory in the wonderful present, to have got rid of all prejudices, to have no strong beliefs except in material progress, to be tolerant of all tendencies but fanaticism, this was its highest boast. And though this self-complacent wisdom received some rude shocks in the crash of revolution with which the last century closed, and though the soul and spirit that are in man, long unheeded, then once more awoke and made themselves heard, that one-sided and soulless intelligence, if weakened, was not destroyed. It was carried over into this century in the brisk but barren criticism of the early "Edinburgh Review." And at this very moment there are symptoms enough on every side that the same spirit, after having received a temporary repulse, has once more regained the ascendant.

The same manner of thought which we have attempted to describe as it existed in our own country, dominated in others during the same period. So well is it known in Germany that they have a name for it, which we want. They call it by a term which means the Illumination or Enlightenment, and they have marked the notes by which it is known. Some who are deep in German lore tell us that Europe has produced but one power really counteractive of this Illumination, or tyranny of the mere understanding, and that is, the philosophy which began with Kant and culminated in Hegel. And they affect no small scorn for any attempt at reaction which has originated elsewhere. Nevertheless, at the turn of the century, there did arise men nearer home, who felt the defect in the thought of the preceding age, and did much to supply it; who strove to base philosophy on principles of universal reason; and who, into thought and sentiment, dwarfed and starved by the effects of Enlightenment, poured the inspiration of soul and spirit. The men who mainly did this in England were Wordsworth and Coleridge. These are the native champions of spiritual truth against the mechanical philosophy of the Illumination. Of the former of the two, I have already spoken. In something of the same way I propose to place now before my readers some account of the friend of Wordsworth, whom his name naturally recalls, a man not less original nor remarkable — Samuel Taylor Coleridge. And yet, though the two were friends, and shared together many mental sympathies, between the lives and characters of the philosophic poet and the poetic philosopher there was more of contrast than of likeness. The one, robust and whole in body as in mind, resolute in will, and single in purpose, knowing little of books and of other men's thoughts, and caring less for them, set himself, with his own unaided resources, to work out the great original vein of poetry that was within him, and stopped not, nor turned aside, till he had fulfilled his task, had enriched English literature with a new poetry of the deepest and purest ore, and thereby made the world forever his debtor. The other, — master of an ampler and more varied though not richer field, of quicker sympathies, less self-sustained, but touching life and thought at more numerous points, eager to know all that other men had thought and known, and working as well on a basis of wide erudition as on his own internal resources, but with a body that did him grievous wrong, that, far from obeying, frustrated his better aspirations, and a will faltering, and irresolute to follow out the behests of his surpassing intellect, — only drove in a shaft here and there into the vast mine of thought that was in him, and died leaving samples rather of what he might have done, than any full and rounded achievement, — yet samples so rich, so varied, so suggestive, that to thousands they have been the quickeners of new intellectual life, and to this day they stand unequaled by anything his country has since produced. In one point, however, the friends are alike. They both turned aside from professional aims, devoted themselves to pure thought, set themselves to counterwork the mechanical and utilitarian bias of their time, and became the great spiritualizers of the thought of their countrymen, the fountain-heads from which has flowed most of what is high and unworldly and elevating in the thinking and speculation of the succeeding age.

It is indeed strange, that of Coleridge's philosophy, once so much talked of, and really so important in its influence, no comprehensive account has been ever attempted. The only attempt in this direction that I know of, is that made six years after Coleridge's death, and now more than twenty years ago, by one who has since become the chief expounder of that philosophy which Coleridge spent most of his life in combating. In a well-known essay, Mr. Mill, while fully acknowledging that no other Englishman, save only his own teacher Bentham, had left so deep an impress on his age, yet turns aside from making a full survey of Coleridge's whole range of thought, precluded, as he confesses, by his own radical opposition to Coleridge's fundamental principles. After setting forth clearly the antagonistic schools of thought which, since the dawn of philosophy, have divided opinion as to the origin of knowledge, and after declaring his own firm adhesion to the sensational school, and his consequent inability to sympathize with Coleridge's metaphysical views, he passes from this part of the subject, and devotes the rest of his essay mainly to the consideration of Coleridge as a political philosopher. This, however, is but one, and that by no means the chief department of thought, to which Coleridge devoted himself. Had Mr. Mill felt disposed to give to the other and more important of Coleridge's speculations, — his views on metaphysics, on morals, and on religion, — as well as to his criticisms and his poetry, the same masterly treatment which he has given to his politics, any further attempt in that direction might have been spared. But it is characteristic of Mr. Mill, that, though gifted with a power which no other writer of his school possesses, of entering into lines of thought, and of apparently sympathizing with modes of feeling most alien to his own, he still, after the widest sweep of appreciation, returns at last to the ground from which he started, and there entrenches himself within his original tenets as firmly as if he had never caught a glimpse of those other and higher truths, with which his own principles are inconsistent.

Before entering on the intellectual result of Coleridge's labors, and inquiring what new elements he has added to British thought, it may be well to pause for a moment, and review briefly the well-known circumstances of his life. This will not only add a human interest to the more abstract thoughts which follow, but may perhaps help to make them better understood. And if, in contrast with the life of Wordsworth, and with its own splendid promise, the life of Coleridge is disappointing even to sadness, it has not the less for that a mournful interest; while the union of transcendent genius with infirmity of will and irregular impulses, the failure and the penitential regret, lend to his story a humanizing, even a tragic pathos, which touches our common nature more closely than any gifts of genius.

The vicarage of Ottery St. Mary's, Devonshire, was the birthplace and early home of Samuel Taylor Coleridge. As in Wordsworth we saw that his whole character was in keeping with his native Cumberland, — the robust northern yeoman, only touched with genius, — so the character of Coleridge, so far as it had any local hue, seems more native to South England. Is it fanciful to imagine that there was something in that character which accords well with the soft mild air, and the dreamy loveliness that rests on the blue coombes and sea-coves of South Devon? He was born on the 21st of October 1772, nearly two years and a half after Wordsworth's birth, the youngest child of ten by his father's second marriage with Anne Bowden, said to have been a woman of strong practical sense, thrifty, industrious, very ambitious for her sons, but herself without any "tincture of letters." Plainly not from her, but wholly from his father, Samuel Taylor took his temperament. The Rev. John Coleridge, sometime head-master of the Free Grammar School, afterwards vicar of the parish of Ottery St. Mary's, is described as, for his age, a great scholar, studious, immersed in books, altogether unknowing and regardless of the world and its ways, simple in nature and primitive in manners, heedless of passing events, and usually known as "the absent man." In a Latin grammar which he wrote for his pupils, he changed the case which Julius Cæsar named, from the ablative to the Quale-quare-quidditive, just as his son might have done had he ever taken to writing grammars. He wrote dissertations on portions of the Old Testament, with the same sort of discursiveness which his son afterwards showed on a greater scale. In his sermons he used to quote the very words of the Hebrew Scriptures, and the country people would exclaim admiringly, "How fine he was! He gave us the very words the Spirit spoke in." Of his absent fits and his other eccentricities, many stories were long preserved in his own neighborhood, which Coleridge used to tell to his friends at Highgate, till the tears ran down his face at the remembrance. Among other well-known stories, it is told that once when he had to go from home for several days, his wife packed his portmanteau with a shirt for each day, charging him strictly to be sure and use them. On his return, his wife, on opening the portmanteau, was surprised to find no shirts in it. On asking him to account for this, she found that he had duly obeyed her commands, and had put on a shirt every day, but never taken off one. There were all the shirts, not in the portmanteau, but on his own back. With all these eccentricities, he was a good and unworldly Christian pastor, much beloved and respected by his own people. Though Coleridge was only seven years old when his father was removed by a sudden death, he remembered him to the last with deep reverence and love. "O that I might so pass away, if, like him, I were an Israelite without guile! The image of my father — my revered, kind, learned, simple-hearted father — is a religion to me."

During his childhood, he tells us, he never took part in the plays and games of his brothers, but sought refuge by his mother's side, to read his little books and listen to the talk of his elders. If he played at all, it was at cutting down nettles with a stick, fancying them the seven champions of Christendom. He had, he says, the simplicity and docility of a child, but he never thought or spoke as a child.

But childhood with him, such as it was, did not last long. At the age of nine he was removed to a school in the heart of London, Christ's Hospital, "an institution," says Charles Lamb, "to keep those who yet hold up their heads in the world from sinking." The presentation to this charity school, no doubt a great thing for the youngest of so many sons, was obtained through the influence of Judge Buller, formerly one of his father's pupils. "O what a change," writes Coleridge in after years, "from home to this city school; depressed, moping, friendless, a poor orphan, half-starved!" Of this school, Charles Lamb, the school companion, and through life the firm friend of Coleridge, has left two descriptions in his delightful Essays. Everything in the world has, they say, two sides; certainly Christ's Hospital must have had. One cannot imagine any two things more unlike than the picture which Lamb draws of the school in his first essay, and that in the second. The first sets forth the look which the school wore to Lamb himself, a London boy, with his family close at hand, ready to welcome him at all hours, to send him daily supplies of additional food, and with influential friends among the trustees, who, if he had wrongs, would see them righted. The second shows the stepdame side it turned on Coleridge, an orphan from the country, with no friends at hand, forlorn, half starved, "for in those days the food of the Blue-coats was cruelly insufficient for those who had no friends. to supply them." Any one who cares to see these things sketched off as no other could sketch them, may turn to Lamb's essay, "Christ's Hospital Five-and-Thirty Years Ago." "To this late hour of my life," he represents Coleridge as saying, "I trace impressions left by the recollection of those friendless holidays. The long warm days of summer never return, but they bring with them a gloom from the haunting memory of those whole-day leaves, when, by some strange arrangement, we were turned out for the livelong day upon our own hands, whether we had friends to go to or none. I remember those bathing excursions to the New River. How merrily we would sally forth into the fields, and strip under the first warmth of the sun, and wanton like young dace in the streams, getting us appetites for noon, which those of us that were penniless (our scanty morning crust long since exhausted) had not the means of allaying; the very beauty of the day, and the exercise of the pastime, and the sense of liberty setting a keener edge upon them! How faint and languid, finally, we would return towards nightfall to our desired morsel, half rejoicing, half reluctant that the hours of our uneasy liberty had expired." In one of these bathing excursions Coleridge swam the New River in his clothes, and let them dry on his back in the fields. This laid the first seeds of those rheumatic pains and that prolonged bodily suffering which never afterwards left him, and which did so much to frustrate the large promise of his youth.

In the lower school at Christ's the time was spent in idleness, and little was learnt. But even then Coleridge was a devourer of books, and this appetite was fed by a strange accident, which, though often told, must here be repeated once again. One day as the lower schoolboy walked down the Strand, going with his arms as if in the act of swimming, he touched the pocket of a passer-by. "What, so young and so wicked!" exclaimed the stranger, at the same time seizing the boy for a pickpocket. "I am not a pickpocket; I only thought I was Leander swimming the Hellespont." The capturer, who must have been a man of some feeling, was so struck with the answer, and with the intelligence as well as simplicity of the boy, that instead of handing him over to the police, he subscribed to a library, that Coleridge might get thence in future his fill of books. In a short time he read right through the catalogue and exhausted the library. While Coleridge was thus idling his time in the lower school, Middleton, an elder boy, afterwards writer on the Greek article, and Bishop of Calcutta, found him one day sitting in a corner and reading Virgil by himself, not as a lesson, but for pleasure. Middleton reported this to Dr. Bowyer, then head-master of the school, who, on questioning the master of the lower school about Coleridge, was told that he was a dull scholar, could never repeat a single rule of syntax, but was always ready to give one of his own. Henceforth Coleridge was under the head-master's eye, and soon passed into the upper school to be under his immediate care. Dr. Bowyer was one of the stern old disciplinarians of those days, who had boundless faith in the lash. Coleridge was one of those precocious boys who might easily have been converted into a prodigy, had that been the fashion at the time. But, "Thank Heaven," he said, "I was flogged instead of flattered." He was so ordinary looking a boy, with his great black head, that Bowyer, when he had flogged him well, generally bestowed on him an extra cut, "For you are such an ugly fellow." When he was fifteen, Coleridge, in order to get rid of school, wished to be apprenticed to a shoemaker and his wife, who had been kind to him. On the day when some of the boys were to be apprenticed to trades, Crispin appeared and sued for Coleridge. The head-master, on hearing the proposal, and Coleridge's assent, hurled the tradesman from the room with such violence, that had this last been litigiously inclined, he might have sued the doctor for assault. And so Coleridge used to joke, "I lost the opportunity of making safeguards for the understandings of those who will never thank me for what I am trying to do in exercising their reason."

While Coleridge was at school, one of his brothers was attending the London Hospital, and from his frequent visits there the Blue-coat boy imbibed a love of surgery and doctoring, and was for a time set on making this his profession. He devoured English, Latin, and Greek books on medicine voraciously, and had by heart a whole Latin medical dictionary. But this dream gave way, or led on to a rage for metaphysics, which metaphysical reading finally landed him in Voltaire's "Philosophical Dictionary," after perusing which he sported infidel. When this new turn reached Bowyer's ears, he sent for Coleridge. "So, sirrah! you are an infidel, are you? Then I'll flog your infidelity out of you." So saying, the doctor administered the severest, and, as Coleridge used to say, the only just flogging he ever received.

Of this stern scholastic Lamb has left the following portrait: —

"He had two wigs, both pedantic, but of different omen. The one serene, smiling, powdered, betokening a mild day. The other, an old, discolored, unkempt, angry caxon, denoting frequent and bloody execution. Woe to the school when he made his morning appearance in his 'Passy,' or passionate wig. Nothing was more common than to see him make a headlong entry into the school-room from his inner recess or library, and with turbulent eye, singling out a lad, roar out, ''Ods my life, sirrah!' his favorite adjuration, 'I have a great mind to whip you,' then with as sudden a retracting an impulse fling back into his lair, and then, after a cooling relapse of some minutes (during which all but the culprit had totally forgotten the context), drive headlong out again, piecing out his imperfect sense, as if it had been some devil's litany, with the expletory yell, 'and I *will*, too.' In his gentler moods he had resort to an ingenious method, peculiar, for what I have heard, to himself, of whipping a boy and reading the 'Debates' at the same time — a paragraph and a lash between. . . . . Perhaps," adds Lamb, "we cannot dismiss him better than with the pious ejaculation of Coleridge" (the joke was no doubt Lamb's own) "when he heard that his old master was on his death-bed, 'Poor J. B., may all his faults be forgiven, and may he be wafted to bliss by little cherub boys, all head and wings, with no bottoms to reproach his sublunary infirmities.' "

How much of all this may be Lamb's love of fun one cannot say. Coleridge always spoke of Dr. Bowyer with grateful affection. In his literary life he speaks of having enjoyed the inestimable advantage of a very sensible, though severe master; one who taught him to prefer Demosthenes to Cicero, Homer and Theocritus to Virgil, and Virgil to Ovid; who accustomed his pupils to compare Lucretius, Terence, and the purer poems of Catullus, not only with "the Roman poets of the silver, but even with those of the Augustan era, and on grounds of plain sense and universal logic, to see the superiority of the former in the truth and nativeness both of their thoughts and diction." This doctrine was wholesome though rare in those days, not so common even now, so much so that some have supposed that in these and other lessons with which Coleridge credited Dr. Bowyer, he was but reflecting back on his master his own afterthoughts.

While Coleridge was being thus wholesomely drilled in the great ancient models, his own poetic power began to put forth some buds. Up to the age of fifteen, his school verses were not beyond the mark of a clever schoolboy. At sixteen, however, the genius cropped out. The first ray of it appears in a short allegory, written at the latter age, and entitled "Real and Imaginary Time." The opening lines are —

"On the wide level of a mountain's head,
I knew not where; but 'twas some faery place."

In that short piece, short and slight as it is, there is a real touch of his after spirit and melody.

During those years when he was in the upper school, metaphysics and controversial theology struggled for some time with poetry for the mastery; but at last, under the combined influence of a first love and of Bowles's poems, he was led clear of the bewildering maze, and poetry for some years was paramount. It may seem strange now that Bowles's sonnets and early poems, which Coleridge then met with for the first time, should have produced on him so keen an impression of novelty. But so it often happens that what was, on its first appearance, quite original, when we look back upon it in later years, after it has been absorbed into the general taste, seems to lose nearly all its freshness. There can be no doubt of the powerful effect that Bowles had on Coleridge's dawning powers; that he opened the young poet's eyes to what was false and meretricious in the artificial school from Pope to Darwin, and made him feel that here, for the first time in contemporary poetry, natural thought was combined with natural diction — heart reconciled with head. To those who care for these things, it would be worth while to turn to the first chapter of Coleridge's "Literary Life," and see there the first fermenting of his poetic taste and principles. But during those last school years, while his mind was thus expanding, and while his existence was a more tolerable, in some respects even a happy one, he was suffering severely in that body, which throughout life was such a clog to him. Full half his time from seventeen to eighteen was passed in the sick-ward, afflicted with jaundice and rheumatic fever, inherent it may be in his constitution, but doubtless not lessened by those swimmings over the New River in his clothes. But, above these sufferings, which were afterwards so heavily to weigh him down, Coleridge, during his early years, was enabled by buoyancy of heart to rise, and to hide them from ordinary observers. Having dwelt thus long on Coleridge's school-days, because they are very fully recorded, and contain as in miniature both the strength and the weakness of the full-grown man, I may close them with Lamb's description of Coleridge as he appeared in the retrospect of Lamb's school companions: —

"Come back to my memory like as thou wert in the dayspring of my fancies, with hope like a fiery column before thee — the dark pillar not yet turned — Samuel Taylor Coleridge, Logician, Metaphysician, Bard! How have I seen the casual passer through the cloisters stand still, entranced with admiration (while he weighed the disproportion between the speech and the garb of the young Mirandula), to hear thee unfold, in thy deep and sweet intonations, the mysteries of Iamblichus or Plotinus; for even then thou waxedst not pale at such philosophic draughts; or reciting Homer in his Greek, or Pindar; while the walls of the old Grey Friars reëchoed the accents of the inspired charity boy!"

It is hardly possible to conceive two school-times more unlike than this of Coleridge at Christ's, pent up in the heart of London city, and that of Wordsworth at Hawkshead, free of Esthwaite Mere, and all the surrounding solitudes. And yet each, as well in habits and teaching as in outward scenery and circumstance, answers strangely to the character and after lives of the two friends.

Coleridge entered Jesus College, Cambridge, in February 1791, just a month after Wordsworth had quitted the University. On neither of the poets had their University much effect. For neither was that the place and the hour. Coleridge for a time, under the influence of his elder friend Middleton, was industrious, read hard, and obtained the prize for the Greek Sapphic ode. It was on some subject about slavery, and was better in thought than in Greek. Afterwards he tried for the Craven Scholarship, in which contest his rivals were Keat, afterwards head-master of Eton, Bethell, who became an M. P. for Yorkshire, and Butler, the future head of Shrewsbury School and Bishop of Lichfield. The last-named won the scholarship. Out of sixteen or seventeen competitors, Coleridge was selected along with the above three; but he was not the style of man to come out great in University competitions. He had not that exactness and readiness which are needed for those trials; and he wanted entirely the competitive ardor which is with many so powerful an incentive. After this there is no more notice of regular work. His heart was elsewhere — in poetry, with Bowles for guide; in philosophy, with Hartley, who had belonged to his own college; plunging into politics too, which then filled all ardent young minds even to intoxication. For the French Revolution was then in its first frenzy, promising liberty, virtue, regeneration to the old and outworn world. Into that vortex of boundless hope and wild delirium what high-minded youth could keep from plunging? Not Coleridge. "In the general conflagration," he writes, "my feelings and imagination did not remain unkindled. I should have been ashamed rather than proud of myself if they had." Pamphlets were pouring from the press on the great subjects then filling all men's minds; and whenever one appeared from the pen of Burke or other man of power, Coleridge, who had read it in the morning, repeated it every word to his friends gathered round their small supper-tables. Presently one Frend, a Fellow of Jesus College, being accused of sedition, of defamation of the Church of

England, and of holding Unitarian doctrines, was tried by the authorities, condemned, and banished the University. Coleridge sided zealously with Frend, not only from the sympathy which generous youth always feels for the persecuted, but also because he had himself adopted those Unitarian and other principles for which Frend suffered. Hence arose a growing disaffection, which must have weakened his attachment to his University. Other circumstances supervened, which in his second year of residence, brought his Cambridge career to a sudden close.

The loss of Middleton, his trusty friend and guide, who, failing in the final examination, quitted the University without obtaining a fellowship; and the pressure of some college debts, less than £100, incurred through his own inexperience, drove Coleridge into despondency. He went to London, and wandered hopelessly about the streets. At night he sat down on the steps of a house in Chancery Lane, where, being soon surrounded by swarms of beggars, real or feigned, he emptied to them the little money that remained in his pockets. In the morning, seeing an advertisement — "Wanted, Recruits for the 15th Light Dragoons," he said to himself, "Well, I have hated all my life soldiers and horses; the sooner I cure myself of that the better." He enlisted as Private Comberbach, a name, the truth of which he himself was wont to say, his horse must have fully appreciated. A rare sight it must have been to see Coleridge perched on some hard-set, rough-trotting trooper, and undergoing his first lessons in the riding-school, with the riding master shouting out to the rest of the awkward squad, "Take care of that Comberbach; he'll ride over you." For the grooming of his horse and other mechanical duties Coleridge was dependent on the kindness of his comrades, with whom he was a great favorite. Their services he repaid by writing all their letters to their wives and sweethearts. At last the following sentence, written up in the stable under his saddle, "Eheu, quam infortunii miserrimum est fuisse felicem," revealed his real condition to a captain who had Latin enough to translate the words, and heart enough to feel them. About the same time an old Cambridge acquaintance passing through Reading on his way to join his regiment, met Coleridge in the street in dragoon uniform, stopped him when he would have passed, and informed his friends. After about four months' service he was bought off, returned to Cambridge, stayed there but a short time, and finally left in June 1794, without taking a degree.

Then followed what may be called his Bristol period. This included his first friendship with Southey, their dream of emigration, their marriage, Coleridge's first attempts at authorship, and his many ineffectual plans for settling what he used to call the Bread and Cheese Question. On leaving Cambridge he had gone to Oxford, and there met with Southey, still an undergraduate at Balliol, whose friendship, quickly formed, became one of the main hinges on which Coleridge's after life turned. Their tastes and opinions on religion and politics were then at one, though their characters were widely different. Southey, with far less genius than Coleridge, possessed that firmness of will, that definite aim and practical wisdom, the want of which were the bane of Coleridge's life. Southey's high and pure disposition and consistent conduct, combined with much mental power and literary acquirement, made Coleridge feel, as he had not done before, the duty and dignity of bringing actions into accordance with principles, both in word and deed. In after years Southey was to Coleridge a faithful monitor in word, and a friend firm and self-denying in deed. In morality of action, it must be owned that he rose as much above Coleridge, as in genius he fell below him. But at their first meeting, pure and high-minded as Southey was, he had not so fixed his views, or so systematically ordered his life, as he afterwards did. He too, like Coleridge and Wordsworth, had been stirred at heart by the moral earthquake of the French Revolution. Enthusiastically democratic in politics and Unitarian in religion, he at once responded to the day-dream of Pantisocracy, which Coleridge opened to him at Oxford. This was a plan of founding a community in America, where a band of brothers, cultivated and pure-minded, were to have all things in common, and selfishness was to be unknown. The common land was to be tilled by the common toil of the men; the wives, for all were to be married, were to perform all household duties; and abundant leisure was to remain over for social intercourse, or to pursue literature, or in more pensive moods —

> "Soothed sadly by the dirgeful wind,
> Muse on the sore ills they had left behind."

The banks of the Susquehanna were to be this earthly paradise, chosen more for the melody of the name than for any ascertained advantages. Indeed, they hardly seem to have known exactly where their paradise lay. Southey soon left Balliol, and the two friends went to Bristol, Southey's native town, there to prepare for carrying out the Pantisocratic dream. Such visions have been not only dreamed since then, but acted on by enthusiastic youths, and the result leaves no reason to regret that the project of Coleridge and Southey never got further than being a dream. Want of money was, as usual, the immediate cause of the failure; everything else had been provided for, but when it came to the point it was found that neither the two leaders, nor any of the other friends who had embarked in the scheme, had money enough to pay their passage to America. Southey was the first to see how matters stood, and to recant. At this Coleridge was greatly disgusted, and gave vent to his disappointment in no measured language. The scheme was abandoned early in 1795, and the two young poets, having been for some time in love with two sisters of a Bristol family, were married, Coleridge in October of that year to Sarah Fricker, and Southey six weeks later to her sister Edith.

Marriage, of course, brought the money question home to Coleridge more closely than Pantisocracy had done. The three or four following years were occupied with attempts to solve it. But his ability was not of the money making order, nor did his habits, natural or acquired, give even such ability as he had a fair chance in the toil for bread. First he tried lecturing to the Bristol folks on the political topics of the time, and on religious questions. But either the lectures did not pay, or Coleridge did not stick to them steadily, so they were soon given up, and afterwards published as "Conciones ad populum," Coleridge's first prose work. Attacking with equal vehemence Pitt, the great minister of the day, and his opponents, the English Jacobins, Coleridge showed in this his earliest, as in his latest works, that he could not be warranted to run quietly in the harness of any party, and that those who tried to set him to this work were sure of an upset. Coleridge's next enterprise was the publication of a weekly miscellany; the contents were to range over nearly the same subjects as those now discussed in the best weeklies, and the aim was to be, as announced in the motto, that "all may know the truth, and that the truth may make us free." But powerful as he would have been as a contributor, Coleridge was not the man to conduct such an undertaking, least of all to do so single-handed. The most notable thing about "The Watchman" was the tour he made through the Midland county towns with a flaming prospectus, "Knowledge is power," to try the political atmosphere. It was during this tour that Coleridge encountered the Birmingham tallow-chandler, whom he describes with hair like candlewicks, and face pinguinitescent, for it was a melting day with him. After Coleridge had harangued the man of dips for half an hour, and run through every note in the whole gamut of eloquence, now reasoning, now declaiming, now indignant, now pathetic, on the state of the world as it is, compared with what it should be; at the first pause in the harangue the tallow-chandler interposed: "And what might the cost be?" "Only *fourpence* (O the anti-climax, the abysmal bathos of that fourpence!) — only fourpence, sir, each number." "That comes to a deal of money at the end of a year; and how much did you say there was to be for the money?" "Thirty-two pages, sir! large octavo, closely printed." "Thirty and two pages? Bless me! except what I does in a family way on the Sabbath, that's more than I ever reads, sir, all the year round. I am as great a one as any man in Brummagem, sir, for liberty and truth, and all that sort of things, but as to this (no offense, I hope, sir) I must beg to be excused."

Notwithstanding this repulse, Coleridge returned to Bristol triumphant with above a thousand subscribers' names, having left on the minds of all who heard his wonderful conversation an impression that survived long after "The Watchman" was forgotten. The first number appeared on the 1st of March, the tenth and last on the 13th of May, 1796. From various causes, delay in publishing beyond the fixed day, offense given to the religious subscribers by an essay against fast-days, to his democratic patrons by inveighing against Jacobinism and French philosophy, to the Tories by abuse of Pitt, to the Whigs by not more heartily backing Fox, the subscription list rapidly thinned, and he was glad to close the concern at a dead loss of money to himself, not to mention his wasted labor. Though this failure was to him a very serious matter, he could still laugh heartily at the ludicrous side of it. He tells how one morning, when he had risen earlier than usual, he found the servant girl lighting the fire with an extravagant quantity of paper. On his remonstrating against the waste, "La, sir!" replied poor Nanny, "why, it is only Watchmen."

The third of the Bristol enterprises was the publication of his "Juvenile Poems," in the April of 1796, while "The Watchman" was still struggling for existence. For the copyright of these he received thirty guineas, from Joseph Cottle, a Bristol bookseller, who to his own great credit undertook to publish the works of Southey, of Coleridge, and of Wordsworth, at a time when those higher in the trade would have nothing to say to them. If Cottle long afterwards, when their names had waxed great, published a somewhat gossiping book of reminiscences, and gave to the public many petty details which a wiser man would have withheld, it should always be remembered, to his honor, that he showed true kindness and liberality towards these men, especially towards Coleridge, when he greatly needed it, and that he had a genuine admiration of their genius for its own sake, quite apart from its marketable value. No doubt, if any one wishes to see the seamy side of genius, he will find it in the letters and anecdotes of Coleridge preserved in Cottle's book.

Other plans for a livelihood were ventilated during his Bristol sojourn, such as writing for the "Morning Chronicle" and taking private pupils, but as these came to nought, I need only notice one other line in which Coleridge at this time occasionally employed himself, not without some thought of making it a permanent profession. We have seen that before leaving Cambridge he had become a Unitarian, and so he continued till about the time of his visit to Germany. While he was in Bristol he was engaged from time to time to preach in the Unitarian chapels in the neighborhood. The subjects which he there discussed seem to have been somewhat miscellaneous, and the reports of his success vary. Nothing can be more dreary, if it were not grotesque, than Cottle's description of his first appearance as a preacher in a Unitarian chapel in Bath. On the appointed Sunday morning, Coleridge, Cottle, and party drove from Bristol to Bath in a post-chaise. Coleridge mounted the pulpit in blue coat and white waistcoat, and for the morning service, choosing a text from Isaiah, treated his audience to a lecture against the Corn Laws; in the afternoon, he gave them another on the Hair-Powder Tax. The congregation on the latter occasion consisted of seventeen, of whom several walked out of the chapel during the service. The party returned to Bristol disheartened, Coleridge from a sense of failure, the others with a dissatisfying sense of a Sunday wasted. Compare this with Hazlitt's account of his appearance some time afterwards before a Birmingham congregation: —

"It was in January, 1798, that I rose one morning before daylight, to walk ten miles in the mud to hear this celebrated person preach. Never, the longest day

I have to live, shall I have such another walk as that cold, raw, comfortless one. When I got there the organ was playing the 100th Psalm, and when it was done, Mr. Coleridge arose and gave out his text, "He departed again into a mountain himself alone." As he gave out this text, his voice rose like a steam of rich distilled perfumes; and when he came to the two last words, which he pronounced loud, deep, and distinct, it seemed to me, who was then young, as if the sound had echoed from the bottom of the human heart, and as if that prayer might have floated in solemn silence through the universe. The preacher then launched into his subject, like an eagle dallying with the wind. The sermon was upon peace or war, upon Church and State — not their alliance, but their separation; on the spirit of the world and the spirit of Christianity — not as the same, but as opposed to one another. He talked of those who had inscribed the Cross of Christ on banners dripping with human gore. He made a poetical and pastoral excursion, and, to show the fatal effects of war, drew a striking contrast between the simple shepherd-boy, driving his team a-field, or sitting under the hawthorn, piping to his flock as though he should never be old; and the same poor country lad, crimped, kidnapped, brought into town, made drunk at an alehouse, turned into a wretched drummer-boy, with his hair sticking on end with powder and pomatum, a long cue at his back, and tricked out in the finery of the profession of blood.

"'Such were the notes our own loved poet sung.'

"And for myself, I could not have been more delighted if I had heard the music of the spheres. Poetry and Philosophy had met together, Truth and Genius had embraced, under the eye and sanction of Religion. This was even beyond my hopes."

Which of the two was right in his estimate of Coleridge's preaching, Cottle or Hazlitt? Or were both right, and is the difference to be accounted for by Coleridge, like most men of genius, having his days now above himself, now below? With one more passage from Hazlitt, descriptive of Coleridge's talk at that time, I may close his Bristol life: —

"He is the only person I ever knew who answered to the idea of a man of genius. He is the only person from whom I ever learned anything. There is only one thing he might have learned from me in return, but *that* he has not. He was the first poet I ever knew. His genius at that time had angelic wings, and fed on manna. He talked on forever; and you wished him to talk on forever. His thoughts did not seem to come with labor and effort; but as if borne on the gusts of genius, and as if the wings of imagination lifted him off his feet. His voice rolled on the ear like a pealing organ, and its sound alone was the music of thought. His mind was clothed with wings; and raised on them he lifted philosophy to heaven. In his descriptions, you then saw the progress of human happiness and liberty in bright and never ending succession, like the steps of Jacob's ladder, with airy shapes ascending and descending. And shall I who heard him then, listen to him now? Not I! That spell is broke; that time is gone forever; that voice is heard no more: but still the recollection comes rushing by, with thoughts of long past years, and rings in my ears with never-dying sound."

It is pitiful to turn from such high-flown descriptions to the glimpses of poverty and painful domestic cares with which his letters of this date abound. Over these one would gladly draw the veil. Whoso wishes to linger on them may turn him to Cottle. There are many more incidents of this time which I can but name: his residence for some months in a rose-covered cottage in the neighboring village of Clevedon; the birth of his first son, whom he named Hartley, for love of that philosopher whom Coleridge then admired as the wisest of men; his complete reconciliation with Southey on the return of the latter from Portugal. One little entry, in a letter of November 1796, is sadly memorable as the first appearance of

> "The little rift within the lute,
> Which soon will make the music mute."

He complains of a violent neuralgic pain in the face, which for the time was like to overpower him. "But," he writes, "I took between sixty and seventy drops of laudanum, and sopped the Cerberus." That sop was soon to become the worst Cerberus of the two.

It was early in 1797 that Coleridge removed with his family from Bristol, and pitched his tent in the village of Nether Stowey, under the green hills of Quantock. One of the kindest and most hospitable of his friends, Mr. Poole, had a place hard by; and Coleridge having in June made a visit to Wordsworth at Racedown, persuaded this young poet, and his scarcely less original sister, to adjourn thence to the neighboring mansion of Alfoxden. With such friends for daily intercourse, with the most delightful country for walks on every side, and with apparently fewer embarrassments, Coleridge here enjoyed the most genial and happy years that were ever vouchsafed to his changeful existence. "Wherever we turn we have woods, smooth downs, and valleys with small brooks running down them, through green meadows to the sea. The hills that cradle these valleys are either covered with ferns and bilberries or oak woods. Walks extend for miles over the hill-tops, the great beauty of which is their wild simplicity; they are perfectly smooth, without rocks." Over these green hills of Quantock the two young poets wandered for hours together, rapt in fervid talk; Coleridge no doubt the chief speaker, Wordsworth more silent, not less suggestive. Never before or since have these downs heard such high converse. "His society I found an invaluable blessing, and to him I looked up with equal reverence as a poet, a philosopher, and a man." So wrote Coleridge in after years. By this time Wordsworth had given himself wholly to poetry as his work for life. Alfoxden saw the birth of many of the happiest, most characteristic of his shorter poems. Coleridge had some years before this, when he first fell in with Wordsworth's "Descriptive Sketches," found even in these the opening of a new vein. He himself, too, had from time to time turned aside from more perplexing studies, and found poetry to be its own exceeding great reward. But in this Nether Stowey time Coleridge came all at once to his poetic manhood. Whether it was the freedom from the material ills of life which he found in the aid and kindly shelter of Mr. Poole, or the secluded beauty of the Quantock, or the converse with Wordsworth, or all combined, there cannot be any doubt that this was, as it has been called, his *annus mirabilis*, his poetic prime. This was the year of "Genevieve," "The Dark Ladie," "Kubla Khan," "France," the lines to Wordsworth on first hearing "The Prelude" read aloud, the "Ancient Mariner," and the first part of "Christabel," not to mention many other poems of less mark. The occasion which called forth the two latter poems, to form part of a joint volume with Wordsworth, has been already noticed. If Coleridge could only have maintained the high strain he then struck, with half the persistency of his brother poet, posterity might perhaps have had more reason to regret that he should ever have turned to other subjects. During all his time at Nether Stowey he kept up a fire of small letters to Cottle in Bristol, at one time about poems or other literary projects, at another asking Cottle to find him a servant-maid, "simple of heart, physiognomically handsome, and scientific in vaccimulgence!" When they had composed poems enough to form one or more joint volumes, Cottle is summoned from Bristol to visit them. Cottle took Wordsworth in his gig from Bristol to Alfoxden, picking up Coleridge at Nether Stowey. They had brought the viands for their dinner with them in the gig: a loaf, a stout piece of cheese, and a bottle of brandy. As they neared their landing place, a beggar whom they helped with some pence, returned their kindness by helping himself to the cheese from the back of the gig. Arrived at the place Coleridge unyoked the horse, dashed down the gig-shafts with a jerk that rolled the brandy bottle from the seat, and broke it to pieces before their eyes. Then Cottle set to unharnessing the horse, but could not get off the collar. Wordsworth next essayed it, with no better success. At last Coleridge came to the charge, and worked away with such violence that he nearly thrawed the poor horse's head off. He too was forced to desist, with a protest that "the horse's head must have grown since the collar was put on." While the two poets and their publisher were standing thus nonplussed, the servant girl happened to pass through the stable yard, and seeing their perplexity, exclaimed, "La, master you don't go about the work the right way; you should do it like this." So saying, she turned the collar upside down, and slipped it off in a trice.

Then came the dinner, "a superb brown loaf, a dish of lettuces, and, instead of the brandy, a jug of pure water." The bargain was struck, and Cottle undertook the publication of the first edition of the famous "Lyrical Ballads," which appeared in Midsummer, 1798. About the same time the two Messrs. Wedgewood settled on Coleridge £150 a year for life, which made him think no more of Unitarian chapels, and enabled him to undertake, what he had for some time desired, a continental tour. In September of that year the two poets bade farewell, Wordsworth and his sister to Alfoxden, Coleridge to Nether Stowey, and together all three set sail for Hamburg.

So ended the Nether Stowey time, to Coleridge the brief blink of a poetic morning which had no noon; to Wordsworth but the hopeful dawn of a day which completely fulfilled itself.

Landed at Hamburg, Wordsworth was interpreter, as he had French, Coleridge nothing but English and Latin. After an interview with the aged poet Klopstock, the two young poets parted company, Wordsworth, with his sister, settling at Goslar, there to compose, by the German fire-stoves, the poems on "Matthew," "Nutting," "Ruth," "The Poet's Epitaph," and others, in his happiest vein; while Coleridge made for Ratzeburg, where he lived for four months in a pastor's family, to learn the language, and then passed on to Göttingen to attend lectures and consort with German students and professors. Among the lectures were those of Blumenbach on Natural History, while Eichhorn's lectures on the New Testament were repeated to him from notes by a student who had himself taken them down. Wordsworth kept sending Coleridge the poems he was throwing off during this prolific winter, and Coleridge replied in letters full of hope that their future homes might be in the same neighborhood: "Whenever I spring forward into the future with noble affections, I always alight by your side." His whole time in Germany seems to have overflowed with exuberant spirits and manifold life. "Instead of troubling others with my own crude notions, I was better employed in storing my head with the notions of others. I made the best use of my time and means, and there is no period of my life to which I look back with such unmingled satisfaction."

He had passed within a zone of thought new to himself, and up to that time quite unknown in England; one of the great intellectual movements which occur but rarely, and at long intervals, in the world's history. The philosophic genius of Germany which awoke in Kant during the latter part of last century was an impulse the most original, the most far-reaching, and the most profound, which Europe has seen since the Reformation. It has given birth to linguistic science, has recast metaphysics, and has penetrated history, poetry, and theology. For good or for evil, it must be owned that, under the shadow of this great movement, the world is now living, and is likely to live more or less for some time to come. Perhaps we should not call it German philosophy, for philosophy is but one side of a great power which is swaying not only the world's thought, but those feelings which are the parents of its thoughts, as well as of its actions and events. If asked to give in a sentence the spirit of this great movement, most men in this country would feel constrained to answer, as the great German sage is reported to have answered Cousin, "These things do not sum themselves up in single sentences." If any one still insists on a formula, he must seek it from some adroit French critic who will clench the whole thing for him in a phrase, or at most a sentence. Into this great atmosphere, define it how you will, then seething and fermenting, it was that Coleridge passed. Most of his fourteen months were, no doubt, given to acquiring the language, but he could not mingle with those professors and students without catching some tincture of that way of thought which was then busy in all brains. It was not, however, till after his return to England that he studied Kant and other German philosophers. His name will ever be historically associated with the first attempt to introduce these new thoughts to the English mind, which, having been for more than a century steeped to repletion in Lockeism, was now sadly in need of other aliment. Some have reviled Coleridge because he did not know that whole cycle of thought so fully as they suppose that they themselves do. As if anything so all-embracing as German philosophy can be taken in completely at once ; as if the first delver in any mine ever yet extracted the entire ore. But to such impugners it were enough to say, We shall listen with more patience to your accusations, when you have done one half as much to bring home the results of German thought to the educated British mind now, as Coleridge did in his day.

The first fruits, however, of his newly acquired German were poetic, not philosophic. Arriving in London in November, 1799, he set to work to translate Schiller's "Wallenstein," and accomplished in three weeks what many competent judges regard as, notwithstanding some inaccuracies, the finest translation of any poem into the English language. It is a free translation, with here and there some lines of Coleridge's own added where the meaning seemed to him to require it. At the time, the translation fell almost dead from the press, but since that day it has come to be prized as it deserves.

In the autumn of 1799, Coleridge joined Wordsworth on a tour among the lakes, that tour on which the latter fixed on the Town-End of Grasmere for his future home. This was Coleridge's first sight of English mountains. Rydal and Grasmere, he says, gave him the deepest delight; Haweswater kept his eyes dim with tears. During the last days of the year, Wordsworth, with his sister, walked over the Yorkshire fells, and settled in their new home. From this time forward, Coleridge wrote for the "Morning Post," off and on, till the close of 1802. About Coleridge's contributions to that paper, there has been maintained, since his death, a debate which hardly concerns us here. Enough to say, that having originally agreed with Fox in opposing the French war in 1800, and having at that time written violently against Pitt in the "Morning Post" and elsewhere, he was gradually separated from the leader of the opposition by the independent view he took against Napoleon, as the character of the military despot gradually unfolded itself. Coleridge passed over to the Tories, as he himself says, "only in the sense in which all patriots did so at that time, by refusing to accompany the Whigs in their almost perfidious demeanor towards Napoleon. Anti-ministerial they styled their policy, but it was really anti-national. It was exclusively in relation to the great feud with Napoleon that I adhered to the Tories. But because this feud was so capital, so earth-shaking, that it occupied all hearts, and all the councils of Europe, suffering no other question almost to live in the neighborhood, hence it happened that he who joined the Tories in this was regarded as their ally in everything. Domestic politics were then in fact forgotten."

But though he was constrained to come round to Pitt's foreign policy, he never, that I know, recanted the invectives with which he assailed that minister in 1800. There is still extant, among "The Essays on his Own Times," a well-known character of Pitt from the pen of Coleridge, which appeared in the "Morning Post." Coleridge, in general fair-minded and far-seeing, had one or two strange and unaccountable antipathies to persons, which Wilson mentions, and this against Pitt was perhaps the strongest and the blindest. On the day that the character of Pitt appeared, the character of Bonaparte was promised for "to-morrow," but that to-morrow never arrived. What that portrait would have been may perhaps be gathered from a paragraph on the same subject, contained in Appendix B to the first "Lay Sermon." The will, dissevered from conscience and religion, "becomes Satanic pride and rebellious self-idolatry in the relations of the spirit to itself, and remorseless despotism relatively to others; the more hopeless as the more obdurate by the subjugation of sensual impulses, by its superiority to toil and pain and pleasure; in short, by the fearful resolve to find in itself alone the one absolute motive of action, under which all other motives from within and from without must be either subordinated or crushed. . . . . This is the character which Milton has so philosophically, as well a-ssublimely, embodied in the Satan of his 'Paradise Lost'—Hope in which there is no cheerfulness; steadfastness within and immovable resolve, with outward restlessness and whirling activity; violence with guile; temerity with cunning; and, as the result of all, interminableness of object with perfect indifference of means — these are the marks that have characterized the masters of mischief, the liberticides, and mighty hunters of mankind, from Nimrod to Bonaparte. . . . . By want of insight into the possibility of such a character, whole nations have been so far duped as to regard with palliative admiration, instead of wonder and abhorrence, the Molochs of human nature, who are indebted for the larger portion of their meteoric success to their total want of principle, and who surpass the generality of their fellow-creatures in one act of courage only, that of daring to say with their whole heart, 'Evil, be thou my good!' All system is so far power; and a systematic criminal, self-consistent and entire in wickedness, who entrenches villainy within villainy, and barricades crime by crime, has removed a world of obstacles by the mere decision that he will have no other obstacles but those of force and brute matter."

It must have been early in 1801 that Coleridge turned his back for a time on London and the "Morning Post," to transfer his family to the Lakes, and settle them at Greta Hall. The landlord of it was a Mr. Jackson, the "Master" of Wordsworth's poem of the "Wagoner." From this house, destined to become Southey's permanent earthly home, Coleridge writes to Southey, then in Portugal, this description of it: "In front we have a giant's camp, an encamped army of tent-like mountains, which, by an inverted arch, gives a view of another vale [meaning, I suppose, the range of peaks which close the head of the Newlands' vale]. On our right the lovely vale and wedge-shaped lake of Bassenthwaite; and on our left, Derwentwater and Lodore in full view, and the fantastic mountains of Borrowdale. Behind us the massy Skiddaw, smooth, green, high, with two chasms, and a tent-like ridge in the larger. A fairer scene you have not seen in all your wanderings." There Southey soon joined Coleridge, and the two kindred families shared Greta Hall together, a common home with two doors.

Coleridge was now at the full manhood of his

powers; he was about thirty, and the time was come when the marvelous promise of youth ought to have had its fulfillment. He was surrounded with a country which, if any could, might have inspired him, with friends beside him who loved and were ready in any way to aid him. But the next fifteen years, the prime strength of his life, when his friends looked for fruit, and he himself felt that it was due, were all but unproductive. The "Ode to Dejection," written at the beginning of the Lake time, and "Youth and Age," written just before its close, with two or three more short pieces, are all his poetry of this period, and they fitly represent the sinking of heart and hope which were now too habitual with him. What was the cause of all this failure? Bodily disease, no doubt, in some measure, and the languor of disease depressing a will by nature weak and irresolute. But more than these, there was a worm at the root that was sapping his powers, and giving fatal effect to his natural infirmities. This process had already set in, but it was some years yet before the result was fully manifest. During these first years at the Lakes, though Greta was his home, Coleridge, according to De Quincey, was more often to be found at Grasmere. This retirement, for such it then was, had for him three attractions, a loveliness more complete than that of Derwentwater, an interesting and pastoral people not to be found at Keswick, and above all, the society of Wordsworth. It was about this time that there arose the name of the Lake School, a mere figment of the "Edinburgh Review," which it invented to express its hatred of three original writers, each unlike the other, and all agreeing only in one thing, their opposition to the hard and unimaginative spirit which was then the leading characteristic of the "Edinburgh." How unlike

Wordsworth and Coleridge really were in their way of thinking and working may be now clearly seen by comparing the works they have left behind. And as for Southey and Wordsworth, they had but little in common, and were not even on friendly terms till more than ten years after the Lake School was first talked of. Likely enough Coleridge found Wordsworth more original and suggestive than Southey. But the singleness and wholeness of moral purpose which inspired the lives of both his friends, must have been to Coleridge a continual rebuke; and Southey, as being a near relation, and a closer observer of the domestic unhappiness caused by Coleridge's neglects, had perhaps added to the silent reproof of his own example more open remonstrance.

In August, 1803, Wordsworth and his sister visited Coleridge at Keswick, and took him with them on that first tour in Scotland of which Wordsworth, and his sister too, have left such imperishable memorials. Most of the way they walked, from Dumfries up Nithsdale, over Crawfordmuir by the Falls of Clyde, and so on to Loch Lomond. Coleridge being in poor health and worse spirits than usual, and somewhat too much in love with his own dejection, left his two companions somewhere about Loch Lomond to return home. But either at this or some other time not specially recorded, he must have got further north, for we find him, in his second "Lay Sermon," speaking of his solitary walk from Loch Lomond to Inverness, and describing the impression made upon him both by the sight of the recently unpeopled country, and by the story he heard from an old Highland widow near Fort Augustus, of the wrongs she herself, her kinsfolk and her neighbors, had suffered in those sad clearances. But if Scotland woke in him no poetry on this his first and perhaps only visit, and if Scotchmen have had some severe things said of them by him, they can afford to pardon them. The land is none the less beautiful for not having been sung by him; and if from the people he could have learned some of that shrewdness of which they have enough and to spare, his life would have been other and happier than it was.

If the Lake country had suited Coleridge's constitution, and if he had turned to advantage the scenery and society it afforded, in no part of England, it might seem, could he have found a fitter home. But the dampness of the climate brought out so severely the rheumatism from which he had suffered since boyhood, that he was forced to seek a refuge from it on the shores of the Mediterranean, — a doubtful measure, it is said, for one in his state of nerves. Arriving at Malta in April, 1804, he soon became known to the Governor, Sir Alexander Ball, and during a change of secretaries Coleridge served for a time as a temporary secretary. The official task-work, and not less the official parade, expected from him, which he never attempted to maintain, were highly distasteful to him, and he gladly resigned, as soon as a new secretary came out. He made, however, the friendship of the Governor, whose character he has painted glowingly in "The Friend." Whether Sir Alexander Ball merited this high encomium I cannot say, but Professor Wilson mentions that Coleridge's craze for the three B's, Ball, Bell, and Bowyer, was a standing joke among his friends. The health he sought at Malta he did not find. The change at first seemed beneficial, but soon came the reaction, — "limbs like lifeless tools, violent internal pains, laboring and oppressed breathing." For relief from these he had recourse to the sedative, which he had begun to use so far back as 1796, and the habit became now fairly confirmed. Leaving Malta in September, 1805, he came to Rome, and there spent some time in seeing what every traveller sees, but what Coleridge would see with other eyes and keener insight than most men. Full observations on these things he noted down for after use. There, too, he made the acquaintance of the German poet Tieck, of an American painter, Allston, and of Humboldt, the brother of the great traveller. Gilman informs us that Coleridge was told by Humboldt that his name was on the list of the proscribed at Paris, owing to an article which he (Coleridge) had written against Bonaparte in the "Morning Post;" that the arrest had already been sent to Rome, but that one morning Coleridge was waited on by a noble Benedictine, sent to him by the kindness of the Pope, bearing a passport signed by the Pope, and telling him that a carriage was ready to bear him at once to Leghorn. Coleridge took the hint; at Leghorn embarked on board of an American vessel sailing for England; was chased by a French ship; and was, during the chase, forced by the captain to throw overboard all his papers, and among them his notes and observations made in Rome. So writes Coleridge's biographer. Wilson laughs at the thought of the Imperial eagle stooping to pursue such small game as Coleridge. And certainly it does seem hardly credible that Bonaparte should have so noted the secrets of the London newspaper press, or have made such efforts to lay hands on one stray member of that corps. De Quincey, however, argues from Bonaparte's character and habits that the thing was by no means improbable.

It is hardly worth while to attempt to trace all the changes of his life for the next ten years after his return from Malta. Sometimes at Keswick, where his family still lived; sometimes with Wordsworth at the Town-End of Grasmere; sometimes in London, living in the office of the "Courier," and writing for it; sometimes lecturing at the Royal Institution, often, according to De Quincey, disappointing his audience by non-appearance; anon an inmate in Wordsworth's new home at Allan Bank, while "The Excursion" was being composed; then taking final farewell of the Lakes in 1810, travelling with Basil Montagu to London, and leaving his family at Keswick, for some years, under care of Southey; domiciled now with Basil Montagu, now with a Mr. Morgan at Hammersmith, or Calne, now with other friends in or not far from London; so passed with him those homeless, aimless, wasted years of middle manhood. No doubt there were bright spots here and there, when his marvelous powers found vent in lecturing on some congenial subject, or flowed forth in that stream of thought and speech which was his native element. During these wanderings he met now and then with the wits of the time, either in rivalry not of his own seeking, or in friendly intercourse. Scott has recorded a rencounter he had with Coleridge at a dinner party, when some London *littérateurs* sought to lower Scott by pitting Coleridge against him. Coleridge had been called on to recite some of his own unpublished poems, and had done so. Scott, called on to contribute his share, refused, on the plea that he had none to produce, but offered to recite some clever lines which he had lately read in a newspaper. The lines were the unfortunate "Fire, Famine, and Slaughter," of which Coleridge was the then unacknowledged author. It is amusing to see the two sides of the story; the easy, off-hand humor with which Scott tells it in a letter, or in his journal; and the laborious self-defense with which

Coleridge ushers in the lines in his published poems. More friendly was his intercourse with Lord Byron, who, while he was lessee of a London theatre, had brought forward Coleridge's "Remorse," and had taken much interest in its success. This brought the two poets frequently into company, and in April, 1816, Coleridge thus speaks of Byron's appearance: "If you had seen Lord Byron you could scarcely disbelieve him. So beautiful a countenance I scarcely ever saw; his teeth so many stationary smiles; his eyes the open portals of the sun — things of light, and made for light; and his forehead, so ample, and yet so flexible, passing from marble smoothness into a hundred wreaths and lines and dimples, correspondent to the feelings and sentiments he is uttering." But lecturing, or conversation, or intercourse with brother poets, even taken at their best, are but a poor account to give of the prime years of such genius as Coleridge was intrusted with.

The record of his writings from 1801 till 1816 contains only one work of real importance. This was "The Friend," a periodical of weekly essays, intended to help to the formation of opinions on moral, political, and artistic subjects, grounded upon true and permanent principles. Undertaken with the countenance of, and with some slight aid from, Wordsworth, it began to be published in June, 1809, and ceased in March, 1810, because it did not pay the cost of publishing, which Coleridge had imprudently taken on himself. The original work having been much enlarged and recast, was published again in its present three-volume form in 1818. Even as it now stands, the ground-swell after the great French Revolution tempest can be distinctly felt. It is full of the political problems cast up by the troubled waters of the then recent storm, and of the attempt to discriminate between the first truths of morality and maxims of political expediency, and to ground each on their own proper basis. No one can read this work without feeling the force of Southey's remark: "The vice of 'The Friend' is its round-aboutness." But whoever will be content to bear with this and to read right on, will find all through fruit which will more than repay the labor, with essays here and there which are nearly perfect both in matter and in form. But its defects, such as they are, must have told fatally against its success when it appeared as a periodical. It was Coleridge's misfortune in this, as in so many of his works, to have to try to combine two things, hard, if not impossible to reconcile, — popularity that will pay, and thought that will elevate. The attempt to dig deep, and to implant new truths which can only be taken in by painful thought, finds small favor with most readers of periodicals. Few writers have attained present popularity and enduring power, and least of all could Coleridge do so. "The Friend" contains in its present, and probably it did in its first shape, clear indications of the change that Coleridge's mind had gone through in philosophy, as well as in his religious belief. But of this we shall have to speak again. This middle portion of Coleridge's life may, perhaps, be not inaptly closed by the description of his appearance and manner, as these appeared to De Quincey when he first saw him in 1807: —

"I had received directions for finding out the house where Coleridge was visiting; and in riding down a main street of Bridgewater, I noticed a gateway corresponding to the description given me. Under this was standing and gazing about him a man whom I will describe. In height he might seem to be about five feet eight (he was in reality about an inch and a half taller, but his figure was of an order which drowns the height); his person was tall and full, and tended even to corpulence; his complexion was fair, though not what painters technically style fair, because it was associated with black hair; his eyes were large and soft in their expression; and it was from the peculiar appearance of haze or dreaminess which mixed with their light that I recognized my object. This was Coleridge. I examined him steadfastly for a minute or more, and it struck me that he saw neither myself nor any other object in the street. He was in a deep reverie, for I had dismounted and advanced close to him before he had apparently become conscious of my presence. The sound of my voice, announcing my name, first awoke him; he started, and for a moment seemed at a loss to understand my purpose or his own situation. There was no *mauvaise honte* in his manner, but simple perplexity, and an apparent difficulty in recovering his position amongst daylight realities. This little scene over, he received me with a kindness of manner so marked that it might be called gracious. The hospitable family with whom he was domesticated all testified for Coleridge deep affection and esteem; sentiments in which the whole town of Bridgewater seemed to share. . . . .

"Coleridge led me to the drawing-room, rang the bell for refreshments, and omitted no point of a courteous reception. . . . . That point being settled, Coleridge, like some great Orellana, or the St. Lawrence, that, having been checked and fretted by rocks or thwarting islands, suddenly recovers its volume of waters, and its mighty music, swept at once, as if returning to his natural business, into a continuous strain of eloquent dissertation, certainly the most novel, the most finely illuminated, and traversing the most spacious fields of thought, by transitions the most just and logical that it was possible to conceive. . . . . To many people, and often I have heard the complaint, he seemed to wander; and he seemed then to wander the most when in fact his resistance to the wandering instinct was greatest, namely, when the compass and huge circuit by which his illustrations moved, travelled furthest into remote regions, before they began to revolve. Long before this coming round commenced, most people had lost him, and naturally enough supposed that he had lost himself. They continued to admire the separate beauty of the thoughts, but did not see their relations to the dominant theme. However, I can assert, upon my long and intimate knowledge of Coleridge's mind, that logic the most severe was as inalienable from his modes of thinking as grammar from his language."

Admirable as in the main the essay is from which this sketch is taken, it contains some things which one could wish unwritten. De Quincey dwells on some alleged faults of Coleridge with a loving minuteness which the pure love of truth can hardly account for; and with regard to the great and all-absorbing fault, the habit of opium-taking, his statements are directly opposed to those made by Coleridge himself, and by his friends who had the best means of knowing the truth. He says that Coleridge first took to opium, "not as a relief from bodily pains or nervous irritations, for his constitution was naturally strong and excellent, but as a source of luxurious sensations." Here De Quincey falls into two errors. First, Coleridge's constitution was not really strong. Though full of life and energy, his body was also full of disease, which gradually poisoned the springs of life. His letters bear witness to this, by the many complaints of ill health which they contain, before he ever touched opium. Again, as we have already seen, what he sought in opium was not pleasurable sensations, but freedom from pain, — an antidote to the nervous agitations under which he suffered. But whatever may have been the beginning of the habit, the result of continued indulgence in it was equally disastrous. We have already seen the letter which notes his first recourse to the fatal drug in 1796. As his ailments increased, so did his use of it. At Malta, opium-taking became a confirmed habit, and from that time for ten years it quite overmastered him. In 1807, the year when De Quincey first met him, he writes of himself as "rolling rudderless," with an increasing and overwhelming sense of wretchedness. The craving went on growing, and his consumption of the drug had, by 1814, reached a quite appalling height. Cottle, then, on meeting Coleridge, saw what a wreck he had become, discovered the fatal cause, and took courage to remonstrate by letter. Coleridge makes no concealment, pleads guilty to the evil habit, and confesses that he is utterly miserable. Sadder letters were perhaps never written than those cries out of the depths of his agony. He tells Cottle that he had learned what "sin is against an imperishable being, such as is the soul of man; that he had had more than one glimpse of the outer darkness and the worm that dieth not; that if annihilation and the possibility of heaven were at that moment offered to his choice, he would prefer the former." More pitiful still is that letter to his friend Wade: "In the one crime of opium, what crime have I not made myself guilty of? Ingratitude to my Maker; and to my benefactors injustice; and unnatural cruelty to my poor children. . . . . After my death, I earnestly entreat that a full and unqualified narrative of my wretchedness, and of its guilty cause, may be made public, that at least some little good may be effected by the direful example." It is painful to dwell on these things, nor should they have been reproduced here, had it been possible to have given a true picture of the man, without touching on this, the dark side of his character.

Strange and sad as it is to think that one so gifted should have fallen so low, it is hardly less strange that from that degradation he should ever have been enabled to rise. The crisis seems to have come about the time when those letters passed between Cottle and him in 1814. For some time there followed a struggle against the tyrant vice, by various means, but all seemingly ineffectual. At last he voluntarily arranged to board himself with the family of Mr. Gilman, a physician, who lived at Highgate, in a retired house, in an airy situation surrounded by a large garden. It was in April, 1816, that he first entered this house at Highgate, which continued to be his home for eighteen years till his death. The letter in which he opens his grief to Mr. Gilman, and commends himself to his care, is very striking, showing at once his strong desire to overcome the inveterate habit, and his feeling of inability to do so, unless he were placed under a watchful eye and external restraint. In this home he learned to abandon opium, and here, though weighed down by ever increasing bodily infirmity, and often by great mental depression, he found on the whole —

> "The best quiet to his course allowed."

That the vice was overcome might be inferred from the very fact that his life was prolonged. And though statements to the contrary have been made from quarters whence they might least have been expected, there is, as I have learned from the most trustworthy authorities still living, no ground for these statements. The friends of Coleridge, who have had best access to the truth, believe that at Highgate he obtained that self-mastery which he sought. No doubt, the habit left a bane behind it, a body shattered, a mind shorn of much of its strength for continuous effort, ever-recurring seasons of despondency and visitings of self-reproach for so much life wasted, so great powers given, so little achieved. No man ever felt more painfully than he the contrast between —

"The petty Done, the Undone vast."

But still, under all these drawbacks, he labored earnestly to redeem what of life remained; and most of what is satisfactory to remember of his life belongs to those last eighteen years. It was a time of gathering up of the fragments that remained — of saving splinters washed ashore from the mighty wreck. To this time, such as it is, we owe most of that by which Coleridge is now known to men, and by which, if at all, he has benefited his kind.

During those years the great religious change that had been long going on was completed and confirmed. As far back as 1800 his adherence to the Hartleian philosophy and his belief in Unitarian theology had been shaken. By 1805 he was in some sense a believer in the Trinity, and had entered on a closer study of Scripture, especially of St. Paul and St. John. There were in him, as De Quincey observed, the capacity of love and faith, of self-distrust, humility, and child-like docility, waiting but for time and sorrow to mature them. Such a discipline the long ineffectual struggle with his infirmity supplied. The sense of moral weakness, and of sin, working inward contrition, made him seek for a more practical, supporting faith than he had known in his early years. And so he learned that, while the consistency of Christianity with right reason and the historic evidence of miracles are the outworks, yet the vital centre of faith lies in the believer's feeling of his great need, and the experience that the redemption which is in Christ meets that need; that it is the "sorrow rising from beneath and the consolation meeting it from above," the actual trial of the faith in Christ, which is its ultimate and most satisfying evidence. With him, too, as with so many before, it was *credidi, ideoque intellexi.* The Highgate time was also the period of his most prolonged and undisturbed study. Among much other reading, the Old English divines were diligently perused and commented on; and his criticisms and reflections on them fill nearly the whole of the third and fourth volumes of his "Literary Remains." A discriminating, often a severe critic of these writers, he was still a warm admirer, in this a striking contrast to Arnold, who certainly unduly depreciated them.

Almost the whole of his prose works were the product of this time. First the "Two Lay Sermons," published in 1816 and 1827. Then the "Biographia Literaria," published in 1817, though in part composed some years before. In 1818 followed the recast and greatly enlarged edition of "The Friend;" and in 1825 he gave to the world the most mature of all his works, the "Aids to Reflection." Incorporated especially with the earlier part of this work, are selections from the writings of Archbishop Leighton, of which he has said that to him they seemed "next to the inspired Scriptures, yea, as the vibration of that once-struck hour remaining on the air." The main substance of the work, however, contains his own thoughts on the grounds of morality and religion, and of the relation of these to each other, along with his views on some of the main doctrines of the faith. The last work that appeared during his lifetime was that on "Church and State," published in 1830. After his death appeared his posthumous works, namely, the four volumes of "Literary Remains," and the small volume on the inspiration of Scripture, entitled "Confessions of an Inquiring Spirit."

It is by these works alone, incomplete as many of them are, that posterity can judge of him. But the impression of overflowing genius which he left on his contemporaries was due not so much to his writings as to his marvelous talk. Printed books have made us undervalue this gift, or at best regard it more as a thing of display than as a genuine thought-communicating power. But as an organ of teaching truth, speech is older than books, and for this end Plato, among others, preferred the living voice to dead letters. Measured by this standard, Coleridge had no equal in his own, and few in any age. How his gift of discourse in his younger days arrested Hazlitt and De Quincey, has been already seen; and in his declining years at Highgate, when bodily ailments allowed, during the pauses of study and writing, fuller and more continuous than ever the mighty monologue streamed on. Some faint echoes of what then fell from him have been caught up and preserved in the well-known "Table-Talk," by his nephew and son-in-law, Henry Nelson Coleridge, who in his preface has finely described the impression produced by his uncle's conversation on congenial listeners. To that retirement at Highgate flocked as on a pilgrimage most of what was brilliant in intellect or ardent in youthful genius at that day. Edward Irving, Julius Hare, Sterling, and many more who might be named, were among his frequent and most devoted listeners. Most came to listen, wonder, and learn. But some came and went to shrug their shoulders, and pronounce it unintelligible, as Chalmers; or in after years to scoff, as Mr. Carlyle. Likely enough this latter came craving a solution of some pressing doubt or bewildering enigma; and to receive instead a prolonged and circuitous disquisition must to his then mood of mind have been tantalizing enough. But was it well done, O great Thomas! for this, years afterwards, to jeer at the old man's enfeebled gait, and caricature the tones of his voice?

In the summer of 1833 Coleridge was seen for the last time in public, at the meeting of the British Association at Cambridge. Next year, on the 25th of July, he died in Mr. Gilman's house in The Grove, Highgate, which had been so long his home, and was laid hard by in his last resting-place within the old churchyard by the roadside.

Twelve days before his death, not knowing it to be so near, he wrote to his godchild this remarkable letter,[1] which, gathering up the sum of his whole life's experience, reads like his unconscious epitaph on himself: —

"My dear Godchild, — . . . . Years must pass before you will be able to read with an understanding heart what I now write; but I trust that the all-gracious God, the Father of our Lord Jesus Christ, the Father of mercies, who by his only begotten Son (all mercies in one sovereign mercy) has redeemed you from the evil ground, and willed you to be born out of darkness, but into light; out of death, but into life; out of sin, but into righteousness, even into the Lord our

[1] This letter was written on the 13th, and he died on the 25th day of July.

Righteousness, — I trust that He will graciously hear the prayers of your dear parents, and be with you as the spirit of health and growth in body and mind.

". . . . I, too, your godfather, have known what the enjoyments and advantages of this life are, and what the more refined pleasures which learning and intellectual power can bestow; and with the experience which more than threescore years can give, I now, on the eve of my departure, declare to you (and earnestly pray that you may hereafter live and act on the conviction) that health is a great blessing, competence obtained by honorable industry a great blessing, and a great blessing it is to have kind, faithful, and loving friends and relatives; but that the greatest of all blessings, as it is the most ennobling of all privileges, is to be indeed a Christian. But I have been likewise, through a large portion of my later life, a sufferer, sorely afflicted with bodily pains, languors, and infirmities; and for the last three or four years have, with a few and brief intervals, been confined to a sick-room, and at this moment, in great weakness and heaviness, write from a sick-bed, hopeless of a recovery, yet without prospect of a speedy removal; and I, thus on the very brink of the grave, solemnly bear witness to you, that the Almighty Redeemer, most gracious in his promises to them that truly seek Him, is faithful to perform what He hath promised, and has preserved, under all my pains and infirmities, the inward peace that passeth all understanding, with the supporting assurance of a reconciled God, who will not withdraw his Spirit from me in the conflict, and in his own time will deliver me from the Evil One.

"O, my dear godchild! eminently blessed are those who begin early to seek, fear, and love their God, trusting wholly in the righteousness and mediation of their

Lord, Redeemer, Saviour, and everlasting High Priest, Jesus Christ.

"O, preserve this as a legacy and bequest from your unseen godfather and friend, S. T. COLERIDGE."

And now, perhaps, this sketch cannot close more fitly than in the affectionate words of his nephew, the faithful defender of the memory of his great uncle: —

"Coleridge! blessings on his gentle memory! Coleridge was a frail mortal. He had indeed his peculiar weaknesses as well as his unique powers; sensibilities that an averted look would rack, a heart which would beat calmly in the tremblings of an earthquake. He shrank from mere uneasiness like a child, and bore the preparatory agonies of his death-attack like a martyr. He suffered an almost life-long punishment for his errors, whilst the world at large has the unwithering fruits of his labors, and his genius, and his sufferings."

If I have traced in any measure aright the course of Coleridge's life, no more is needed to show what these failings and errors were. It more concerns us to ask what permanent fruit of all that he thought, and did, and suffered under the sun, there still remains, now that he has lain more than thirty years in his grave. To answer this fully is impossible in the case of any man, much more in the case of one who has been a great thinker rather than a great doer; for many of his best ideas have so melted into the general atmosphere of thought, that it is hard to separate them from the complex whole, and trace them back to their original source. But the abler men of his own generation were not slow to confess how much they owed to him. In poetry, Sir Walter Scott acknowledged himself as indebted to him for the opening key-note of "The Lay of the Last Minstrel." In the metre, sentiment, and drapery of that first canto, it is not difficult to trace the influence of "Christabel," then unpublished, but well known. Wordsworth, aloof from his contemporaries, and self-sufficing as he was, felt Coleridge to be his equal — "the only wonderful man I have ever known." Arnold, at a later day, called him the greatest intellect that England had produced within his memory, and shared with, perhaps learned from him, some of his leading thoughts, as that the identification of the church with the clergy was "the first and fundamental apostasy." Dr. Newman pointed to Coleridge's works long since as a proof that the minds of men in England were then yearning for something higher and deeper than what had satisfied the last age. Julius Hare speaks of him as "the great religious philosopher, to whom the mind of our generation in England owes more than to any other man." Mr. Maurice has everywhere spoken with deeper reverence of him than of any other teacher of these latter times. Even Mr. Mill has said that "no one has contributed more to shape the opinions among younger men, who can be said to have any opinions at all."

But what need to note the impression he made here and there on single men, however eminent? He was the spirit-quickener not only of this man or that, but of his whole age. The greatest men of his time were the most susceptible of his influence, and the first to feel it — Wordsworth, Scott, Byron, Irving, Wilson, Hazlitt, even Carlyle — on these, as has been lately said, he laid his spell, and "spoke through them." And partly through them, partly by his own immediate agency, he has since entered into the inner thought of every reflective man. For his was the most germinative mind England has this century given birth to.

Like a vast seed-field it lay, till the winds of inspiration wafted over it, blowing the seeds of his new thought over all the land. Incommensurable as Scott and Coleridge in all other respects are, lying as they do at the very opposite poles of thought, in one thing they are alike — the width of their operation. If the one by the vastness of his objective work changed the whole surface of society, not less widely or powerfully did the other by his penetrating subjectivity leaven it in its inmost depths. No really great man can be fully represented by his books, but few great men have left in their books so inadequate expressions of themselves as Coleridge has done. The living presence with the winged words, vivifying the minds of all hearers, has long been gone, and of all that matchless discourse, no trace remains but the few faint notices of those who heard it. Therefore, from the living eloquence to the silent books, we are forced reluctantly to turn, since these, though but a moiety of what he was, are all the permanent record of him that remains.

These works are but fragments of his speculation, and this forms one difficulty in rightly estimating them. Another, and perhaps greater, lies in the width over which they range. Most original thinkers have devoted themselves to but a few lines of inquiry. Coleridge's thought may be almost said to have been as wide as life. To apply to himself the word which he first coined, or rather translated from some obscure Byzantian, to express Shakespeare's quality, he was a "myriad-minded man." He touched being at almost every point, and wherever he touched it, he opened up some new shaft of truth, and his books contain some fragment of what he saw. He who would fully estimate Coleridge's contributions to thought would have to consider him at least in these several aspects, as a poet, as a critic, as a political philosopher, as a moralist, and as a theologian. But without hazarding anything like so large an attempt, a few brief remarks may be offered on what he has done in some of these so widely different fields.

It was as a poet that Coleridge was first known, and the wish has many times been expressed that he had stuck to poetry, and never tried philosophy. No doubt he had imagination enough, as some one has said, to have furnished forth a thousand poets, and "Christabel" will probably be read longer than any prose work he has written. This, however, belongs both to the substance and the form of all poetry that is perfect after its kind. But vast and vivid as Coleridge's imagination was, may not this power be as legitimately employed in interpenetrating and quickening the reason, and revivifying domains of philosophy, which are apt to grow narrow or dead through prosaic formalism, as in purely poetic creation? Moreover, there were perhaps in Coleridge some special powers of fine analysis and introvertive speculation, which seem to have predestined him for other work than poetry; just as there were some special wants, arising either from natural temperament or early education, which marred his poetic completeness. He had never lived much in the open air; he had no large storehouse of facts or images, either drawn from observation of outward nature, or from more than common acquaintance with any modes of life or sides of human character, such as Wordsworth and Scott in different ways had. It was not the nature of his mind to dwell lovingly on concrete things, but rather, from its strong generalizing bias, to be borne off continually into the abstract. Therefore I cannot think that Coleridge, though he might have more delighted, would have done better service to mankind, if he had stuck wholly to poetry, or that he did otherwise than fulfill his destiny by giving way to the philosophic impulse.

His daughter has said that he had four poetic epochs, representing, more or less, boyhood, early manhood, middle, and declining life. To trace these carefully is not for this place. The juvenile poems, those of the first epoch, though showing here and there hints of the coming power, contain, as a whole, nothing which would make them live, were it not for what came afterwards. He himself has said that these poems are disfigured by too great exuberance of double epithets, and by general turgidity. These mark, perhaps, the tumult of his thick-thronging thoughts, struggling to utter themselves with force and freshness, yet not quite disengaged from the old commonplaces of poetic diction, "eve's dusky car," and such-like, and from those frigid personifications of abstract qualities in which the former age delighted. Of these early poems, one of the most interesting is that on the death of Chatterton, in which, though the form somewhat recalls the odes of Collins and Gray, his native self here and there breaks through. Some of them are pensive with his early sorrow, others fierce and turbid with his revolutionary fervor. The longest and most important, styled "Religious Musings," though Bowles ranked it high, might easily, notwithstanding some fine thoughts, suggest one of his rhapsodies in a Unitarian chapel cut into blank verse. The religious sentiments it contains are frigid and bombastic; the politics denunciatory of existing things, of—

> "Warriors, lords, and priests, all the sore ills
> That vex and desolate our mortal life."

They contain, however, some true thoughts, well put, though tinged with his Revolution dreams, on the good and evil that have sprung out of the institution of property, and a fine apostrophe to all the sin-defiled and sorrow-laden ones, whose day of deliverance yet waits.

It had been well if the poems of the second period, which were mostly written during the Bristol and Nether Stowey periods, and now make up the chief part of the "Sibylline Leaves," had been arranged in the order in which they were composed. This would have thrown much light on them, arising as they do either out of the events of the time or of Coleridge's personal circumstances. Compared with those of the former period, the stream flows more even and unbroken. The crude philosophy has all but disappeared, the blank verse is now more fused and melodious, the rhythm of thought more mellow, the religious sentiment, where it does appear, no longer reasoning, but meditative, is more chastened and deep. These poems it must have been, which were to De Quincey "the ray of a new morning, a revealing of untrodden worlds, till then unsuspected amongst men." Such Wilson found them, and so in a measure they have been to many since. In re-reading them, after an interval of years, this is perhaps felt less vividly. Is it that time has diminished the keen sense of their originality; that the new fragrance they once gave forth has so filled the poetic atmosphere that it makes itself now less distinctly felt? However this may be, such accidents of personal feeling do not affect their real worth. Of two fine poems written at Clevedon, the one on the "Æolian Harp" contains a passage that may be compared with the well-known so-called Pantheistic passage in Wordsworth's "Tintern Abbey." The other, "Reflections on leaving a place of Retirement," breathes a beautiful though too brief spirit of happiness and content. In the same gentle vein are the "Lines to his Brother George," and "Frost at Midnight," in finely balanced and beautifully modulated blank verse. But higher and of wider compass are the three political poems, the ode on "The Departing Year," written at the close of 1796, "France," an ode, written in February, 1797, and "Tears in Solitude," in 1798. The last of these opens and closes with some of his best blank verses, full of lambent light and his own exquisite music, though the middle is troubled with somewhat intemperate politics, pamphleteeringly expressed. The ode on "France," when his fond hopes of the Revolution had ended in disappointment, is a strain of noblest poetry. It opens with a call on the clouds, the waves, the sun, the sky, all in nature that is most free, to bear witness —

> "With what deep worship I have still adored
> The spirit of divinest Liberty."

And closes with these grand lines : —

> "O Liberty! with profitless endeavor
> Have I pursued thee many a weary hour;
> But thou nor swell'st the victor's strain, nor ever
> Didst breathe thy soul in forms of human power;
> Alike from all, howe'er they praise thee
> (Nor prayer nor boastful name delays thee),
> Alike from Priestcraft's harpy minions,
> And factious Blasphemy's obscener slaves,
> Thou speedest on thy subtle pinions,
> The guide of homeless winds, the playmate of the waves!
> And there, I felt thee! on that sea-cliff's verge,
> Whose pines, scarce travelled by the breeze above,
> Had made one murmur with the distant surge!
> Yes! while I stood and gazed, my temples bare,
> And shot my being through earth, sea, and air,
> Possessing all things with intensest love,
> O Liberty, my spirit felt thee there!"

Equal, perhaps, to any of the above, are the lines he addressed to Wordsworth, after hearing that poet read aloud the first draft of "The Prelude:" —

"An Orphic song indeed,
A song divine, of high and passionate thoughts,
To their own music chanted! . . . .
And when, O friend! my comforter and guide!
Strong in thyself, and powerful to give strength,
Thy long-sustainèd song finally closed,
And thy deep voice had ceased — yet thou thyself
Wert still before my eyes, and round us both
That happy vision of beloved faces —
Scarce conscious, and yet conscious of its close,
I sat, my being blended in one thought
(Thought was it? or aspiration? or resolve?)
Absorbed, yet hanging still upon the sound —
And when I rose, I found myself in prayer."

Of the "Ancient Mariner" and "Christabel," the two prime creations of the Nether Stowey period, nothing need be said. Time has now stamped these with the signet of immortality. The view with which these two masterpieces were begun, as the brother poets walked on the green heights of Quantock, has been detailed elsewhere. Coleridge was to choose supernatural or romantic characters, and clothe them from his own imagination with a human interest and a semblance of truth. It would be hard to analyze the strange witchery that is in both, especially in "Christabel;" the language so simple and natural, yet so aerially musical, the rhythm so original, yet so fitted to the story, and the glamour over all, a glamour so peculiar to this one poem. The first part belongs to Quantock, the second was composed several years later at the Lakes, yet still the tale is but half told. Would it have gained or lost in power had it been completed?

It has been asked whether there is in Coleridge's poetry any trace of the peculiar vein of thought which afterwards appeared in him as philosophy. There is first a delicacy and subtlety of thought and imagery strange to English poets for at least two centuries. It is in him we find —

> "The stilly murmur of the distant sea
> Tells us of silence."

His, too, is —

> "A dream remembered in a dream,"

and his —

> "Her voice that even in its mirthful mood
> Hath made me wish to steal away and weep."

In him too it is that the vision of Mont Blanc awakens that idealism —

> "Most dread and silent mount! I gazed upon thee
> Till thou, still present to my bodily sense,
> Hadst vanished from my thought; entranced in prayer,
> I worshipped the Invisible alone."

But besides these separate subtleties, are they mistaken who see in the unearthly weirdness of the "Ancient Mariner," and the mysterious witchery of "Christabel" those very mental elements in solution which, condensed and turned inward, would find their most congenial place in "the exhausting atmosphere of transcendental ideas?"

His third poetic epoch includes his whole sojourn at the Lakes, and the fourth the remainder of his life. The poems of these two periods are few altogether, and what there are, more meditative than formerly, sometimes even hopelessly dejected. "Youth and Age," written just before leaving the Lakes, with a strangely aged tone for a man of only seven or eight and thirty, has a quaint beauty; to adapt its own words, it is like sadness, that "tells the jest without the smile." There are some pieces of this time, however, in another strain, as the beautiful lines called "The Knight's Tomb," and "Recollections of Love." After the Lake time, there was still less poetry; only when, as in the "Visionary Hope" and the "Pains of Sleep," the too frequent despondency or severe suffering of his later years sought relief in brief verse. Yet, belonging to the third or fourth periods, there are short gnomic lines, in which, if the visionary has disappeared, the wisdom wrought by time and meditation is excellently condensed. Such are these:—

"Frail creatures are we all; to be the best
Is but the fewest faults to have;
Look thou then to thyself, and leave the rest
To God, thy conscience, and the grave."

Or the Complaint and Reply:—

"How seldom, friend! a good great man inherits
Honors or wealth with all his toil and pains.
It sounds like stories from the land of spirits,
If any man obtain that which he merits,
Or any merit that which he obtains."

REPLY.

"For shame, dear friend! forego this canting strain;
What wouldst thou have the good great man obtain?
Wealth, titles, salary, a gilded chain;
Or throne of corses which his sword had slain?
Goodness and greatness are not means, but ends!
Hath he not always treasures, always friends,
The good great man! — Three treasures, life, and light,
And calm thoughts, regular as infants' breath;
And three firm friends, more sure than day and night, —
Himself, his Maker, and the Angel Death."

If from his own poetry we pass to his judgments on the poetry of others, we shall see an exemplification of the adapted adage, "Set a poet to catch a poet." Here for once were fulfilled the necessary conditions of a critic or judge, in the highest sense; that is, a man possessing in himself abundantly the originative poetic faculty which he is to judge of in others, combined with that power of generalization and delicate, patient analysis which, if poets possess, they but seldom express in prose. This is but another way of saying, that before a man can pass worthy judgment on a thing, he must know that thing at first and not at second hand. The other kind of critic is he who, though with little or none of the poetic gift in himself, has yet, from a careful study of the great master-models of the art, deduced certain canons by which to judge of poetry universally. But a critic of this kind, as the world has many a time seen, whenever he is called upon to estimate some new and original work of Art, like to which the past supplies no models, is wholly at fault. His canons no longer serve him, and the native sympathetic insight he has not. To judge aright in such a case takes another order of critic; one who knows after another and more immediate manner of knowing; one who does not judge merely by what the past has done, but who, by the poet's heart within him, is made quick to welcome whatever new thing, however seemingly irregular, the young time may bring forth. Such a critic was Coleridge. An imagination richer and more penetrative than that of most poets of his time; a power of philosophic reflection and of subtle discrimination, almost over-active; a sympathy and insight of marvelous universality; and a learning "laden with the spoils of all times," — these things made him the greatest — I had almost said the only truly philosophic — critic England had yet seen.

Of his critical power, the two most eminent examples are his chapters on Wordsworth's poetry in the "Biographia Literaria," and his notes on Shakespeare in the "Literary Remains." If a man wished to learn what genuine criticism should be, where else in our country's literature would he find so worthy a model as in that dissertation on Wordsworth? An excellent authority has lately said that the business of criticism is "to know the best thing that is known or thought in the world, and to make this known to others." In these chapters on Wordsworth, Coleridge has done something more than this. In opposition to the blind and utterly worthless criticism which Jeffrey then represented, he thought out for himself, and laid down the principles on which Wordsworth or any poet such as he should be judged, and showed these principles to be grounded, not on caprices of the hour, but on the fundamental and permanent elements which human nature contains. He gave definitions of poetry in its essential nature, and showed more accurately than Wordsworth in his preface, wherein poetry really differs from prose. Let any one who wishes to see the truth on these matters turn to Coleridge's description of the poet and his work, as they are in their ideal perfection. Then how truly and with what fine analysis he discriminates between the language of prose and of metre! How good is his account of the origin of metre! "This I would trace to the balance in the mind, effected by that spontaneous effort which strives to hold in check the workings of passion." There is more to be learned about poetry from a few pages of that dissertation, confined though it is to a specific kind of poetry, than from all the reviews that have been written in English on poets and their works from Addison to the present hour. Nor is the result of the whole a mere defense or indiscriminating eulogy on Wordsworth, rudely as that poet was then assailed by those who were also Coleridge's own revilers. From several of Wordsworth's theories about poetry he dissents entirely, especially from the whole of his remarks on the sameness of the language of prose and verse. At times, too, he finds fault with his practice, and lays his finger on faulty passages and defective poems here and there, in which he traces the influence of false theory; while the true merits of these poems he places not on mere blind preference or individual taste, but on a solid foundation of principles. These principles few or none at that time acknowledged, but they have since won the assent of all competent judges. Canons of judgment they are, not mechanical, but living. They do not furnish the reader with a set of rules which he can take up and apply ready made. But they require, before they can be used aright, to be assimilated by thought — made our own inwardly. They open the eye to see, generate the power of seeing for one's self, call forth from within a living standard of judgment, which is based on truth and nature.

Again, turning to his criticisms on Shakespeare and the Drama. They are but brief notes, scattered leaves, written by himself or taken down by others, from lectures given mainly in London. His lectures were in general wholly oral, and are said to have been best when delivered with no scrap of paper before him. But short as these notes are, they mark, and helped to cause, a revolution in men's ways of thinking about Shakespeare. First he taught, and himself exemplified, that he who would understand Shakespeare must not, Dr. Johnson-wise, seat himself on the critical throne, and thence deliver verdict, as on an inferior, or at best a mere equal; but that he has need to come before all things with reverence, as for the poet of all poets, and that, wanting this, he wants one of the senses the "language of which he is to employ." Again, Coleridge was the first who clearly saw through and boldly denounced the nonsense that had been talked about Shakespeare's irregularity and extravagance. Before his time it had been customary to speak of Shakespeare as of some great abnormal creature, some fine but rude barbarian, full of all sorts of blemishes and artistic solecisms, which were to be tolerated for the sake of the beauties with which they were interlaid. In the face of all this, he ventured to ask, "Are then the plays of Shakespeare's works of rude and uncultivated genius, in which the splendor of the parts compensates for the barbarous shapelessness and irregularity of the whole? Or is the form equally admirable with the matter, and the judgment of the poet not less deserving our admiration than his genius?" The answer which he gave to his own question, and which he enforced with manifold argument, is in effect that the judgment of Shakespeare is as great as his genius; "nay, that its genius reveals itself in his judgment as in its most exalted form." In arguing against those who at that time "were still trammeled with the notion of the Greek unities, and who thought that apologies were due for Shakespeare's neglect of them," he showed how the form of Shakespeare's dramas was suited to the substance, not less than the form of the Greek dramas to their substance. He pointed out the contrast between mechanical form superinduced from without, and organic form growing from within; that if Shakespeare or any modern were to hold by the Greek dramatic unities, he would be imposing on his creations a dead form copied from without, instead of letting them shape themselves from within, and clothe themselves with their own natural and living form, as the tree clothes itself with its bark. Another point which Coleridge insists on in these lectures and throughout his works, a point often unheeded, sometimes directly denied, is the close connection between just taste and pure morality, because true taste springs out of the ground of the moral nature of man. I cannot now follow him into detail, and show the new light which he has thrown on Shakespeare's separate plays, and on his leading characters. But it may be noticed in passing, that Hamlet was the character in the exposition of which Coleridge first proved his Shakespearean insight. In the "Table Talk" he says, "In fact, I have a smack of Hamlet in myself." If any one wishes to see what a really masterly elucidation of a subtle character is, let him turn to the remarks on Hamlet in the second volume of the "Literary Remains." This and other of Coleridge's Shakespearean criticisms have been claimed for Schlegel. But most of these had, I believe, been given to the world in lectures before Schlegel's book appeared; and as to this exposition of Hamlet, Hazlitt bears witness that he had heard it from Coleridge before his visit to Germany in 1798. That view of Hamlet has long since become almost a commonplace in literature, but the idea of it was first conceived and expressed by Coleridge. Some of the other criticisms may be more subtle than many may care to follow. But any one who shall master these notes on Shakespeare, taken as a whole, will find in them more fine analysis of the hidden things of the heart, more truthful insight into the workings of passion, than are to be found in whole treatises of psychology.

Any survey of Coleridge's speculations would be incomplete if it did not include some account of his political philosophy, which holds so prominent a place among them. Not that he ever was a party politician, — his whole nature recoiled from that kind of work, — but his mind was too universal in its range, his sympathy with all human interests too strong, to have allowed him to pass by these questions. But the thorough and comprehensive survey of this department of Coleridge's thought, which occupies the greater part of

Mr. Mill's well-known essay, makes any discussion of this subject here superfluous. There is however one important point to which this distinguished writer fails to advert. He speaks of Coleridge as an original thinker, but "within the bounds of traditional opinions," and as looking at received beliefs merely from within their pale. But it must surely have been known to Mr. Mill that Coleridge, during his youth and early manhood, stood as entirely outside of established opinions, and looked at existing institutions as purely from without as it was possible to do. No extremest young radical of the present hour, when intellectual radicalism has once again become a fashion, can question received beliefs more freely, or assail the established order more fearlessly, than Coleridge did in his fervid youth. The convictions on politics and religion, therefore, in which he ultimately rested, are entitled to the weight, whatever it be, of having been formed by one who all his life long sought truth from every quarter, who for many years of his life stood not within, but entirely outside of traditionary beliefs; and who, when his thought had gone full circle, became conservative, if that word is to be applied to him, not from self-interest or expediency, or from weariness of thinking, but after ample experience and mature reflection. With this one remark on his political side I pass on.

Criticism, such as I have described above, presupposes profound and comprehensive thought on questions not lying within, but based on wider principles beyond, itself. His critical studies, if nothing else, would have driven Coleridge back on metaphysics. But it was the same with whatever subject he took up, whether art or politics, morals or theology. Everywhere he strove to reach the bottom, — to grasp the living idea which gave birth to the system or institution, and kept it alive.

Even in those of his works, as the "Literary Life," "The Friend," and the "Lay Sermons," which most enter into practical details, the granite every here and there crops out, the underlying philosophy appears. But that searching for fundamental principles, which seems to have been in him from the first an intellectual necessity, was increased by the morbidly introvertive turn of mind which, at some stages of his life, had nearly overbalanced him. In an often quoted passage from the "Ode to Dejection," written at Keswick in 1802, he laments the decay within himself of the shaping imagination, and says that —

> . . . "By abstruse research to steal
> From my own nature all the natural man;
> This was my sole resource, my only plan,
> Till that which suits a part infects the whole,
> And now is almost grown the habit of my soul."

This passage opens a far glimpse into his mental history. It shows how metaphysics, for which he had from the first an innate propension, became from circumstances almost an unhealthy craving. What then was his ultimate metaphysical philosophy? This is not set forth systematically in any of his works, but we are left to gather it, as best we can, from disquisitions scattered through them all. And here, that unphilosophical readers may more clearly see Coleridge's place in the world of thought, I must recur to a few elementary matters, which will seem trite enough to philosophical adepts.

Every one knows that from the dawn of thought down to the present hour, the question as to the origin of knowledge has been the Sphinx's riddle to philosophers. This strange thing named Thought, what is it? This wondrous fabric we call Knowledge, whence comes it? It is a web woven out of something, but is it wholly or chiefly woven from outward materials, or mainly wrought by self-evolving powers from within? Or, if due to the combined action of these, what part does each contribute? How much is due to the raw material, how much to the weaver who fashions it? These questions, even if they be insoluble, will never cease to provoke the curiosity of every new generation of thoughtful men. There always has been a set of thinkers who have regarded outward things as the fixed reality which impresses representations of itself on mind as on a passive recipient. There has always existed also another set, which has held the mind to be a free creative energy, evolving from itself the laws of its own thinking, and stamping on outward things the forms which are inherent in its own constitution. The one school have held that outward things are genetic of knowledge, and that what are called laws of thought are wholly imposed on the mind by qualities which belong primarily to outward things. The others have maintained that it is the mind which is genetic, and that it in reality makes what it sees. This great question, as Mr. Mill has well said, "would not so long have remained a question, if the more obvious arguments on either side had been unanswerable." There must, however, be a point of view, if we could reach it, from which these opposing tendencies of thought shall be seen to combine into one harmonious whole. But the man who shall achieve this final synthesis, and the age which shall witness it, are probably still far distant. Philosophic thought in Great Britain has in the main leaned towards the external side, towards that extreme which makes the mind out of the senses, and maintains experience to be the ultimate ground of all belief. This way of thinking, so congenial to the prevailing English temper, dates from at least as far back as

Hobbes, but was first fairly established, almost like a part of the British Constitution, by the famous essay of Locke. In his polemic against innate ideas he asserted two sources of all knowledge. "Our observation," he says, "employed either about external sensible things, or about the internal operations of our minds perceived and reflected on by ourselves, is that which supplies our understandings with materials of thinking." The latter of these two sources, here somewhat vaguely announced, was never very strongly insisted on by Locke himself, and was by his followers speedily discarded. The full development of Locke's system is seen most clearly in Hume, who divided all the mind's furniture into impressions or lively perceptions, as when we see, hear, hate, desire, will; and ideas or faint perceptions, which are copies of our sensible or lively impressions. So that with him all the materials of thought are derived from outward sense, or inward sentiment or emotion.

Contemporary with Hume, and like him a follower of Locke, Hartley appeared at Cambridge, and carried out the same views to still more definite issues. He gathered up and systematized the materialistic views which were at that time floating about his University. Being, like Locke, a physician, he imported into his system a much larger amount of his professional knowledge, and sought to explain the movements of thought by elaborate physiological theories. He held that vibrations in the white medullary substance of the brain are the immediate causes of sensation, and that these first vibrations give birth to vibratiuncles or miniatures of themselves, which are conceptions, or the simple ideas of sensible things. In another point he differed from Locke, in that, discarding Reflection, he brought more prominently forward Association, as the great weaving power of the mental fabric, which compounds all our ideas, and gives birth to all our faculties.

Such theories as these were the chief philosophical aliment to be found in England when Coleridge was a young man. At Cambridge, having entered Hartley's college, where the name of that philosopher was still held in honor, Coleridge became his ardent disciple. In the "Religious Musings," after Milton and Newton, he speaks of Hartley as —

> "He of mortal kind
> Wisest: the first who marked the ideal tribes
> Up the fine fibres to the sentient brain."

Materialistic though his system was, Hartley was himself a believer in Christianity, and a religious man. His philosophical system came to be in high favor with Priestley and the Unitarians towards the end of last century; so that when Coleridge became a Hartleian, he adopted Necessitarian views of the will, and Unitarian tenets in religion. A Materialist, a Necessitarian, a Unitarian, such was Coleridge during his Cambridge and Bristol sojourn. But it was not possible that he should be permanently holden of these things. There were ideal lights and moral yearnings within him which these could never satisfy. The piece of divinity that was in him would not always do homage to Materialism.

Before he visited Germany he had begun to awake out of his Hartleianism. It had occurred to him that all association — Hartley's great instrument — "presupposes the existence of the thought and images to be associated." In short, association cannot account for its own laws. All that association does is to use these laws, or latent *a priori* forms, to wit, contiguity of time and place, resemblance, contrast, so as to bring particular things under them. When two things have been thus brought together under one law — say contiguity in time — they may get so connected in thought that it becomes difficult to conceive them apart. But it never can be impossible so to conceive them; that is, to separate them in thought. Further, he began to see that the hypothesis of all knowledge, being derived from sense, does not get rid of the need of a living intellectual framework, which makes these copies from sensible impressions. To take his own illustration, the existence of an original picture, say Raphael's Transfiguration, does not account for the existence of a copy of it; but rather the copyist must have put forth the same powers, and gone through the same process, as the first painter did when he made the original picture. Or take that instance, which is a kind of standing Hougoumont to sensational and idealistic combatants, — I mean causality, or the belief that every event must have a cause. Sensationalists, from Hume to Mr. Mill, have labored to derive this, the grand principle of all inductive reasoning, from invariable experience. Mr. Mill's theory, the latest and most accredited from that side, thus explains it. He says that we arrive, by simple enumeration of individual instances, first at one and then at another particular uniformity, till we have collected a large number of such uniformities, or groups of cases in which the law of causation holds good. From this collection of the more obvious particular uniformities, in all of which the law of causation holds, we generalize the universal law of causation, or the belief that all things whatever have a cause; and then we proceed to apply this law so generalized as an inductive instrument to discover those other particular laws which go to make up itself, but which have hitherto eluded our investigation. Thus, according to this philosopher, we arrive at the universal law by generalizing from many laws of inferior generality. But as these last do not rest on rigid induction, but only on simple enumeration of instances, the universal law cannot lay claim to any greater cogency than the inferior laws on which it rests. One authenticated instance in which the law of causality does not hold may upset our belief in the universal validity of that law. And Mr. Mill accepts this consequence. He finds no difficulty in conceiving that there may be worlds in which it is so upset — in which events succeed each other at random, and by no fixed law. But this is really a *reductio ad absurdum*. This world of causeless disorder, which Mr. Mill finds no difficulty in conceiving, is simply inconceivable by any intelligence. If such a world were proved to exist, we should be compelled to believe that for this absence of order there is a cause, or group of causes ; just as we know there is a cause, or group of causes, for the presence of that order which we know to exist as far as our knowledge extends. This necessity to think a cause for every existence or event, a necessity which we cannot get rid of, forms the essential peculiarity of the notion of causality ; marking it out as a necessary form of thought, born from within, and not gathered from experience. That which is created by experience is strengthened by the same. But this belief that every event must have a cause, is one which, as soon as we have clearly comprehended the terms, we feel to be inevitable. Experience, no doubt, first brings this cognition out into distinct consciousness ; but as soon as we reflect on it, we discover that it must have been present as a constituent element of that very experience. Of causality, then, it may be said, what an able young metaphysician has lately said of time and space, "Themselves cognitions generalized from experience, and, in that point of view, later than experience; they are discovered to have been also elements of those very cognitions of experience from which they have been generalized, present in them as constituent elements, undistinguished before analysis. . . . . They are elements of any and every particular experience, entering into every one of them as its necessary form." Or, as Coleridge put it, "Though first revealed to us by experience, they must yet have preëxisted in order to make experience itself possible; even as the eye must exist previously to any particular act of seeing, though by sight only can we know that we have eyes." And again, "How can we make bricks without straw, or build without cement? We learn things, indeed, by occasion of experience; but the very facts so learned force us inward on the antecedents that must be presupposed in order to render experience itself possible."

These and such like thoughts were sure to arise in a mind naturally so open to the idealistic side of thought as that of Coleridge, and to shake to pieces the materialistic fabric in which he had for a time ensconced himself. And not merely intellectual misgivings would work this way, but the soul's deeper cravings. Driven by hunger of heart, he wandered from the school of Locke and Hartley, successively on through those of Berkeley, Leibnitz, and, I believe, Spinoza, and finding in them no abiding place, began to despair of philosophy. To this crisis of his history probably apply these words: —

"I found myself all afloat. Doubts rushed in, broke upon me from the fountains of the great deep, and fell from the windows of heaven. The fontal truths of natural religion and the books of revelation alike contributed to the flood; and it was long ere my 'ark touched on an Ararat and rested.' "

About this time he fell in with the works of the German and other mystics — Tauler, Böhmen, George Fox, and William Law, and in them he found the same kind of help which Luther had found in Tauler: —

"The writings of these mystics acted in no slight degree to prevent my mind from being imprisoned within the outline of any single dogmatic system. They helped to keep alive the heart within the head; gave me an indistinct yet stirring presentiment that all the products of the mere reflective faculty partook of death, and were as the rattling twigs and sprays in winter, into which a sap was yet to be propelled from some root to which I had not as yet penetrated, if they were to afford my soul food or shelter. If they (the mystics) were a moving cloud of smoke to me by day, yet were they a pillar of fire throughout the night, during my wanderings through the wilderness of doubt, and enabled me to skirt, without crossing, the sandy deserts of utter unbelief."

It was in the company of these men that he first got clear of the trammels of the mere understanding, and learned that there is higher truth than that faculty can compass and circumscribe. The learned seemed to him for several generations to have walked entirely by the light of this mere understanding, and to have confined their investigations strictly within certain conventional limits, beyond which lay all that is most interesting and vital to man. To enthusiasts, illiterate and simple men of heart, they left it to penetrate towards the inmost centre, "the indwelling and living ground of all things." And then he came to this conviction, which he never afterwards abandoned, that if the intellect will acknowledge a higher and deeper ground than it contains within itself, if, making itself the centre of its system, it seeks to square all things by its own laws, it must, if it follows out fearlessly its own reasoning, land in Pantheism or in some form of blank unbelief.

While his mind was seething with these thoughts it was that he first studied the works of Kant, and these he says, took hold of him as with a giant's hand. Henceforth his metaphysical creed was moulded mainly by the Kantian principles. This is not the place to attempt to enter on the slightest exposition of these. But, to speak popularly, it may be said that the gist of Kant's system is not to make the mind out of the senses as Hume had done, but the senses out of the mind. As Locke and Hume had started from without, so he started from within, making the one fixed truth, the only ground of reality, to consist, not in that which the senses furnish, but in that which the understanding supplies to make sensible knowledge possible. His prime question was, How is experience possible? And this possibility he found in the *a priori* forms of the sensory, time and space, and in the *a priori* forms or categories of the understanding, which by their activity bind together into one the multifarious and otherwise unintelligent intimations of sense. It is sense that supplies the understanding with the raw material; this the understanding passes through its machinery, and, by virtue of its inherent concept-forms, reduces it to order, makes it conceivable and intelligible. But the understanding is limited in its operation to phenomena of experience, and whenever it steps beyond these and applies its categories to supersensible things, it lands itself in contradictions. It cannot arrive at any other truth than that which is valid within man's experience.

Ultimate truths, valid for all intelligents, if such there be, are beyond its reach.

Had Kant's philosophy stopped here, it would not have done much more for Coleridge than Locke's and Hartley's had done. It was because Kant asserted the existence in man of another power, distinct from and higher than understanding, namely Reason, that Coleridge found him so helpful. The term *Reason* Kant employed in another than our ordinary sense, as the faculty of ultimate truths or necessary principles. He distinguished, however, between Reason in its speculative and in its practical use. Speculative Reason he held to be exclusively a regulative faculty, having only a formal and logical use. This use is to connect our judgments together into conclusions, according to the three forms of reasoning — the categorical, the hypothetical, and the disjunctive. These three methods are the ideas of Speculative Reason by which it strives to produce unity and perfectness among the judgments of the understanding. As long as the ideas of Speculative Reason are thus used to control and bring into unity the conceptions of the discursive understanding, they are used rightly, and within their own legitimate sphere. But whenever Speculative Reason tries to elevate these regulative ideas into objects of theoretical knowledge, whenever it ascribes objective truth to these ideas, it leads to contradiction and falsehood. In other words, Speculative Reason Kant held to be true in its formal or logical, but false in its material application. As the understanding, with its categories, has for its object and only legitimate sphere the world of sense, so Speculative Reason, with its ideas, has for its exclusive sphere of operation the conceptions of the understanding, and beyond this these ideas have no truth or validity. It was not, however, by these views, either of Understanding or of Speculative Reason, that Kant came to the help of the highest interests of humanity, but by his assertion of the existence in man of the Practical Reason which is the sufficient warrant for our belief in moral and supersensuous truth. Some have maintained this to be an afterthought added on somewhat discordantly to the rest of Kant's system. But, be this as it may, Kant held that the moral law revealed itself to man as a reality through his Practical Reason — a law not to be gathered from experience, but to be received as a fundamental principle of action for man, evidencing itself by its own light. This moral law requires for its action the truth of three ideas, that of the soul, of immortality, and of God. These ideas are the postulates of the practical reason, and are true and certain, because, if they are denied, morality and free-will, man's highest certainties, become impossible. They are, however, to man truths of moral cogency — of practical faith, though Kant did not use this last expression, — rather than objects of scientific certitude.

This distinction between the Understanding and the Reason Coleridge adopted from Kant, and made the groundwork of all his teaching. But the distinction between Speculative and Practical Reason, which was with Kant radical, Coleridge did not dwell on, nor bring into prominence. He knew and so far recognized Kant's distinction, that he spoke of Speculative Reason as the faculty of concluding universal and necessary truths from particular and contingent appearances, and of Practical Reason as the power of proposing an ultimate end, that is, of determining the will by ideas. He does not, however, seem to have held by it firmly. Rather, he threw himself mainly on Kant's view of Practical Reason, and carried it out with a boldness which Kant would have probably disallowed. Kant's strong assertion that there was at least one region of his being in which man comes into contact with supersensible truth, with the reality of things, this, set forth not vaguely, but with the most solid reasoning, was that which so attracted Coleridge. But in the use which Coleridge made of this power, and the range he assigned it, he went much beyond his master. He speaks of Reason as an immediate beholding of supersensible things, as the eye which sees truths transcending sense. He identifies Reason in the human mind, as Kant perhaps would have done, with Universal Reason; calls it impersonal; indeed, regards it as a ray of the Divinity in man. In one place he makes it one with the light which lighteth every man, and in another he says that Reason is "the presence of the Holy Spirit to the finite understanding, at once the light and the inward eye." "It cannot be rightly called a faculty," he says, "much less a personal property of any human mind." We cannot be said to possess Reason, but rather to partake of it; for there is but one Reason, which is shared by all intelligent beings, and is in itself the universal or Supreme Reason. "He in whom Reason dwells can as little appropriate it as his own possession, as he can claim ownership in the breathing air, or make an inclosure in the cope of heaven." Again, he says of Reason, that "it has been said to be more like to sense than to understanding; but in this it differs from sense: the bodily senses have objects differing from themselves; Reason, the organ of spiritual apprehension, has objects consubstantial with itself, being itself its own object, — that is, self-contemplative." And, again, "Reason substantiated and vital, one only, yet manifold, overseeing all, and going through all understanding, without being either the sense, the understanding, or the imagination, contains all three within itself, even as the mind contains its own thoughts, and is present in and through them all; or as the expression pervades the different features of an intelligent countenance."

In much of the above, Coleridge has not only gone beyond Kant's cautious handling of Practical Reason, but has given to the German's philosophical language a religious, and even a Biblical, coloring of his own. Nay, in regarding Reason as the power of intuitive insight into moral and spiritual truths, he has approached nearer to some of the German philosophers who came after Kant. Though Coleridge made so much of this distinction between Reason and Understanding, and of Reason as the organ of spiritual truth, and though throughout his later works he is continually insisting on it as a fundamental principle, yet he cannot be said to have made it secure against the objections of assailants.

It is a theory to account for certain great facts of mental experience, and like every theory it must be tested by its fitness to explain the facts, and to solve the chief difficulties they present. The facts are these. Amid the objects of thought we find a large number of which we can form distinct, well-rounded conceptions, and from these conceptions so formed, we can deduce accurate trains of reasoning. Another portion of the things which occupy our thoughts are of such a nature that, if truths at all, they are transcendent truths. The best conceptions we can form of them we feel to be defective and inadequate, not presenting to us the idea as it truly is, but only hinting it through "feeble analogies and approximations." Such objects of thought, it is often said, we apprehend, but cannot comprehend. To this latter category belong the fundamental truths of morals and religion, those primal faiths on which man's spiritual nature rests. But the logical faculty ever tends, if left to itself, to ignore or even deny the reality of this whole order of truths, because they cannot be reduced to that clear-cut precision after which this faculty ever strives. And philosophers, whose vocation it is to exercise this faculty, and in all subjects to seek for reasoned truth, are prone to become the victims of the instrument which they use, and to deny the existence, for us at least, of whatever cannot be shaped into clear conceptions, and made fast in the grip of conclusive logic. They ever tend to circumscribe the orb of belief, and to narrow it within exactly the same limits as the orb of logical conception. If this tendency had full way, what place would be found for all the higher side of man's being, for those truths by which the spirit lives, those primal truths which, though transcendent, and hard to grasp, —

"Are yet the master light of all our seeing?"

It was to vindicate the validity of these truths, and to show that though man's thought cannot fully compass them, they are not less real, and far more vital, than the conclusions of the most irrefragable logic, that Coleridge insisted so earnestly on his doctrine of the distinction between Reason and Understanding.

That in making this distinction he was striving to utter a deep spiritual truth, which lies at the bottom of all human thought, I fully believe. But whether he has succeeded in uttering it in the best, most unassailable shape, may well be made a question. It is not easy to meet the old challenge, "Name a certain number of propositions which are products to the Reason, and as many more which belong to the Understanding, that we may compare the two sets, and learn to appreciate the distinction." Since all truths, from whatever source they come, must, before they can be reduced to definite conceptions, and expressed in propositions, first have passed through the moulds of the understanding, it seems hardly possible to produce a single truth, unless it be the law of contradiction, and the other necessary laws of formal logic, which is the pure mint of the reason, unalloyed by contact with the understanding. A close examination would, I believe, show that what Coleridge called truths of the reason are mainly those moral and spiritual faiths, the possession of which makes man a moral being. Though they are born undoubtedly in another region than the understanding, yet before they can become distinct objects of reflection, they must have been shaped by intellectual moulds, and expressed in linguistic terms, which, as regards the truths themselves, are but poor and inadequate accommodations. Coleridge recognized the necessity of this process, but maintained that it was to him no argument against a truth of reason, if, after passing through the logical process, it issued in propositions which seem illogical and contradictory. To this, one of the uninitiated might naturally reply, "It may be so; but if your truths of the reason when attempted to be logically expressed issue in contradictions, by what test am I to distinguish such a truth of reason from absolute nonsense?" A satisfactory reply to such a querist I do not know that Coleridge has ever furnished. On the whole, it would seem that Reason, as he used it, is but another and perhaps not better name for what, in vague popular phrase, is known as man's moral and spiritual nature. His truths of Reason are that which is essential and primitive in this nature,— those elemental truths, which we cannot adequately grasp, but on which we are in the last resort constrained to fall back, as the ultimate ground of all belief — indeed, as the very substratum of our being. If to vindicate fully this transcendent side of being, to show how it is cogitable, and in harmony with logical thought and with all other truth, if this be the great aim of philosophy, it cannot be said that Coleridge has fully accomplished it. On the other hand, at a time when philosophy had almost forgotten the problem, and discarded the higher truths as mere fanatical chimeras, to have brought the question once more into court, to have reasserted the reality and the preëminence of the spiritual verities, to have pressed for their admittance into and reconciliation with men's ordinary ways of thinking; this was good service, and this service Coleridge did.

A good example of the way in which Coleridge applied his metaphysical principles to philosophic questions will be found in the Essays on Method, in the third volume of "The Friend." He there attempts to reconcile Plato's view of the Idea as lying at the ground of all investigation with Bacon's philosophy of induction, and to prove that, though they worked from opposite ends of the problem, they are not really opposed. In all inductive investigations, Coleridge contends, the mind must contribute something, the mental initiative, the *prudens quæstio*, the idea; and this, when tested or proved by rigorous scientific processes, is found to be a law of nature. What in the mind of the discoverer is a prophetic idea, is found in nature to be a law, and the one answers, and is akin to the other. What Coleridge has there said of the mental initiative which lies at the foundation of induction, Dr. Whewell has taken up and argued out at length in his works on Induction. Mr. Mill has as stoutly redargued it from his own point of view, and their polemic still waits a solution. But I must pass from these pure metaphysical questions to notice some of the ways in which Coleridge applied his principles to moral and religious questions.

In the "Literary Remains" there is a remarkable essay on Faith, which contains a suggestive application of these principles. Faith he defines to be fealty or fidelity to that part of our being which cannot become an object of the senses; to that in us which is highest, and is alone unconditionally imperative. What is this? Every man is conscious of something within him which tells him he ought, which commands him, to do to others as he would they should do to him. Of this he is as assured as he is that he sees and hears; only with this difference, that the senses act independently of the will; whereas, the conscience is essentially connected with the will. We can, if we will, refuse to listen to it. The listening or the not listening to conscience is the first moral act by which a man takes upon him or refuses allegiance to a power higher than himself, yet speaking within himself. Now, what is this in each man, higher than himself, yet speaking within him? It is Reason, supersensuous, impersonal, the representative in man of the will of God; and demanding the allegiance of the individual will. Faith then is fealty to this rightful superior; "allegiance of the moral nature to Universal Reason, or the will of God; in opposition to all usurpation whether of appetite, or of sensible objects, or of the finite understanding," or of affection to others, be it even the purest love of the creature. And conscience is the inward witness to the presence in us of the divine ray of reason, "which is the irradiative power, the representative of the Infinite." An approving conscience is the sense of harmony of the personal will of man with that impersonal light which is in him, representative of the will of God. A condemning conscience is the sense of discord or contrariety between these two. Faith, then, consists in the union and interpenetration of the Reason and the individual will. Since our will and moral nature enter into it, faith must be a continuous and total energy of the whole man. Since Reason enters into it, faith must be a light — a seeing, a beholding of truth. Hence faith is a spiritual act of the whole being; it is "the source and germ of the fidelity of man to God, by the entire subjugation of the human will to Reason, as the representative in Him of the divine will." Such is a condensation, nearly in Coleridge's own words, of the substance of that essay. Hard words and repulsive these may seem to some, who feel it painful to analyze the faith they live by. And no doubt the simple childlike apprehension of the things of faith is better and more blessed than all philosophizing about them. They who have good health and light breathing, whose system is so sound that they know not they have a system, have little turn for disquisitions on health and respiration. But, just as sickness and disease have compelled men to study the bodily framework, so doubt and mental entanglement have forced men to go into these abstruse questions in order to meet the philosophy of denial with a counter philosophy of faith. The philosophy is not faith, but it may help to clear away sophistications that stand in the way of it.

For entering into speculations of this kind, Coleridge has been branded as a transcendentalist, — a word with many of hideous import. But abstruse and wide of practice as these speculations may seem, it was for practical behoof mainly that Coleridge undertook them. "What are my metaphysics?" he exclaims;

"merely the referring of the mind to its own consciousness for truths which are indispensable to its own happiness." Of this any one may be convinced who shall read with care his "Friend" or his "Lay Sermons." One great source of the difficulty, or, as some might call it, the confusedness of these works, is the rush and throng of human interests with which they are filled. If he discusses the ideas of Reason, or any other like abstract subject, it is because he feels its vital bearing on some truth of politics, morality, or religion, the clear understanding of which concerns the common weal. And here is one of his strongest mental peculiarities, which has made many censure him as unintelligible. His eye flashed with a lightning glance from most abstract truth to the minutest practical detail, and back again from this to the abstract principle. This makes that, when once his mental powers begin to work, their movements are on a vastness of scale, and with a many-sidedness of view, which, if they render him hard to follow, make him also stimulative and suggestive of thought beyond all other modern writers.

When Coleridge first began to speculate, the sovereignty of Locke and his followers in English Metaphysics was not more supreme than that of Paley in Moral Philosophy. Both were Englishmen of the round robust English stamp, haters of subtleties, abhorrent of idealism, resolute to warn off any ghost of scholasticism from the domain of common-sense philosophy. And yet both had to lay down dogmatic decisions on subjects into which, despite the burliest common sense, things infinite and spiritual will intrude. How resolute was Coleridge's polemic against Locke and all his school, we have seen. Not less vigorous was his protest against Paley as a moralist, and that at a time when few voices were raised against the common-sense Dean.

For completely rounded moral systems Coleridge indeed professed little respect, ranking them for utility with systems of casuistry or auricular confession. But of vital principles of morality, penetrating to the quick, few men's writings are more fruitful. A standing butt for Coleridge's shafts was Paley's well-known definition of virtue as "the doing of good to mankind, in obedience to the will of God, and for the sake of everlasting happiness." Or, as Paley has elsewhere more broadly laid down the same principle, "we are obliged to do nothing, but what we ourselves are to gain or lose something by, for nothing else can be a violent motive." Against this substitution, as he called it, of a scheme of selfish prudence for moral virtue, Coleridge was never weary of raising his voice. Morality, as he contended, arises out of the Reason and Conscience of man; prudence out of the Understanding, and the natural wants and desires of the individual; and though prudence is the worthy servant of morality, the master and the servant must not be confounded. The chapter in "The Friend," in which he argues against the Utilitarian system of ethics, and proves that general consequences cannot be the criterion of the right and wrong of particular actions, is one of the best reasoned and most valuable which that work contains. The following are some of the arguments with which he contends against "the inadequacy of the principle of general consequences as a criterion of right and wrong, and its utter uselessness as a moral guide." Such a criterion is vague and illusory, for it depends on each man's notion of happiness, and no two men have exactly the same notion. And even if men were agreed as to what constitutes the end, namely, happiness, the power of calculating consequences, and the foresight needed to secure the means to the end, are just that in which men most differ. But morality ought to be grounded on that part of their nature, namely, their moral convictions, in which men are most alike, not on the calculating understanding, in which they most differ. Again, such a criterion confounds morality, which looks to the inward motive, with law, which regards only the outward act. Indeed, the need of a judgment of actions according to the inward motive, forms one of the strongest arguments for a future state. For in this world our outward actions, apart from their motives, must needs determine our temporal welfare. But the moral nature longs for, and Scripture reveals, a more perfect judgment to come, wherein not the outward act but the inward principle, the thoughts and intents of the heart, shall be made the ground of judgment. Again, this criterion is illusory, because evil actions are often turned to good by that Providence which brings good out of evil. If, then, consequences were the sole or chief criterion, then these evil actions ought to be, because of their results, reckoned good. Nero persecuted the Christians, and so spread Christianity: is he to be credited with this good result? Again, to form a notion of the nature of an action multiplied indefinitely into the future, we must first know the nature of the original action itself. And if we already know this, what need of testing it by its remote consequences? If against these arguments it were urged that general consequences are the criterion, not of the agent but of the action, Coleridge would reply that all actions have their whole worth and main value from the moral principle which actuates the agent. So that if it could be shown that two men, one acting from enlightened self-love, the other from pure Christian principle, would observe towards all their neighbors throughout life exactly the same course of outward conduct, yet these two, measured by a true moral standard, would stand wide apart in worth. By these and such like arguments Coleridge opposes the Paleyan and every other form of Utilitarian ethics. Instead of confounding morality with prudence, he everywhere bases morality on religion. "The widest maxims of prudence," he asserts, "are arms without hearts, when disjoined from those feelings which have their fountain in a living principle." That principle lies in the common ground where morality and religion meet, and from which neither can be sundered without destruction to both. The moral law, every man feels, has a universality and an imperativeness far transcending the widest maxims of experience; and this because it has its origin in Reason, as described above, in that in each man which is representative of the Divine Will, and connects him therewith. Out of Reason, not from experience, all pure principles of morality spring, and in it they find their sanction. This is a truth which Coleridge reiterated in every variety of form.

But while he is thus strong in placing the foundation of individual morality in Reason, in his sense of that word, he repudiates those theories which would draw from the same source the first principles of political government. In opposition to these theories, he held that each form of government is sufficiently justified, when it can be shown that it is suitable to the circumstances of the particular nation. Therefore no one form of government can lay claim to be the sole rightful one. Thus to prudence or expediency Coleridge assigns a place in political questions which he denies to it in moral ones. Full of power is his whole argument against Rousseau, Paine, and others of that day, who maintained the social contract and the rights of man, and, laying the grounds of political right exclusively in Reason, held that nothing was rightful in civil society which could not be deduced from the primary laws of reason. "Who," asked Rousseau, "shall dare prescribe a law of moral action for any rational being, considered as a member of a state, which does not flow immediately from that reason which is the fountain of all morality?" Whereto Coleridge replies, Morality looks not to the outward act, but to the internal maxim of actions. But politics look solely to the outward act. The end of good government is so to regulate the actions of particular bodies of men, as shall be most expedient under given circumstances. How then can the same principle be employed to test the expediency of political rules and the purity of inward motives? He then goes on to show that, when Rousseau asserted that every human being possessed of Reason had in him an inalienable sovereignty, he applied to actual man — compassed about with passions, errors, vices, and infirmities — what is true of the abstract Reason alone; that all he asserted of "that sovereign will, to which the right of legislation belongs, applies to no human being, to no assemblage of human beings, least of all to the mixed multitude that makes up the people; but entirely and exclusively to Reason itself, which, it is true, dwells in every man potentially, but actually and in perfect purity in no man, and in no body of men." And this reasoning he clinches by an instance and an argument, often since repeated, though we know not whether Coleridge was the first to employ it. He shows that the constituent assembly of France, whenever they tried to act out these principles of pure Reason, were forced to contravene them. They excluded from political power children, though reasonable beings, because in them Reason is imperfect; women, because they are dependent. But is there not more of Reason in many women, and even in some children, than in men dependent for livelihood on the will of others, the very poor, the infirm of mind, the ignorant, the depraved? Some reasonable beings must be disfranchised. It comes then to a question of degrees. And how are degrees to be determined? Not by pure reason, but by rules of expedience, founded on present observation and past experience. But the whole of Coleridge's reasoning against Rousseau and Cartwright's universal suffrage is well worth the attention of those advanced thinkers of the present day, who are beginning once again, after a lapse of nearly a century, to argue about political rights on grounds of abstract reason. They will there find, if they care to see it, the whole question placed not on temporary arguments, but on permanent principles.

But keen as was Coleridge's interest in political and moral subjects, the full bent of his soul, and its deepest meditations, were given to the truths of the Christian revelation, as bearing most profoundly on the well-being of man. From none of his works are these thoughts absent; but the fullest exposition of his religious views is to be found in the "Aids to Reflection," his maturest work, and in the third and fourth volumes of the "Literary Remains." Before, however, adverting to these opinions, it may be well to remember, that, much as Coleridge thought and reasoned on religion, it was his firm conviction, founded on experience, that the way to an assured faith, that faith which gives life and peace, is not to be won by dint of argument. "Evidences of Christianity!" he exclaims, "I am weary of the word. Make a man feel the *want* of it; rouse him, if you can, to the self-knowledge of the need of it, and you may safely trust it to its own evidence, remembering always the express declaration of Christ himself: 'No man cometh to me, unless the Father leadeth him.'" So it was with himself. Much as he philosophized, philosophy was not his soul's haven; not thence did his help come. It may have cleared away outlying hindrances, but it was not this that led him up to the stronghold of hope. Through the wound made in his own spirit, through the brokenness of a heart humbled and made contrite by the experience of his own sin and utter helplessness, entered in the faith which gave rest, the peace which "settles where the intellect is meek." Once his soul had reached the cidatel, his ever busy eye and penetrating spirit surveyed the nature of the bulwarks, and examined the foundations, as few before had done. And the world has the benefit, whatever it may be, of these surveys. But though Coleridge was a religious philosopher, he discriminated clearly between the philosophy and the religion. He knew well, and often insisted, that religion is life rather than science, and that there is a danger, peculiar to the intellectual man, of turning into speculation what was given to live by. He knew that the intellect, busy with ideas about God, may not only fail to bring a man nearer the divine life, but may actually tend to withdraw him from it. For the intellect takes in but the image of the truth, and leaves the vital impression, the full power of it, unappropriated. And hence it comes that those truths which, if felt by the unlearned at all, go straight to the heart and are taken in by the whole man, are apt, in the case of the philosopher and the theologian, to stop at the vestibule of the understanding, and never to get further. This is a danger peculiar to the learned, or to those who think themselves such. The trained intellect is apt to eat out the child's heart, and yet the "except ye become as little children" stands unrepealed. Coleridge knew this well. In his earliest interview with De Quincey, he said, "that prayer with the whole soul is the highest energy of which the human heart is capable, and that the great mass of worldly men, and of learned men, are absolutely incapable of prayer." And only two years before his death, after a retrospect of his own life, to his nephew, who sat by his bedside one afternoon, he said, "I have no difficulty in forgiveness. . . . Neither do I find or reckon the most solemn faith in God as a real object the most arduous act of reason and will. O no! it is to pray, to pray as God would have us: that is what at times makes me turn cold to my soul. Believe me, to pray with all your heart and strength, with the reason and the will, to believe vividly that God will listen to your voice through Christ, and verily do the thing He pleaseth thereupon — this is the last, the greatest achievement of a Christian's warfare on earth." "And then he burst into tears, and begged me to pray for him."

It has been said that the great object of his theological speculations was to bring into harmony religion and philosophy. This assertion would mislead if it were meant to imply that he regarded these as two coordinate powers, which could be welded together into one reasoned system. It would perhaps be more true to say that his endeavor was, in his own words, to remove the doubts and difficulties that cannot but arise whenever the understanding, the mind of the flesh, is made the measure of spiritual things. He labored to remove religion from a merely mechanical or intellectual, and to place it on a moral and spiritual foundation. His real aim was, notwithstanding that his love for scholastic distinctions might seem to imply the contrary, to simplify men's thoughts on these things, to show that spiritual truth is, like the light, self-evidencing, that it is preconformed to man's higher nature, as man's nature is preconformed to it.

As he had to contend against Lockeian metaphysics and Paleyan ethics, so he had to do strenuous battle against a theology mainly mechanical. He awoke upon an age when the belief in God was enforced in the schools as the conclusion of a lengthened argument; when revelation was proved exclusively by miracles, with little regard to its intrinsic evidence; and when both natural and revealed truths were superinduced from without, as extraneous, extra-moral beliefs, rather than taught as living faiths evidenced from within. In opposition to this kind of teaching, which had so long reigned, Coleridge taught that the foundation truth of all religion, faith in the existence of God, was incapable of intellectual demonstration — that as all religion, so this corner-stone of religion, must have a moral origin. To him that belief was inherent in the soul, as Reason is inherent, indeed a part of Reason, in the sense he gave to that word, as moral in its nature, and the fountain of moral truth. His creed on this subject he thus expresses: —

"Because I possess Reason, or a law of right and wrong, which, uniting with the sense of moral responsibility, constitutes my conscience, hence it is my absolute duty to believe, and I do believe, that there is a God, that is, a Being in whom supreme Reason and a most holy will are one with infinite power; and that all holy will is coincident with the will of God, and therefore secure in its ultimate consequences by his omnipotence. The wonderful works of God in the sensible world are a perpetual discourse, reminding me of his existence, and a shadowing out to me his perfections. But as all language presupposes, in the intelligent hearer or reader, those primary notions which it symbolizes, ... even so, I believe that the notion of God is essential to the human mind ; that it is called forth into distinct consciousness principally by the conscience, and auxiliarily by the manifest adaptation of means to ends in the outward creation. It is therefore evident to my Reason, that the existence of God is absolutely and necessarily insusceptible of a scientific demonstration, and that Scripture so represents it. For it commands us to believe in one God. Now all commandment necessarily relates to the will ; whereas all scientific demonstration is independent of the will, and is demonstrative only in so far as it is compulsory on the mind, *volentem, nolentem.*"

Thus we see that with regard to the first truth of all religion, Coleridge places its evidence in conscience and the intuitive reason. Carrying the same manner of thinking into revealed religion, he gave to its inherent substance the foremost place as evidence, while to historical proofs and arguments from miracles he assigned the same subordinate place as, in reference to the existence of God, he assigned to arguments from design.

His view upon this subject also is better given in his own language. It could hardly be expressed in fewer, and certainly not in better words. The main evidence, he thinks, are " the doctrines of Christainity, and the correspondence of human nature to these doctrines, illustrated, *first*, historically, as the production of a new world, and the dependence of the fate of the planet upon it ; *second*, individually, from its appeal to an ascertained fact, the truth of which every man possessing Reason has an equal power of ascertaining within himself ; namely, a will, which has more or less lost its own freedom, though not the consciousness that it ought to be and may become free; the conviction that this cannot be achieved without the operation of a principle co-natural with itself; the experience in his own nature of the truth of the process described by Scripture, as far as he can place himself within the process, aided by the confident assurances of others as to the effects experienced by them, and which he is striving to arrive at. All these form a practical Christian. To such a man one main test of the truth is his faith in its accompaniment by a growing insight into the moral beauty and necessity of the process which it comprises, and the dependence of that process on the causes asserted. Believe, and if thy belief be right, that insight which changes faith into knowledge, will be the reward of that belief."

Subordinate to the internal evidence in Coleridge's view — buttresses, but not corner-stones — are the facts of the existence and of the history of Christianity, and also of the miracles which accompanied its first appearance. These are necessary results, rather than primary proofs of revelation. "As the result of the above convictions, he will not scruple to receive the particular miracles recorded, inasmuch as it is miraculous that an incarnate God should not work what must to mere men appear as miracles; inasmuch as it is strictly accordant with the ends and benevolent nature of such a Being to commence the elevation of man above his mere senses by enforcing attention first, through an appeal to those senses." Thus, according to him, miracles are not the adequate and ultimate proof of religion, not the keystone of the arch, but rather "compacting stones in it, which give while they receive strength."

It thus appears that Coleridge's theology was more

or less a recoil from one in which miracles had been pushed into undue, almost exclusive, prominence, one in which the proof of religion was derived mainly from the outward senses. In accordance with his pre-eminently subjective mode of thought, he was convinced that to subjugate the senses to faith, the passive belief to the moral and responsible belief, was one main end of all religion. Whether Coleridge struck the balance rightly between outward and inward evidence, whether he gave to miracles that place which is their due; whether, in his zeal for the inward truths, he estimated as they deserve the miraculous facts which, whatever they may be to some over-subtilized intellects, have been, and always must be, to the great mass of men, the main objective basis on which the spiritual truths repose, — these are questions on which I shall not now enter. My aim here is not so much to criticise, as to set forth, as fairly as may be, what his views really were.

We have seen then that Coleridge held the adaptation of Christianity to man's need, and to his whole moral nature, to be the strongest evidence of its truth. And this naturally suggests the question, How far did he regard man's moral convictions to be the test of revelation as a whole, or of any particular doctrine of revelation? Did he wish to square down the truths of revelation to the findings of human conscience? To answer this question is the more necessary, because Mr. Mill, in the few remarks on Coleridge's religious opinions with which he closes his essay, has asserted that he "goes as far as the Unitarians in making man's reason and moral feelings a test of revelation; but differs *toto cœlo* from them in their rejection of its mysteries, which he regards as the highest philosophical truths." It would be strange, indeed, if Coleridge, who certainly ought to have known both his own views and those of the Unitarians, should have so far deluded himself as to protest against them unweariedly for this very fault, that they made man the measure of all things, while in this matter he himself was substantially at one with them. The truth is, that those who speak most strongly about Reason being the measure of faith, mean by the word Reason much the same as Coleridge meant by Understanding — the faculty of definite conceptions, the power of clearly comprehending truths. And in their mouths the proposition means that nothing is to be believed in religion, or in anything else, which man's understanding cannot fully grasp, clearly conceive, definitely express, satisfactorily explain. Now Coleridge used the term Reason in a sense different from this, nay opposed to it. He held, whether rightly or no I do not now inquire, but he held that there is a power in man to apprehend spiritual truths which he cannot comprehend, — something that brings him into close relation, I had almost said contact, with supersensible reality, — and to this power he gave the name of Reason. And the intimations of moral and spiritual things, which he believed that he received through this power, he accepted readily, though he could not understand nor explain them. Even with regard to the first truth of religion, the existence, personality, and moral nature of God, he held that this is to be received on moral grounds, and regarded as a settled truth "not by the removal of all difficulties, or by any such increase of insight as enables a man to meet all skeptical objections with a full and precise answer; but because he has convinced himself that it is folly as well as presumption to expect it; and because the doubts and difficulties disappear at the beam when tried against the weight of the reasons in the other scale." Again, of the fall of man, he says that it is a mystery too profound for human insight; and of the doctrine of the Trinity, that it is an absolute truth transcending our human means of understanding or demonstrating it. These, and numerous other such like sayings, might be adduced, not to speak of the whole scope of his philosophy, to show that it was no obstacle to his belief in the truth, that it transcended his comprehension. Nay, more, so far was he from desiring to bring down all religious truths to the level of human comprehension, that he everywhere enforced it as a thing antecedently to be expected, that the fundamental truths should be mysteries, and declared that he would have found it hard to believe them if they had not been so.

What then did he mean when he maintained, as he certainly did, that "in no case can true Reason and a right faith oppose each other?" We have seen that Reason with Coleridge was the link by which man is joined on to a higher order, the source whence he draws in all of moral truth and of religious sentiment which he possesses. It was the harmony of revelation with this faculty of apprehending universal spiritual truths which was to him the main ground for originally believing in revelation, and therefore he held that no particular doctrine of revelation can contradict the findings of that faculty on the evidence of which revelation as a whole is originally received. In other words, no view of God's nature and of his dealings with men, no interpretation of any doctrine, or of any text of Scripture, can be true, which contradicts the clear intimations of enlightened conscience. And the substance of revelation and the dictates of conscience so answer to each other, that the religious student, under the guidance of the Divine Spirit, may expect to gain an ever-growing insight into their harmony. Opposed to this doctrine of Coleridge, on the one hand, is the teaching of those who, believing in revelation, deny to man any power of apprehending spiritual truths, and hold that the first truths of religion must be received simply as authoritative data from without. Equally opposed, on the other hand, are the views of those who, though admitting in some sense the truth of revelation, yet make man's power of understanding the entire measure of all that is to be received as revealed. The creed which is bounded either theoretically or practically within this latter limit must needs be a scanty one.

The truth seems to be that, both in the things of natural and revealed religion, the test that lies in man's moral judgment seems more a negative than a positive one. We are not to believe about God anything which positively contradicts our first notions of righteousness and goodness, for to do so would be to cut away the original moral ground of our belief in his existence and character. Thus far our moral judgments carry us, but not much further. No rational man who believes in God at all will try to square all the facts that meet him in the natural and the moral world to his sense of right and wrong. Life is full of inscrutable facts which cannot be made by us to fit into any moral standard of ours. All that the moral judgment has a right to say with regard to them is to refuse to believe any proposed interpretation of them which contradicts the plain laws of right and wrong, any interpretation which makes God unrighteous on account of such facts, and to wait patiently in full faith that a time will come when we shall see these now inexplicable facts to have been fully consistent with the most perfect righteousness. And the same use which we make of our moral judgment in regard to the facts that meet us in life, we are bound to make of it with regard to the doctrines of revelation. We may not be able now to see moral light through all of these, but we are to refuse any interpretation of them which does violence to the moral judgment. In both cases, however, we have reason to expect that, to those who honestly and humbly use the light they have, more light will be given, — a growing insight into, or at least a trustful acquiescence in, facts which at first were too dark and perplexing. There are in this region two extremes, equally to be shunned. One is theirs, who in matters of religion begin by discrediting the natural light, — by putting out the eye of conscience, — that they may the more magnify the heavenly light of revelation, or rather their own interpretations thereof. The other is seen in those who, enthroning on the judgment-seat the first off-hand findings of their own, and that perhaps no very enlightened conscience, proceed to arraign before this bar the statements of Scripture, and to reject all which does not seem to square with the verdicts of the self-erected tribunal. There is a more excellent way than either, a way not definable perhaps by criticism, but to be found by spiritual wisdom. There are those who, loath to do violence to the teachings either of Scripture or of conscience, but patiently and reverently comparing them together, find that the more deeply they are pondered, the more they do, on the whole, reflect light one on the other. To such the words of Scripture, interpreted by the experience of life, reveal things about their own nature which once seemed incredible. And the more they know of themselves and their own needs, the more the words of Scripture seem to enlarge their meaning to meet these. But as to the large outlying region of the inexplicable that will still remain in the world, in man, and in Holy Writ, they can leave all this, in full confidence that when the solution, soon or late, shall come, it will be seen to be in profound harmony with our highest sense of righteousness, and with that word which declares that "God is light, and in him is no darkness at all." Such, though not expressed in Coleridge's words, I believe to be the spirit of his teaching.

What then is to be said of those passages in his works in which he speaks of the mysteries of faith and the highest truths of philosophy as coincident; in which he says that he received the doctrine of the Logos not merely on authority, but because of its to him exceeding reasonableness; in which he speaks as if he had an intellectual insight into the doctrine of the Trinity, and draws out formulas of it in strange words hard to understand? Whatever we may think of these sayings and formulas, it is to be remembered that Coleridge never pretended that he could have discovered the truths apart from revelation. If after practically accepting these truths, and finding in them the spiritual supports of his soul, he employed his powers of thought upon them, and drew them out into intellectual formulas more satisfactory to himself than they have for the most part proved to others, yet these philosophizings, made for the purpose of speculative insight, he neither represented as the grounds of his own faith, never obtruded on others as necessary for theirs. He ever kept steadily before him the difference between an intellectual belief and a practical faith, and asserted that it was solely in consequence of the historical fact of redemption that the Trinity becomes a doctrine, the belief in which as real is commanded by our conscience.

In the "Aids to Reflection," the earlier half of the work is employed in clearing away preliminary hindrances; the latter part deals mainly with moral diffi culties that are apt to beset the belief in the Origin Sin and in the Atonement.

With regard to the former doctrine, he shows th the belief of the existence of evil, as a fact, in man an in the world, is not peculiar to Christianity, but is com mon to it with every religion and every philosoph that has believed in a personal God; in fact, to all sy tems but Pantheism and Atheism. The fact the needs no proof, but the meaning of the fact does. A to this, Coleridge rejected that interpretation of orig nal sin, which makes "original" mean "hereditary," c inherited like our bodily constitution from our for fathers. Such, he held, might be disease or calamit but could not be sin, the meaning of which is, th choice of evil by a will free to choose between goo and evil. This fact of a law in man's nature whic opposes the law of God, is not only a fact, but a my tery, of which no other solution than the statement o the fact is possible. For consider: Sin, to be sin, evil originating in, not outside of, the will. And wh is the essence of the will? It is a self-determinin power, having the original ground of its own determ nation in itself; and if subject to any cause from witl out, such cause must have acquired this power of dete mining the will, by a previous determination of the wi itself. This is the very essence of a will. And herei it is contradistinguished from nature, whose essence is to be unable to originate anything, but to be boun in the mechanism of cause and effect. If the will h by its own act subjected itself to nature, has receive into itself from nature an alien influence which has cu tailed its freedom, in so far as it has done this, it h corrupted itself. This is original sin, or sin originatin in the only region in which it can originate — tl Will. This is a fall of man.

You ask, When did this fall take place? Has the will of each man chosen evil for itself; and, if so, when? To this Coleridge would reply that each individual will has so chosen; but as to the when, the will belongs to a region of being, is part of an order of things in which time and space have no meaning; that "the subject stands in no relation to time, can neither be called in time or out of time; but that all relations of time are as alien and heterogeneous in this question as north or south, round or square, thick or thin, are in the affections."

Again you ask, With whom did sin originate? And Coleridge replies, The grounds of will on which it is true of any one man are equally true in the case of all men. The fact is asserted of the individual, not because he has done this or that particular evil act, but simply because he is man. It is impossible for the individual to say that it commenced in this or that act, at this or that time. As he cannot trace it back to any particular moment of his life, neither can he state any moment at which it did not exist. As to this fact, then, what is true of any one man is true of all men. For, "in respect of original sin, each man is the representative of all men."

Such, nearly in his own words, was the way in which Coleridge sought, while fully acknowledging this fact, to construe it to himself, so as to get rid of those theories which make it an infliction from without, a calamity, a hereditary disease; for which, however much sorrow there might be, there could be no responsibility, and therefore no sense of guilt. And he sought to show that it is an evil self-originated in the will; a fact mysterious, not to be explained, but to be felt by each man in his conscience as his own deed. Therefore, in the confession of his faith, he said:—

"I believe (and hold it a fundamental article of Christianity) that I am a fallen creature; that I am myself capable of moral evil, but not of myself capable of moral good; and that an evil ground existed in my will previously to any given act, or assignable moment of time, in my own consciousness. I am born a child of wrath. This fearful mystery I pretend not to understand. I cannot even conceive the possibility of it, but I know that it is so. My conscience, the sole fountain of certainty, commands me to believe it, and would itself be a contradiction were it not so; and what is real must be possible."

And the sequel of the same confession thus goes on: —

"I receive, with full and grateful faith, the assurance of revelation that the Word, which is from eternity with God, and is God, assumed our human nature, in order to redeem me and all mankind from this our connate corruption. My reason convinces me that no other mode of redemption is possible. . . . . I believe that this assumption of humanity by the Son of God was revealed and realized to us by the Word made flesh, and manifested to us in Jesus Christ, and that his miraculous birth, his agony, his crucifixion, death, resurrection, and ascension, were all both symbols of our redemption, and necessary parts of the awful process."

Such was his belief in 1816, marking how great a mental revolution he must have gone through since the days when he was a Unitarian preacher. The steps of that change he has himself but partially recorded. But the abandonment of the Hartleian for a more ideal philosophy, the blight that fell on his manhood, his suffering, and sense of inner misery, then the closer study of the Bible in the light of his own need, and growing intercourse with the works of the elder divines, — all these were steps at least in the transition. But whatever may have wrought this change, no one who knows anything of Coleridge can doubt that in this, as in opinions of lesser import, he was influenced only by the sincerest desire for truth. Great as may have been his moral defects — far as he may have fallen, in some of the homeliest duties, even below common men, this at least must be conceded to him, that he desired the truth, hungered and thirsted for it, pursued it with a life-long earnestness, rare even among the best men. In this search for truth, and in his declaration of it when found, self-interest, party feeling, friendship, had no place with him. He had come to believe in some sort in a Trinity in the Godhead, and admitted more or less the personality of the Logos, for some time before he returned fully to the Catholic faith. The belief in the Incarnation and Redemption by the Cross, as historical facts, were the stumbling-blocks which last disappeared. Therefore his final conviction on this subject, as recorded in the "Aids to Reflection," is the more worthy of regard, as being the last step taken by one who had long resisted, and only after profound reflection submitted himself to this faith. He there lays down, that as sin is the ground or occasion of Christianity, so Redemption is its superstructure; that Redemption and Christianity are equivalent terms. From this he does not attempt to remove the awful mystery, but only to clear away any objections which may spring out of the moral instincts of man against the common interpretation of the doctrine. These are the only difficulties that deserve an answer.

In the Redemption, the agent is the Eternal Word made flesh, standing in the place of man to God, and of God to man, fulfilling all righteousness, suffering, dying, and so dying as to conquer death itself, and for all who shall receive Him. The redemptive or atoning act of this divine Agent has two sides — one that looks Godward, the other that looks manward. The side it turns Godward — that is, the essence of the atoning act, the cause of man's redemption — is "a spiritual and transcendent mystery which passeth all understanding;" its nature, mode, and possibility, transcend man's comprehension. But the side that it turns manward — that is, the effect upon the redeemed — is most simply, and without metaphor, described, as far as it is comprehensible by man, in St. John's words, as the being born anew; as at first we were born in the flesh to the world, so now born in the Spirit of Christ. Christ was made a quickening, that is a life-making Spirit. This, Coleridge believed to be the nearest, most immediate effect on man of the transcendent redemptive act. Closely connected with this first, most immediate effect, are other consequences, which St. Paul has described by four principal metaphors. These consequences, in reference to the sinner, are either the taking away of guilt, as by a great sin-offering, just as to the transgressor of the Mosaic law his civil stain was cleared away by the ceremonial offering of the priest; or the reconciliation of the sinner to God, as the prodigal son is reconciled to the parent whom he has injured; or the satisfying of a debt by the payment of the sum owed to the creditor; or the ransoming of a slave, the bringing him back from slavery, by payment of a price for him. These four figures describe, each in a different way, the result of the great redemptive act on sinful man. This is their true meaning. They are figures intended to bring home to man in a practical way the nature and the greatness of the benefit. Popularly they are transferred back to the mysterious cause, but they cannot be taken as if they really and adequately explained the nature of that cause, without leading to confusions. Debt, satisfaction, payment in full, are not terms by which the essential nature of the atoning act, and its necessity, can be literally and adequately expressed. If, forgetting this, we take these expressions literally, and argue from them, as if they gave real intellectual insight into the nature and mode of that greatest of all mysteries, we are straightway landed in moral contradictions. The nature of the redemptive act, as it is in itself, is not to be compassed nor uttered by the language of the human understanding. Such, as nearly as I can give it, was Coleridge's thought upon this great mystery. Whatever may be the value of this view, one thing is to be observed, that Coleridge did not propound it with any hope of explaining a subject which he believed to be beyond man's power of explanation, but from the earnest desire to clear away moral hindrances to its full acceptance. Such hindrances he believed that human theologies, in their attempts to systemize this and other doctrines of Scripture, were from time to time piling up. It was his endeavor, whether successful or not, in what he wrote on this and on every other religious subject, to clear away these hindrances, and to place the truth in a light which shall commend itself to every man's conscience, a light which shall be consistent with such fundamental Scriptures as these, "I, the Lord, speak righteousness, I declare things that are right;" "God is light, and in Him is no darkness at all." Since his day, men's thoughts have been exercised on the nature of the atonement, as perhaps they never were before. There is one view, of late years advocated in various forms, which regards the atonement as merely such a declaration or exhibition of God's love to sinners, as by the pure power of its clemency awakens them to repentance, and takes away the estrangement of their hearts. This is no doubt part of the truth, but it falls far short of satisfying either man's deeper moral instincts, or those many passages of Scripture which declare that forgiveness of sins is one great need of the soul, and that Christ's death is the means through which forgiveness is made possible. Such interpretations, if taken for the whole, leave out of account the "more behind," which Scripture bears witness to, and man's conscience needs. They take no account of that bearing which Christ's death has toward God, and which Coleridge, while he held it to be incomprehensible, fully believed to exist. On this great question, the nature of the atoning act in its relation to God, some meditations have since Coleridge's time been given to the world, which, while penetrating deeper, seem yet in harmony with that which Coleridge taught. I allude to Mr. Campbell's profound work, "The Nature of the Atonement," in which, though all the difficulties are not cleared up, the author goes further toward satisfying at once many of the expressions of Scripture and the requirements of conscience than any other theological work I know of has done.

Such are a few samples of Coleridge's theological method and manner of thinking. In the wish to set them forth in something of a systematic order, I have done but scanty justice to the fullness and the practical fervor which pervade the "Aids to Reflection," and I have given no notion at all of the prodigality of thought with which his other works run over. It were vain to hope that any words could give an impression of that marvellous range of vision, that richness, that swing of thought, that lightning of genius. Besides his works already noticed, his "Lay Sermons," with their Appendices, and his "Literary Remains," are a very quarry of thought, from which young and reflecting readers may dig wealth of unexhausted ore. But over these I cannot now linger.

Neither can I do more than merely allude to those remarkable letters, published after his death, in which Coleridge approaches the great question of the inspiration of Scripture. Arnold recognized their appearance as marking an era in theology the most important that had occurred since the Reformation ; and the interval that has since passed has not diminished their historical importance. On the views of Scripture there propounded Coleridge himself laid great stress. In the words of his nephew, " he pleaded for them so earnestly, as the only middle path of safety and peace between a godless disregard of the unique and transcendent character of the Bible taken generally, and that scheme of interpretation, scarcely less adverse to the pure spirit of Christian wisdom, which wildly arrays our faith in opposition to our reason, and inculcates the sacrifice of the latter to the former, that to suppress this important part of his solemn convictions, would be to misrepresent and betray him."

When these letters first appeared, they struck the loudest, if not the earliest note, which till then had been heard in England, of that way of thought which has since become known as the Critical School. Recognizing, as these letters did, in the different books of Scripture, various degrees and diverse modes of inspiration, and in all the books the co-presence of the human element with the Divine Word, they startled from their " dogmatic slumbers " the many who had hitherto held a merely mechanical view of the inspiring Spirit. The Critical School, which in this country may be almost said to date its rise from the appearance of these letters, has since then parted into two widely divergent paths. One party have so busied themselves with investigating the earthly accompaniments of time, place, and character, that they seem ever less and less to overhear the divine voice that speaks through these. Those who have taken the other path, while examining closely the "earthen vessel," and its historical formation, have used this study only to enable them to penetrate deeper into the true nature of the heavenly treasure which it enshrines. That these last are the legitimate representatives of the Coleridgean theology, the true inheritors of the principles he taught, will, if I have interpreted him aright, need no further proof.

Having given the fullest scope to his own inquiries on all subjects, yet in a spirit of reverence, he wished others to do the same, believing this to be a condition of arriving at assured convictions of truth. He was full of wise and large-hearted tolerance, — not that tolerance, so common and so worthless, which easily bears with all opinions, because it earnestly holds none, — but that tolerance, attained but by few, which, holding firmly by convictions of its own, and making conscience of them, would neither coerce nor condemn those who most strongly deny them. Heresy he believed to be an error, not of the head, but of the heart. He distinguished between that internal faith which lies at the base of religious character, and can be judged of only by God, and that belief with regard to facts and doctrines, in which good men may err without moral obliquity. His works abound with such maxims as this: "Resist every false doctrine; but call no man heretic. The false doctrine does not necessarily make the man a heretic; but an evil heart can make any doctrine heretical."

These are a few of the contemplations with which Samuel Taylor Coleridge busied himself during the threescore years of his earthly existence. For more than thirty years now he has been beyond them, but these he has left behind for us to use as we may. Those who remember what Coleridge was to their youth, may fear lest in their estimate of him now they should seem to be mere praisers of the past, and yet, if they were to call him the greatest thinker whom Britain has during this century produced, they would be but stating the simple truth. For if any should gainsay this, it might be asked, Whom would you place by his side? What one man would you name who has thrown upon the world so great a mass of original thinking, has awakened so much new thought on the most important subjects? His mind was a very treasure-house of ideas, of which many have gone to enrich the various departments of thought, literary, philosophical, political, and religious; while others still lie imbedded in his works, waiting for those who may still turn them to use. And all he wrote was in the interest of man's higher nature, true to his best aspirations. The one effort of all his works was to build up truth from the spiritual side. He brought all his transcendent powers of intellect to the help of the heart, and soul, and spirit of man against the tyranny of the understanding, that understanding which ever strives to limit truth within its generalizations from sense, and rejects whatever refuses to square with these. This side of philosophy, as it is the deepest, is also the most difficult to build up. Just as in bridging some broad river, that part of the work which has to be done by substructions and piers beneath the water, is much more laborious and important, while it strikes less upon the senses than the arches which are reared in open daylight; so the side of truth which holds by the seen and the tangible, which never quits clear-cut conceptions, and refuses to acknowledge whatever will not come within these, is much more patent and plausible, and, in this country at least, is more likely to command the suffrages of the majority. Owing to the impulse to thought which proceeded from Coleridge, the Sensationalists experienced for a time a brief reaction; for one generation he turned the tide against them; but again they are mustering in full force, and bid fair to become masters of the position. Their chief teachers have for some time — by the merit, it must be owned, of their works — become all but paramount in the most ancient seats of learning. In Oxford, for instance, the only two living authors, a knowledge of whose works is imperatively required of candidates for highest honors, belong to this school. And there is no counteracting authority speaking from the opposite, that is, the spiritual side of philosophy, because no such living voice is amongst us. Whenever such a thinker shall arise, he will have to take up the work which Coleridge left incomplete, and by more patent analysis, and more systematic exposition of the spiritual element which enters into all thought and all objects of thought, to make good as reasoned truth, the ground which Coleridge reached only by far-reaching, but fragmentary intuition. One cannot but sometimes wonder what his thoughts would have been, had he been living now, and looking forth on the wide field of modern speculation, where combatants, more numerous than ever, are, with voices mutually unintelligible, shouting in confused night-battle. And not for the philosophy only, but for the general literature and the politics of our time, what words of admonition would he have had, if he had been still present with us! In his own day the oracle of the Whigs reserved for him its bitterest raillery, while Toryism looked coldly on.

He would hardly, I imagine, have been more popular with the dominant factions now, Liberal or Conservative, for he would not have served the purposes of either. Neither before the intellectual idols of the hour, whatever names they bear, would he have readily bowed down. Rather he would have shown to them their own shortcomings, as seen in the light of a more catholic and comprehensive wisdom. Who can doubt this, when he regards either the spirit of his works, so deep-thoughted and reverent, so little suited for popularity, or the attitude in which he stood towards all the arbiters of praise in his own generation?

But the best thing that can be said of him is, that he was a great religious philosopher. And by this how much is meant? Not a religious man and a philosopher merely, but a man in whom these two powers met and interpenetrated. There are instances enough in which the two stand opposed, mutually denouncing each other; instances too there are in which, though not opposed, they live apart, the philosophy unleavened by the religion. How rare have been the examples, at least in modern times, in which the most original powers of intellect and imagination, the most ardent search for truth, and the largest erudition, have united with reverence and simple Christian faith — the heart of the child with the wisdom of the sage! He who has left behind him a philosophy, however incomplete, in which these elements combine, has done for his fellow-men the highest service human thinker can, has helped to lighten the burden of the mystery.

KEBLE.

THE closing chapter of Lockhart's "Life of Scott" begins with these words: "We read in Solomon, 'The heart knoweth his own bitterness, and a stranger doth not intermeddle with his joy;' and a wise poet of our own time thus beautifully expands the saying —

> "'Why should we faint and fear to live alone,
> Since all alone, so Heaven has willed, we die,
> Nor even the tenderest heart, and next our own,
> Knows half the reasons why we smile or sigh?'"

On glancing to the footnote to see who the wise poet of our own time might be, the reader saw, for the first time perhaps, the name of KEBLE and "The Christian Year." To many, in Scotland at least, this was the earliest announcement of the existence of the poet, and the work which has immortalized him. If some friend soon afterwards happened to bring from England a copy of "The Christian Year," and make a present of it, the young reader could not but be struck by a lyric here and there, which opened a new vein, and struck a note of meditative feeling, not exactly like anything he had heard before. But the little book contained much that was strange and unintelligible, some things even startling. Very vague were the rumors which at that time reached Scotland of the author. Men said he belonged to a party of Churchmen who were making a great stir in Oxford, and leavening the University with a kind of thought which was novel, and supposed to be dangerous. The most definite thing said was that the new school had a general Romanizing tendency. But this must be a mistake or strange exaggeration. Folly and sentimentalism might no doubt go far enough at Oxford. But as for Romanism, the revival of such antiquated nonsense was simply impossible in this enlightened nineteenth century. If such an absurdity were to show itself openly, was there not still extant the "Edinburgh Review" ready to crush it? To many a like folly ere now it had administered the quietus. Would it not deal as summarily with this one too? Such was the kind of talk that was heard when Scott's "Life" appeared in 1838. For more exact information, young men who were inquisitive had to wait, till a few years later gave them opportunities of seeing for themselves, and coming into personal contact with what was actually going on in Oxford.

It was a strange experience for a young man trained anywhere, much more for one born and bred in Scotland, and brought up a Presbyterian, to enter Oxford when the religious movement was at its height. He found himself all at once in the midst of a system of teaching which unchurched himself and all whom he had hitherto known. In his simplicity he had believed that spiritual religion was a thing of the heart, and that neither Episcopacy nor Presbytery availeth anything. But here were men — able, learned, devout-minded men — maintaining that outward rites and ceremonies were of the very essence, and that where these were not, there was no true Christianity. How could men, such as these were reported to be, really go back themselves and try to lead others back to what were but the beggarly elements? It was all very perplexing, not to say irritating. However, there might be something more behind, which a young man could not understand. So he would wait and see what he should see.

Soon he came to know that the only portions of Oxford society unaffected by the new influence, were the two extremes. The older dons, that is, the heads of houses and the senior tutors, were unmoved by it, except to opposition. The whole younger half of the undergraduates generally took no part in it. But the great body that lay between these extremes, that is, most of the younger fellows of colleges, and most of the scholars and elder undergraduates, at least those of them who read or thought at all, were in some way or other busy with the new questions. When in time the new comer began to know some of the men who sympathized with the movement, his first impression was of something constrained and reserved in their manners and deportment. High character and ability many of them were said to have; but to a chance observer it seemed that, in as far as their system had moulded them, it had made them the opposite of natural in their views of things, and in their whole mental attitude. You longed for some free breath of mountain air to sweep away the stifling atmosphere that was about you. This might come partly, no doubt, from the feeling with which you knew that these men must from their system regard you, and all who had the misfortune to be born outside of their sacred pale. Not that they ever expressed such views in your hearing. Good manners, as well as their habitual reserve, forbade this. But, though they did not say it, you knew quite well that they felt it. And if at any time the "young barbarian" put a direct question, or made a remark which went straight at these opinions, they would only look at him, astonished at his rudeness and profanity, and shrink into themselves.

Now and then, however, it would happen that some adherent, or even leading man of the movement, more frank and outspoken than the rest, would deign to speak out his principles, and even to discuss them with undergraduates and controversial Scots. To him urging the necessity of Apostolical Succession, and the sacerdotal view of the Sacraments, some young man might venture to reply, "Well! if all you say be true, then I never can have known a Christian. For up to this time I have lived among people who were strangers to all these things, which, you tell me, are essentials of Christianity. And I am quite sure that, if I have never known a Christian till now, I shall never know one." The answer to this would probably be, "There is much in what you say. No doubt high virtues, very like the Christian graces, are to be found outside of the Christian Church. But it is a remarkable thing, those best acquainted with Church history tell me, that outside of the pale of the Church the saintly character is never found." This *naïf* reply was not likely to have much weight with the young listener. It would have taken something stronger to make him break faith with all that was most sacred in his early recollections. Beautiful examples of Presbyterian piety had stamped impressions on his memory not to be effaced by sacerdotal theories or subtleties of the schools. And the Church system which began by disowning these examples placed a barrier to its acceptance at the very outset.

But however unbelievable their theory, further acquaintance with the younger men of the new school, whether junior fellows or undergraduate scholars, disclosed many traits of character that could not but awaken respect or something more. If there was about many of them a constraint and reserve which seemed unnatural, there was also in many an unworldliness and self-denial, a purity of life and elevation of aim, in some a generosity of purpose and depth of devotion, not to be gainsaid. Could the movement which produced these qualities, or even attracted them to itself, be wholly false and bad? This movement, moreover, when at its height, extended its influence far beyond the circle of those who directly adopted its views. There was not, in Oxford at least, a reading man who was not more or less indirectly influenced by it. Only the very idle or the very frivolous were wholly proof against it. On all others it impressed a sobriety of conduct and a seriousness not usually found among large bodies of young men. It raised the tone of average morality in Oxford to a level which perhaps it had never before reached. You may call it over-wrought and too highly strung. Perhaps it was. It was better, however, for young men to be so, than to be doubters or cynics.

If such was the general aspect of Oxford society at that time, where was the centre and soul from which so mighty a power emanated? It lay, and had for some years lain, mainly in one man — a man in many ways the most remarkable that England has seen during this century, perhaps the most remarkable whom the English Church has produced in any century, — John Henry Newman.

The influence he had gained, apparently without setting himself to seek it, was something altogether unlike anything else in our time. A mysterious veneration had by degrees gathered round him, till now it was almost as though some Ambrose or Augustine of elder ages had reappeared. He himself tells how one day, when he was an undergraduate, a friend with whom he was walking in the Oxford street cried out eagerly, "There's Keble!" and with what awe he looked at him! A few years, and the same took place with regard to himself. In Oriel Lane light-hearted undergraduates would drop their voices and whisper, "There's Newman!" when, head thrust forward, and gaze fixed as though on some vision seen only by himself, with swift, noiseless step he glided by. Awe fell on them for a moment, almost as if it had been some apparition that had passed. For his inner circle of friends, many of them younger men, he was said to have a quite romantic affection, which they returned with the most ardent devotion and the intensest faith in him. But to the outer world he was a mystery. What were the qualities that inspired these feelings? There was of course learning and refinement, there was genius, not indeed of a philosopher, but of a subtle and original thinker, an unequaled edge of dialectic, and these all glorified by the imagination of a poet. Then there was the utter unworldliness, the setting at naught of all things which men most prize, the tamelessness of soul, which was ready to essay the impossible. Men felt that here was —

> "One of that small transfigured band
> Which the world cannot tame."

It was this mysteriousness which, beyond all his gifts of head and heart, so strangely fascinated and overawed, — that something about him which made it impossible to reckon his course and take his bearings, that soul-hunger and quenchless yearning which nothing short of the eternal could satisfy. This deep and resolute ardor, this tenderness yet severity of soul, were no doubt an offense not to be forgiven by older men, especially by the wary and worldly-wise; but in these lay the very spell which drew to him the hearts of all the younger and the more enthusiastic. Such was the impression he had made in Oxford just before he relinquished his hold on it. And if at that time it seemed to persons at a distance extravagant and absurd, they may since have learnt that there was in him who was the object of this reverence enough to justify it.

But it may be asked, What actions or definite results were there to account for so deep and wide-spread a veneration? There were no doubt the numerous products of his prolific pen, his works, controversial, theological, religious. But none of these were so deep in learning as some of Dr. Pusey's writings, nor so widely popular as "The Christian Year;" and yet both Dr. Pusey and Mr. Keble were at that time quite second in importance to Mr. Newman. The centre from which his power went forth was the pulpit of St. Mary's, with those wonderful afternoon sermons. Sunday after Sunday, month by month, year by year, they went on, each continuing and deepening the impression the last had made. As the afternoon service at St. Mary's interfered with the dinner-hour of the colleges, most men preferred a warm dinner without Newman's sermon to a cold one with it, so the audience was not crowded — the large church little more than half filled. The service was very simple, — no pomp, no ritualism; for it was characteristic of the leading men of the movement that they left these things to the weaker brethren. Their thoughts, at all events, were set on great questions which touched the heart of unseen things. About the service, the most remarkable thing was the beauty, the silver intonation, of Mr. Newman's voice, as he read the Lessons. It seemed to bring new meaning out of the familiar words. Still lingers in memory the tone with which he read, "But Jerusalem which is above is free, which is the mother of us all." When he began to preach, a stranger was not likely to be much struck, especially if he had been accustomed to pulpit oratory of the Boanerges sort. Here was no vehemence, no declamation, no show of elaborated argument, so that one who came prepared to hear a "great intellectual effort" was almost sure to go away disappointed. Indeed, I believe that if he had preached one of his St. Mary's sermons before a Scotch town congregation, they would have thought the preacher a "silly body." The delivery had a peculiarity which it took a new hearer some time to get over. Each separate sentence, or at least each short paragraph, was spoken rapidly, but with great clearness of intonation; and then at its close there was a pause, lasting for nearly half a minute; then another rapidly but clearly spoken sentence, followed by another pause. It took some time to get over this, but, that once done, the wonderful charm began to dawn on you. The look and bearing of the preacher were as of one who dwelt apart, who, though he knew his age well, did not live in it. From his seclusion of study, and abstinence, and prayer, from habitual dwelling in the unseen, he seemed to come forth that one day of the week to speak to others of the things he had seen and known. Those who never heard him might fancy that his sermons would generally be about apostolical succession or rights of the Church, or against Dissenters. Nothing of the kind. You might hear him preach for weeks without an allusion to these things. What there was of High Church teaching was implied rather than enforced. The local, the temporary, and the modern were ennobled by the presence of the catholic truth belonging to all ages that pervaded the whole. His power showed itself chiefly in the new and unlooked-for way in which he touched into life old truths, moral or spiritual, which all Christians acknowledge, but most have ceased to feel — when he spoke of "Unreal Words," of "The Individuality of the Soul," of "The Invisible World," of a "Particular Providence;" or again, of "The Ventures of Faith," "Warfare the condition of Victory," "The Cross of Christ the Measure of the World," "The Church a Home for the Lonely." As he spoke, how the old truth became new! how it came home with a meaning never felt before! He laid his finger — how gently, yet how powerfully! — on some inner place in the hearer's heart, and told him things about himself he had never known till then. Subtlest truths, which it would have taken philosophers pages of circumlocution and big words to state, were dropt out by the way in a sentence or two of the most transparent Saxon. What delicacy of style, yet what calm power! how gentle, yet how strong! how simple, yet how suggestive! how homely, yet how refined! how penetrating, yet how tender-hearted! If now and then there was a forlorn undertone which at the time seemed inexplicable, if he spoke of "many a sad secret which a man dare not tell lest he find no sympathy," of "secrets lying like cold ice upon the heart," of "some solitary incommunicable grief," you might be perplexed at the drift of what he spoke, but you felt all the more drawn to the speaker. To call these sermons eloquent would be no word for them; high poems they rather were, as of an inspired singer, or the outpourings as of a prophet, rapt yet self-possessed. And the tone of voice in which they were spoken, once you grew accustomed to it, sounded like a fine strain of unearthly music. Through the stillness of that high Gothic building the words fell on the ear like the measured drippings of water in some vast dim cave. After hearing these sermons you might come away still not believing the tenets peculiar to the High Church system; but you would be harder than most men, if you did not feel more than ever ashamed of coarseness, selfishness, worldliness, if you did not feel the things of faith brought closer to the soul.

There was one occasion of a different kind, when he spoke from St. Mary's pulpit for the last time, not as Parish minister, but as University preacher. It was the crisis of the movement. On the 2d of February, 1843, the Feast of the Purification, all Oxford assembled to hear what Newman had to say, and St. Mary's was crowded to the door. The subject he spoke of was "The theory of Development in Christian Doctrine," a subject which since then has become common property, but which at that time was new even to the ablest men in Oxford. For an hour and a half he drew out the argument, and perhaps the acutest there did not quite follow the entire line of thought, or felt wearied by the length of it, lightened though it was by some startling illustrations. Such was the famous "Protestantism has at various times developed into Polygamy," or the still more famous "Scripture says the sun moves round the earth, Science that the earth moves, and the sun is comparatively at rest. How can we determine which of these opposite statements is true, till we know what motion is?" Few probably who heard it have forgot the tone of voice with which he uttered the beautiful passage about music as the audible embodiment of some unknown reality behind, itself sweeping like a strain of splendid music out of the heart of a subtle argument: —

"Take another instance of an outward and earthly form, or economy, under which great wonders unknown seem to be typified; I mean musical sounds, as they are exhibited most perfectly in instrumental harmony.

There are seven notes in the scale; make them fourteen; yet what a slender outfit for so vast an enterprise! What science brings so much out of so little? Out of what poor elements does some master create his new world! Shall we say that all this exuberant inventiveness is a mere ingenuity or trick of art, like some game or fashion of the day, without reality, without meaning? We may do so; and then, perhaps, we shall also account the science of theology to be a matter of words; yet, as there is a divinity in the theology of the Church, which those who feel cannot communicate, so there is also in the wonderful creation of sublimity and beauty of which I am speaking. To many men the very names which the science employs are utterly incomprehensible. To speak of an idea or a subject seems to be fanciful or trifling, and of the views which it opens upon us to be childish extravagance; yet is it possible that that inexhaustible evolution and disposition of notes, so rich yet so simple, so intricate yet so regulated, so various yet so majestic, should be a mere sound which is gone and perishes? Can it be that those mysterious stirrings of heart, and keen emotions, and strange yearnings after we know not what, and awful impressions from we know not whence, should be wrought in us by what is unsubstantial, and comes and goes, and begins and ends in itself? It is not so! it cannot be. No; they have escaped from some higher sphere; they are the outpourings of eternal harmony in the medium of created sound; they are echoes from our Home; they are the voices of Angels, or the *Magnificat* of Saints, or the living laws of Divine governance, or the Divine attributes; something are they besides themselves, which we cannot compass, which we cannot utter, though mortal man, and he perhaps not otherwise distinguished above his fellows, has the power of eliciting them."

This was preached in the winter of 1843, the last time he appeared in the University pulpit. His parochial sermons had by this time assumed an uneasy tone which perplexed his followers with fear of change. That summer solved their doubt. In the quiet chapel of Littlemore, which he himself had built, when all Oxford was absent during the long vacation, he preached his last Anglican sermon to the country people and only a few friends, and poured forth that mournful and thrilling farewell to the Church of England. The sermon is entitled "The Parting of Friends." The text was "Man goeth forth to his work and his labor until the evening." He went through all the instances which Scripture records of human affection sorely tried, reproducing the incidents almost in the very words of Scripture, — Jacob, Hagar, Naomi, Jonathan and David, St. Paul and the elders of Ephesus, and last, the weeping over Jerusalem, and the "Behold, your house is left unto you desolate," — and then he bursts forth —

"A lesson, surely, and a warning to us all, in every place where He puts his name, to the end of time, lest we be cold towards his gifts, or unbelieving towards his word, or jealous of his workings, or heartless towards his mercies. . . . . O mother of saints! O school of the wise! O nurse of the heroic! of whom went forth, in whom have dwelt memorable names of old, to spread the truth abroad, or to cherish and illustrate it at home! O thou, from whom surrounding nations lit their lamps! O virgin of Israel! wherefore dost thou now sit on the ground and keep silence, like one of the foolish women who were without oil on the coming of the Bridegroom? Where is now the ruler in Sion, and the doctor in the Temple, and the ascetic on Carmel, and the herald in the wilderness, and the preacher in the market-place? Where are thy 'effectual fervent prayers' offered in secret, and thy alms and good works coming up as a memorial before God? How is it, O once holy place, that "the land mourneth, for the corn is wasted, the new wine is dried up, the oil languisheth, because joy is withered away from the sons of men'? 'Alas for the day! how do the beasts groan! the herds of cattle are perplexed, because they have no pasture; yea, the flocks are made desolate.' 'Lebanon is ashamed and hewn down; Sharon is like a wilderness, and Bashan and Carmel shake off their fruits.' O my mother, whence is this unto thee, that thou hast good things poured upon thee and canst not keep them, and bearest children, yet darest not own them? Why hast thou not the skill to use their services, nor the heart to rejoice in their love? How is it that whatever is generous in purpose, and tender or deep in devotion, thy flower and thy promise falls from thy bosom, and finds no home within thine arms? Who hath put this note upon thee, to have 'a miscarrying womb and dry breasts,' to be strange to thine own flesh, and thine eye cruel to thy little ones? Thine own offspring, the fruit of thy womb, who would love thee and would toil for thee, thou dost gaze upon with fear as though a portent, or thou dost loathe as an offense; at best thou dost but endure, as if they had no claim but on thy patience, self-possession, and vigilance, to be rid of them as easily as thou mayest. Thou makest them 'stand all the day idle' as the very condition of thy bearing with them; or thou biddest them begone where they will be more welcome; or thou sellest them for naught to the stranger that passes by. And what wilt thou do in the end thereof?

"Scripture is a refuge in any trouble; only let us

be on our guard against seeming to use it further than is fitting, or doing more than sheltering ourselves under its shadow. Let us use it according to our measure. It is far higher and wider than our need, and it conceals our feelings while it gives expression to them. It is sacred and heavenly; and it restrains and purifies, while it sanctions them. . . . . And O my brethren, O kind and affectionate hearts, O loving friends, should you know any one whose lot it has been, by writing or by word of mouth, in some degree to help you thus to act; if he has ever told you what you knew about yourselves, or what you did not know; has read to you your wants and feelings, and comforted you by the very reading; has made you feel that there was a higher life than this daily one, and a brighter world than that you see; or encouraged you, or sobered you, or opened a way to the inquiring, or soothed the perplexed, if what he has said or done has ever made you take interest in him, and feel well-inclined towards him, remember such a one in time to come, though you hear him not, and pray for him, that in all things he may know God's will, and at all times he may be ready to fulfill it."

Then followed the resignation of his fellowship, the retirement to Littlemore, the withdrawal even from the intercourse of his friends, the unloosing of all the ties that bound him to Oxford, the two years' pondering of the step he was about to take. And at last, when in 1845 he went away to the Church of Rome, he did it by himself, making himself as much as possible responsible only for his own act, and followed by but one or two young friends who would not be kept back. Those who witnessed these things, and knew that, if a large following had been his object, he might, by leaving the Church of England three years earlier, in the plenitude of his power, have taken almost all the flower of young Oxford with him, needed no "Apologia," to convince them of his honesty of purpose.

On these things, looking over an interval of five and twenty years, how vividly comes back the remembrance of the aching blank, the awful pause, which fell on Oxford when that voice had ceased, and we knew that we should hear it no more. It was as when, to one kneeling by night, in the silence of some vast cathedral, the great bell tolling solemnly overhead has suddenly gone still. To many, no doubt, the pause was not of long continuance. Soon they began to look this way and that for new teachers, and to rush vehemently to the opposite extreme of thought. But there were those who could not so lightly forget. All the more these withdrew into themselves. On Sunday forenoons and evenings, in the retirement of their rooms, the printed words of those marvelous sermons would thrill them till they wept "abundant and most sweet tears." Since then many voices of powerful teachers they may have heard, but none that ever penetrated the soul like his.

Such was the impression made by that eventful time on impartial but not uninterested spectators — on those who by early education and conviction were kept quite aloof from the peculiar tenets of High Churchmen, but who could not but acknowledge the moral quickening which resulted from the movement, and the marvelous character of him who was the soul of it.

Dr. Newman himself tells us that all the while the true and primary author of that movement was out of sight. The Rev. John Keble was at a distance from Oxford, in his vicarage at Hursley, there living in his own life, and carrying out in his daily services and parish ministry, those truths which he had first brought forward, and Newman had carried out, in Oxford. But though out of sight, he was not out of mind. "The Christian Year" was in the hands of every one, even the youngest undergraduate. Besides its more intrinsic qualities, the tone of it blended well with the sentiment which the venerable aspect of the old city awakened. It used to be pleasing to try and identify amid the scenery around Oxford some of the spots from which were drawn those descriptions of nature with which the poems are inlaid. During these years the poet-priest's figure was but seldom seen in the streets of Oxford, — only when some great question affecting the Church, some discussion of No. 90, or trial of Mr. Ward, had summoned Convocation together. Once, if my memory serves, I remember to have seen him in the University pulpit at St. Mary's, but his voice was not strong, and did not reach many of the audience. His service to his party had lain in another direction. It was he who, by his character, had first awakened a new tone of sentiment in Oxford, and attracted to himself whatever else was like-minded. He had sounded the first note which woke that sentiment into action, and embodied it in a party. He had kept up, though from a distance, sympathetic intercourse with the chief actors, counseled and encouraged them. Above all, he gave poetry to the movement, and a poetic aspect. Polemics by themselves are dreary work. They do not touch the springs of young hearts. But he who, in the midst of any line of thought, unlocks a fountain of genuine poetry, does more to humanize it and win for it a way to men's affections, than he who writes a hundred volumes, however able, of controversy. Without disparagement to the patristic and other learning of the party, the two permanent monuments of genius which it has bequeathed to England may be said to be Newman's "Parochial Sermons," and Keble's "Christian Year."

All that was known of Keble at that time to the outer world of Oxford was vague and scanty. The few facts here added are taken from what has since been made public by two of his most attached friends, Sir John Coleridge and Dr. Newman, the former in his beautiful letters, memorial of Keble, the latter in his "Apologia." Yet these facts, though few, are well worthy of attention, both because Keble's character is more than his poetry, and because his poetry can only be rightly understood in the light of his character. For there is no poet whose poetry is more truly an image of the man himself, both in his inner nature and in his outward circumstances.

His father, whose name the poet bore, was a country clergyman, vicar of Coln St. Aldwyns, in Gloucestershire, but the house in which he lived, and in which the poet was born, was at Fairford, three miles distant from the cure. John was the second child and elder son of a family which consisted of two sons and two daughters. His mother, Sarah Maule, was, as I have heard, of Scottish extraction. The father, who lived till his ninetieth year, was a man of no common ability. Of him his son, we are told, "always spoke not only with the love of a son, but with the profoundest reverence for his goodness and wisdom." It would seem that this was one of the few clerical homes in England in which the opinions, traditions, and peculiar piety of the Nonjurors lived on into the present century. Unlike most sons distinguished for ability, John Keble never outgrew the period of absolute filial reverence, never questioned a single opinion or prepossession which he had imbibed from his father. Some of his less reverential companions used to think that this was an intellectual loss to him.

The father's ability and scholarship are proved by

his having himself educated his son, and sent him up to Oxford so well prepared, that at the age of fifteen he gained a Corpus scholarship, an honor which seems to have then held the same place in University estimation that Balliol scholarships have long held and still hold. This strictly home training, in the quiet of a Gloucestershire parsonage, placed in the very heart of rural England, under a roof where the old High Church tradition lived on, blending with what was best in modern piety, makes itself felt in every line the poet wrote. On all hands one hears it said that there is no education like that of one of the old English public schools. For the great run of ordinary boys, whether quick-witted and competitive, or lazy and self-indulgent, it may be so; but for natures of finer texture, for all boys who have a decided and original bias, how much is there that the rough handling of a public school would ruthlessly crush? From all the better public schools coarse bullying, I know, has disappeared; but for peculiarity of any kind, for whatever does not conform itself to the "tyrant tradition" — a manly and straightforward one, I admit — they have still but little tolerance. If Keble had once imbibed the public school spirit, "The Christian Year" would either never have been written at all, or it would have been written otherwise than it is.

If he was fortunate in having his boy-education at home, he was not less happy in the college which he entered and the companions he met there. It is the happiness of college life that a young man can command just as much retirement, and as much society as he pleases, and of the kind that he pleases. All readers of Arnold's life will remember the picture there drawn of the Scholars' Common Room at Corpus, by one of the last survivors, the venerable Sir J. Coleridge.

He tells us that, when Keble came into residence, early in 1807, it was but a small society, numbering only about twenty undergraduate scholars, and these rather under the usual age, who lived on the most familiar terms with each other. The Bachelor scholars resided and lived entirely with the undergraduates. Two of Keble's chief friends among the Corpus scholars, though younger in academic standing than himself, were Coleridge (afterwards Judge Coleridge) and Arnold. Keble indeed must have already graduated before Arnold came into residence. Besides these were many other men distinguished in their day in the University, but less known to the outer world. It was a stirring time when Keble was an undergraduate. Within the University the first wakening after long slumber had begun, and competitions for honors had been just established. From without news of the great Peninsular battles was from time to time arriving. Scott's trumpet-blasts of poetry were stirring young hearts. In Corpus Common Room, as elsewhere, the Peninsular battles were fought over again, and the classical and romantic schools of poetry were vehemently discussed. And among these more exciting subjects, the young scholar Coleridge would insinuate the stiller and deeper tones of Wordsworth's lyrical ballads, which, then but little known, he had heard of from his uncle the poet. These two, Scott and Wordsworth, were to the end Keble's first favorites of contemporary poets, and chiefly moulded his taste and style. Most of the scholars were high Tories in Church and State, great respecters of things as they are: none, no doubt, more so than Keble. The great questioner of the prevailing creed was Arnold, who often brought down on his own head the concentrated arguments of the whole Common Room. But youth's genial warmth healed these undergraduate disputes, as, alas! the same controversies could not be healed when taken up by the same combatants at a later day. In that kindly atmosphere Keble's affectionate nature expanded as a flower in the sun. His was a temperament to drink in deeply whatever there was of finest influence in Oxford. No doubt the learning he there gained was something to him, but far more was the vision of the fair city herself, "with high aisle, and solemn cloister, seated among groves, green meadows, and calm streams." These, and the young friendships which they for a few years embosom, are what made Oxford then, and make it even now, the one spot in England wherein "the curlèd darlings of the nation" find romance still realized. Keble seems to have been much the same in character then as in after years. His affection towards the friends he made at Oxford was warm and deep, and lasted in most instances with his life. With what feelings they regarded him may be gathered from the words of his brother scholar at Corpus, who, when their fifty-five years' friendship had come to its earthly close, could say of him, "It was the singular happiness of his nature, remarkable even in his undergraduate days, that love for him was always sanctified, as it were, by reverence — reverence that did not make the love less tender, and love that did but add intensity to the reverence."

In Easter term, 1810, Keble obtained double first class honors, and this success was soon afterwards followed by another still greater — his election to an Oriel fellowship. The Oriel Common Room numbered among its Fellows, then and for some time afterwards, all that was most distinguished in Oxford for mental power and originality. Copleston, Davidson, Whately, then belonged to it, and were among Keble's electors. Arnold, Newman, Pusey, soon afterwards followed as

Fellows of the same college. "Round the fire of the Oriel Common Room," we are told, "there were learned and able, not rarely subtle and disputatious conversations, in which this lad of nineteen was called to take his part. Amid these he sometimes yearned for the more easy, yet not unintellectual society of his old friends at Corpus." He found, no doubt, that undergraduate days are more congenial to warm friendships than the highly rarefied atmosphere of an intellectual Common Room. Where men touch chiefly by the head, they find that this is the seat as frequently of a repulsive as of an attractive force. While he was an undergraduate, and during the early days of his fellowship, he wrote a good many beautiful little poems, which surviving friends still possess, and the year after his election to Oriel he gained the University prizes for the English and Latin essay.

The interval from 1810 to 1815 he spent in Oriel, taking part in college tuition, and acting as an examiner in the Degree Schools. Was it some time during these years, or at a later date, that the incident recorded by Dr. Newman took place? "When one day I was walking in High Street, with my dear earliest friend, with what eagerness did he cry out, 'There's Keble!' and with what awe did I look at him! Then at another time I heard a Master of Arts of my college give an account, how he had just then had occasion to introduce himself on some business to Keble, and how gentle, courteous, and unaffected Keble had been, so as almost to put him out of countenance. Then, too, it was reported, truly or falsely, how a rising man of brilliant reputation, the present Dean of St. Paul's, Dr. Milman, admired and loved him, adding that somehow he was strangely unlike any one else."

In 1815 he was ordained Deacon, the following year

Priest; soon afterwards he left the University, and never again permanently resided there. He had chosen the calling of a clergyman, and though within that field other paths more gratifying to ambition lay open to him, he turned aside from them, and gave himself to parochial work as the serious employment of his life. He became his father's curate, and lived with him at Fairford, engaged in this duty for twenty years, more or less. This rare absence or restraint of ambition, where it might have seemed natural or even right to have gratified it, was quite in keeping with Keble's whole character. "The Church," says Sir J. Coleridge, "he had deliberately chosen to be his profession, and he desired to follow out that in a country cure. With this he associated, and scarcely placed on a lower level, the affectionate discharge of his duties as a son and brother. Calls, temporary calls of duty to his college and University, for a time and at intervals diverted him (he was again Public Examiner from 1821 to 1823); but he always kept these outlines in view, and as the occasion passed away, reverted to them with the permanent devotion of his heart. Traces of this feeling may be found again and again in 'The Christian Year.'"

This book was first given to the world on the 23d of June, 1827, when Keble was in his thirty-fifth year. This, the great work of his life, which will keep his name fresh in men's memory when all else that he has done shall be forgotten, had been the silent gathering of years. Single poems had been in his friends' hands at least as early as 1819. They had urged him to complete the series, and by 1827 this was done. No record of the exact time when each poem was written has yet appeared. I should imagine that more of them were composed at Fairford than at Oxford. The discussion and criticism natural to a University are not generally favorable to poetic creation of any kind, least of all to so meditative a strain as that of Keble. But it may have been that in this, as in other things, he was "unlike any one else." It was only at the urgent entreaty of his friends that he published the little book. He was not anxious about poetic fame, and never thought that these poems would secure it. His own plan was "to go on improving the series all his life, and leave it to come out, if judged useful, only when he should be fairly out of the way." Had this plan been acted on, how many thousands would have been defrauded of the soothing delight these poems have ministered to them! But even those who most strongly counseled the publication, little dreamt what a destiny was in store for that little book. Of course, if the author had kept it by him he might have smoothed away some of its defects, but who knows how much it might have lost too in the process? "No one," we are told, "knew its literary shortcomings better than the author himself. Wisely, and not in pride, or through indolence, he abandoned the attempt at second-hand to amend this inharmonious line, or that imperfect rhyme, or the instances here and there in which his idea may be somewhat obscurely expressed. Wordsworth's acute poetical sense recognized such faults; yet the book was his delight." Probably it was a wise resolve. All emendation of poetry long after its first composition runs the risk of spoiling it. The author has to take up in one mood what was originally conceived in another. His first warm feeling of the sentiment has gone cold, and he cannot at a later time revive it. This is true of all poetry, more especially of that which deals with subtle and evanescent emotions which can never perhaps recur exactly in the same form. Once only in a lifetime may he succeed in catching —

> "Those brief unisons which on the brain
> One tone that never can recur has cast,
> One accent never to return again."

In 1833 Keble was appointed Professor of Poetry at Oxford. The Statutes then required the Professor to give two or three lectures a year in Latin. The ancient language was required to be spoken from this chair longer than from any other, probably from fear of the trash men might talk if fairly unmuzzled. However prudent this may have been when a merely average functionary held the chair, it is greatly to be regretted that when it was filled by a true poet, who was intent on speaking the secret of his own art, he should have been so formidably weighted. The present[1] gifted occupant of that chair has fortunately been set free, and has vindicated the newly acquired freedom by enriching our literature with the finest poetical criticism it has received since the days of Coleridge. But Keble had to work in trammels. He was the last man to rebel against any limitations imposed by the wisdom or unwisdom of our ancestors. Faithfully he buckled himself to the task of translating into well-rounded Latin periods his cherished thoughts on his own favorite subject. Of the theory of poetry embodied in the two volumes of his published lectures, something may yet be said. The Latin is easy and unconstrained, the thought original and suggestive — a great contrast to the more than Ciceronian paragraphs of his predecessor Copleston, bristling as they do to a marvel with epigrammatic Latinity, but underneath that containing little that is not commonplace.

[1] This ought now to be "the late gifted occupant," as it refers to Mr. Matthew Arnold.

There was another duty which fell to Keble as Professor of Poetry, — to choose the subject for the annual Prize Poem at Oxford, to adjudicate along with others the prize to the best of the poems given in, and to look over and suggest corrections in the verses of the successful competitor. Of all these winners of the Newdigate Prize one only has described his interview with Keble, but he one of the most distinguished. Dean Stanley, who gained the Newdigate Prize in, I think, 1837, with his beautiful poem on "The Gypsies," thus describes his first meeting with Keble. By the Dean's kind leave I give it in his own words, taken from his paper on Keble, now published in "Essays on Church and State:" "There are still living those with whom his discharge of one of his duties left a far livelier recollection than his Latin lectures. It was part of his office to correct the poems which during his tenure of it obtained the Newdigate Prize. One of these young authors still retains so fresh and so characteristic a remembrance of his intercourse with the Professor, even then venerable in his eyes, that it may be worth recording. He recalls, after the lapse of more than thirty years, the quiet kindness of manner, the bright twinkling eye illuminating that otherwise inexpressive countenance, which greeted the bashful student on his entrance into the Professor's presence. One touch after another was given to the juvenile verses, substituting for this or that awkward phrase graceful turns of expression all his own: —

"'Is there a spot where earth's *dim daylight* falls,'

has the delicate color of 'The Christian Year' all over. In adding the expression —

"'Where shade, air, *waters*' —

he dwelt with all the ardor of the keenest critic on the

curious subtlety of language, by which 'water' suggests all that is prosaic, and 'waters' all that is poetical.

"'The heavens all gloom, the *wearied earth* all crime;'

how powerfully does this embody the exhaustion of Europe in the fifteenth century! 'The *storied* Sphinx,' 'India's *ocean-floods;*' how vivid are these glances at the phenomena of the East!

'The wandering Israelite, from year to year,
Sees the Redeemer's conquering wheels draw near;"

how thoroughly here is Southey's language caught from the 'Curse of Kehama;' how thoroughly, too, the Judaic as contrasted with the Christian Advent! And it may be added, though not directly bearing on the present topic, how delighted was his youthful hearer to perceive the sympathetic warmth with which, at a certain point in the poem, he said, 'Ah, surely this was suggested by Dr. Arnold's sermon on "The Egyptians whom ye have seen to-day, ye shall see no more again forever."' This allusion was the more felt as showing his recollection of the friend from whom at that time he was so strangely alienated."

In a foot-note Dean Stanley adds that "on glancing at a note to this poem, which cited from Tennyson's 'Palace of Art,' but without naming the poet, the line

"'Who shuts love out shall be shut out from love,'

Keble remarked 'Shakespeare.' The Laureate will forgive this ignorance of his early fame in consideration of the grandeur of the comparison."

In this vivid description one thing Dean Stanley has refrained from giving, the "certain point in his poem" which Keble recognized as suggested by Dr. Arnold's sermon. But the lines are too good to be thus passed over. Taking the view of the Gypsies, as having had their original home in Egypt, the thought occurs to the young poet, that they and the Jews during their Egyptian sojourn must have met. And then he bursts into these fine lines, full of his own pictorial genius : —

> " Long since ye parted by the Red Sea strand,
> Now face to face ye meet in every land,
> Aliens amidst a new-born world to dwell,
> Egypt's lorn people, outcast Israel."

With slight interruptions Keble continued to live with his father at Fairford, and to assist him as his curate till 1835. "In that year this tie was broken. At the very commencement of it the venerable old man, who to the last retained the full use of his faculties, was taken to his rest; and before the end of it Keble became the Vicar of Hursley, and the husband of Miss Charlotte Clarke, second daughter of an old college friend of his father's, who was incumbent of a parish in the neighborhood of Fairford. This was the happy settlement of his life. For himself he had now no ungratified wish, and the bonds then tied were loosened only by death."

Only two years before Keble left Fairford, and at the very time when he entered on his Poetry Professorship, began what is called the Oxford Movement. Of this, Dr. Newman tells us, Keble was the real author. Let us cast a glance back, and see how it arose, and what it aimed at. With what feelings Newman, when an undergraduate, looked at Keble, we have seen. Some years afterwards, it must have been in 1819 or 1820, Newman was elected to the Oriel Fellowship which Arnold vacated. Of that time he thus writes: "I had to hasten to the Tower to receive the congratulations of all the Fellows. I bore it till Keble took my hand, and then felt so abashed and unworthy of the honor done me, that I seemed quite desirous of sinking into the ground. His had been the first name I had heard spoken of with reverence rather than admiration when I came up to Oxford." This was probably the first meeting of these two. "When I was elected Fellow of Oriel," Dr. Newman continues, "Keble was not in residence, and he was shy of me for years, in consequence of the marks I bore upon me of the evangelical and liberal schools. Hurrell Froude brought us together about 1828. It is one of his sayings preserved in his Remains: 'If I was ever asked what good deed I had ever done, I should say that I had brought Keble and Newman to understand each other.'" The friendship thus cemented was to be fruitful of results for England.

It naturally occurs to ask, How far is "The Christian Year" identified with the principles of the Tractarian movement? On the one hand, "The Christian Year" was published in 1827; the movement did not begin till 1833. The former, therefore, cannot be regarded as in any way a child of the latter. And this accounts for what has often been remarked, how little of the peculiar Tractarian teaching appears in these poems. On the other hand, it is easy to see how the same nature which, in a season of quiet, when controversy was at a lull, shaped out of its own musings "The Christian Year," would, when confronted with opposing tendencies, and forced into a dogmatic attitude, find its true expression in the Tractarian theory. Keble was by nature a poet, living by intuition, not by reasoning; intuition born of, fed by, home affection, tradition, devout religion. His whole being leaned on authority. "Keble was a man who guided himself," says Dr. Newman, "and formed his judgments, not by processes of reason, by inquiry or argument, but, to use the word in a broad sense, by authority." And by authority in its broad sense he means conscience, the Bible, the Church, antiquity, words of the wise, hereditary lessons, ethical truths, historical memories. "It seemed to me as if he felt ever happier when he could speak and act under some such primary and external sanction; and could use argument mainly as a means of recommending or explaining what had claims on his reception prior to proof. What he hated instinctively was heresy, insubordination, resistance to things established, claims of independence, disloyalty, innovation, a critical or censorious spirit." Keble then lived by authority, and hated the dispositions that oppose it. There is a temper of mind which lives by denying authority — a temper whose essence, or at least whose bad side, is to foster these very dispositions which he hated. With that tone of mind, and the men possessed by it, sooner or later he must needs have come into collision. For such a collision, Oxford did not want materials.

During Keble's time of residence, and after he went down, the University had been awakening from a long torpor, and entering on a new era. "The march of the mind," as it was called, was led by a number of active-minded and able men, whose chief rallying point was Oriel Common Room, whose best representative was Whately. These men had set themselves to raise the standard of teaching and discipline in the Colleges and in the University. They were the University Reformers of their day, and to them Oxford, when first arousing itself from long intellectual slumber, owed much. As they had a common aim, to raise the intellectual standard, they were naturally much thrown together, and became the celebrities of the place.

Those who did not belong to their party thought them not free from "pride of reason," an expression then, as now, derided by those who think themselves intellectual, but not the less on that account covering a real meaning. It is, as it has been called, "the moral malady" which besets those who live mainly by intellect. Men who could not in heart go along with them thought they carried liberty of thought into presumption and rationalism. They seemed to submit the things of faith too much to human judgment, and to seek to limit their religious belief by their own powers of understanding. They seemed then, as now, "to halve the gospel of God's grace," accepting the morality, and, if not rejecting, yet making little of the supernatural truths out of which that morality springs. Such at least was the judgment of their opponents. In the presence of men of this stamp, energetic but hard, upright but not over humble or reverent, a man of deep religious seriousness, like Keble, instinctively "shrank into himself." "He was young in years when he became a University celebrity, and younger in mind. He had the purity and simplicity of a child. He had few sympathies with the intellectual party, who sincerely welcomed him as a brilliant specimen of young Oxford. He instinctively shut up before literary display, and pomp, and donnishness, faults which will always beset academical notabilities. He did not respond to their advances. 'Poor Keble,' Hurrell Froude used gravely to say, 'he was asked to join the aristocracy of talent, but he soon found his own level.' He went into the country, but he did not lose his place in the minds of men because he was out of sight." It could not be that Keble and these men could really be in harmony, — they, "sons of Aufklärung," men of mere understanding, bringing all things to the one touchstone of logic and common sense, and content with this; he, a child of faith, with more than half his nature in the unseen, and looking at things visible mainly as they shadow forth and reveal the invisible. They represented two opposite sides of human nature, sides in all but some rare instances antagonistic, and never seemingly more antagonistic that now. Dr. Arnold, indeed, though belonging in the main to the school of liberalism, combined with it more religious warmth than was common in his own party. It is this union of qualities, generally thought incompatible, which perhaps was the main secret of his great influence. But the combination which was almost unique in himself, he can hardly be said, by his example, to have rendered more easy for his followers in the present day.

The Catholic Emancipation was a trying and perplexing time for Keble. With the opponents of the measure in Oxford, the old Tory party of Church and State, he had no sympathy. He saw that they had no principle of growth in them, that their only aim was to keep things as they were. His sympathy for the old Catholic religion, that feeling which had made him say in "The Christian Year,"

"Speak gently of our sister's fall,"

would naturally make him wish to see Catholic disabilities removed. But then he disliked both the men by whom, and the arguments by which, Emancipation was supported. He would rather have not seen the thing done at all, than done by the hands of Whiggery. A few years more brought on the crisis, the inevitable collision. The Earl Grey Administration, flushed with their great Reform victory, went on to lay hands on the English Church, that Church which for centuries had withstood the Whigs. They made their attack on the weakest point, the Irish Church, and suppressed ten of its bishoprics. This might seem to be but a small matter in itself, but it was an indication of more behind. Lord Grey had told the Bishops to set their house in order, and his party generally spoke of the Church as the mere creature of the State, which they might do with as they pleased. The Church must be liberalized, those last fangs must be pulled which had so often proved troublesome to Whiggery. This was too much for Keble. It touched him to the qnick, and made him feel that now the time was come when he must speak and act. By nature he was no politician nor controversialist. He disliked the strife of tongues. But he was a man; he had deep religious convictions; and to change what was ancient and catholic in the Church was to touch the apple of his eye. When he looked to the old Tory party he saw no help in them. To the aggressive spirit they had nothing to oppose but outworn Church and State theories. The Bishops. too were helpless, and spoke slightingly of apostolic succession and the Nonjurors. Was the Establishment principle, then, the only rock on which the Church was built? Keble and his young friends thought scorn of that. This feeling first found utterance in the assize sermon which Keble preached from the University pulpit, on Sunday the 14th of July, 1833, and afterwards published under the title of "National Apostasy." "I have ever considered and kept the day," says Dr. Newman, "as the start of the religious movement of 1833." That sermon itself I have not seen, but the tone of it may be gathered from those lines in the "Lyra Apostolica," in which Keble thus brands the spoliators: —

"Is there no sound about our altars heard
Of gliding forms that long have watched in vain

For slumbering discipline to break her chain,
And aim the bolt by Theodosius feared?
'Let us depart;' these English souls are seared,
Who for one grasp of perishable gold,
Would brave the curse by holy men of old
Laid on the robbers of the shrines they reared;
Who shout for joy to see the ruffian band
Come to reform, where ne'er they came to pray,
E'en where, unbidden, seraphs never trod.
Let us depart, and leave the apostate land
To meet the rising whirlwind as she may,
Without her guardian Angels and her God."

"Robbers of the shrines," "the ruffian band, come to reform, where ne'er they came to pray," that was the trumpet-note which rallied to the standard of the Church whatever of ardor and devotion young Oxford then contained. These virtues had never been greatly countenanced in the Church of England. To staid respectability it has always been, and still is, one of the chief recommendations of that Church, that it is an embodied protest against what one of its own Bishops is said to have denounced as "that most dangerous of all errors — enthusiasm." In the last century she had cast out enthusiasm in the person of Wesley; at the beginning of this, she had barely tolerated it in the Newtons and Cecils, and other fathers of evangelicism. But here was a fresh attempt to reintroduce it in a new form. The young men who were roused by Keble's note of warning — able, zealous, resolute — flung aside with disdain timid arguments from expediency. They longed to do battle with that most prosaic of all political theories, Whiggery, and to smite to the ground the spirit of compromise which had so long paralyzed the Church of England. They set themselves to defend the Church with weapons of ethereal temper, and they found them, as they believed, in reviving her claims to a heavenly origin and a divine prerogative.

That these claims sounded strange to the ears even of Churchmen at that time was to these men no stumbling-block — rather an incentive to more fearless action. True, such a course shut them out from preferment, hitherto the one recognized aim of the abler English Churchmen. But these younger men were content to do without preferment. They had at least got beyond that kind of worldliness. If self still clung to them in any shape, it was in that enlarged and nobler form in which it is one with the glory of the Church Catholic in all ages. The views and aims of the new party soon took shape, in the "Tracts for the Times." If Keble was the starter of the movement, John Henry Newman soon became its leader. In all his conduct of it, one of his great aims was to give to the sentiments and views which had originated with Keble a consistent logical basis. The sequel all men know. The inner working of the movement may be read in the "Apologia."

But deeply as Keble's heart was in the Oxford movement, his place of work was a quiet Hampshire parish. When, in 1835, he left the home of his childhood for the vicarage of Hursley, he found a church there not at all to his mind. It seems to have been a plain, not beautiful, building of flint and rubble. He determined to have a new one built — new all but the tower — and on this object he employed the profits of the many editions of "The Christian Year;" and when the building was finished, his friends, in token of their regard for him, filled all the windows with stained glass. In the words of Sir J. P. Coleridge, "Here daily for the residue of his life, until interrupted by the failing health of Mrs. Keble and his own, did he minister. . . . . He had not, in the popular sense, great gifts of delivery; his voice was not powerful, nor was his ear perfect for harmony of sound; but I think it was difficult not to be impressed deeply both by his reading and his preaching; when he read, you saw that he felt, and he made you feel, that he was the servant of God, delivering his words; or leading you, as one of like infirmities and sins with your own, in your prayer. When he preached it was with an affectionate simplicity and hearty earnestness which were very moving; and the sermons themselves were at all times full of that abundant Scriptural knowledge which was the most remarkable quality in him as a divine; it has always seemed to me among the most striking characteristics of "The Christian Year." It is well known what his belief and feelings were in regard to the Sacraments. I remember on one occasion when I was present at a christening as godfather, how much he affected me, when a consciousness of his sense of the grace conferred became present to me. As he kept the newly-baptized infant for some moments in his arms, he gazed on it intently and lovingly with a tear in his eye, and apparently absorbed in the thought of the child of wrath become the child of grace. Here his natural affections gave clearness and intensity to his belief; the fondest mother never loved children more dearly than this childless man."

During the eventful years that followed the Assize sermon, though his place was still in his country cure, his sympathies and coöperation were with Newman and other friends in Oxford. He contributed some of the more important Tracts; poems of his embodying the sentiments of the party appeared from time to time, and were republished in the "Lyra Apostolica." In 1841, when the famous No. 90 was published, to the scandal of the whole religious world, Keble was one of the few who stood by Newman. What then must his feelings have been when that younger friend, by whom he had so stood, with whom he had so often taken counsel, abandoned the Church of England, and sought refuge in that of Rome? As late as 1863, a friend of his, when walking with him near Hursley, drew his attention to a broken piece of ground — a chalk-pit, as it turned out — hard by. "'Ah!' he said, 'that is a sad place, connected with the most painful event of my life.' I began to fear that it had been the scene of some terrible accident which I had unwittingly recalled to his mind. 'It was there,' he went on, 'that I first knew for certain that J. H. N. had left us. We had made up our mind that such an event was all but inevitable; and one day I received a letter in his handwriting. I felt sure of what it contained, and I carried it about with me through the day, afraid to open it. At last I got away to that chalk-pit, and there, forcing myself to read the letter, I found that my forebodings had been too true; it was the announcement that he was gone.'"

It seems natural to ask how it came that, when Newman left, Keble adhered to the Church of England. They were at one in their fundamental principles. What, then, determined them to go different ways? Of many reasons that occur this one may be given. The two friends, though agreeing in their principles, differed widely in mental structure and in natural temperament. They differed scarcely less in training and circumstances. Keble, as we have seen, cared little for reasoning, and rested mainly on feeling and intuition. Newman, on the other hand, though fully alive to these, added an unresting intellectual instinct which could not be satisfied without a defined logical foundation for what it instinctively held. Not that Keble was without a theory. Taking from Butler the principle that probability is the guide of life, he applied it to theological truth. Butler, by a very questionable process, had employed the maxim of worldly prudence, that probability is the guide of life, as an argument for religion, but mainly in the natural sphere. Keble tried to carry it on into the sphere of revealed truth. The arguments which support religious doctrine, he said, may be only probable arguments judged intellectually; but faith and love, being directed towards their divine Object, and living in the contemplation of that Object, convert these probable arguments into certainties. In fact, the inward assurance, which devout faith has of the reality of its Object, makes doctrines practically certain which may not be intellectually demonstrable. Newman tells us that he accepted this view so far, but, not being fully satisfied with it, tried, in his University sermons and other works, to supplement it with considerations of his own. In time, however, he felt it give way in his hands, and either abandoned it, or allowed it to carry him elsewhere.

But besides difference of mental structure, there were other causes which perhaps determined the divergent courses of the two friends. In the case of Keble, whatever is most sacred and endearing in the English Church had surrounded his infancy and boyhood, and gone with him into full manhood. With him loyalty to Home was hardly less sacred than loyalty to the Faith. These two influences were so intertwined in the inner fibres of his nature that it would have been to him very death to separate them. Of Dr. Newman's early associations I know no more than the little he has himself disclosed. It would appear, however, that the Anglican Church never had so invincible a hold on him as it had on Keble. By few perhaps has it been seen in so winning an aspect as it wore in the rural quiet of that Gloucestershire parsonage which was his early home.

When Newman was gone, on Keble, along with Dr. Pusey, was thrown the chief burden of the toil and responsibility arising out of his position in the Church. Naturally there was great searching of hearts amongst all the followers of the Oxford theology. Keble had to give himself to counsel the perplexed, to strengthen the wavering, and, as far as might be, to heal the breaches that had been made. Throughout the ecclesiastical contests of the last twenty years, though never loud or obtrusive, he yet took a resolute part in maintaining the principles with which his life had been identified. One last extract from Sir J. T. Coleridge's beautiful sketch of his friend, will give all that need here be said of this portion of Keble's life: "Circumstances had now placed him in a position which he would never have desired for himself, but from which a sense of duty compelled him not to shrink. Questions one after another arose touching the faith or the discipline of the Church, and affecting, as he believed, the morals and religion of the people. I need not specify the decisions of courts or the proceedings in Parliament to which I allude; those whose consciences were disturbed, but who shrank from public discussion, and those who stirred themselves in canvassing their propriety, or in counteracting their consequences, equally turned to him as a comforter and adviser in private and in public, and he could not turn a deaf ear to such applications. It is difficult to say with what affectionate zeal and industry he devoted himself to such cares, how much, and at length it is to be feared how injuriously to his health, he spent his time and strength in the labor these brought on him. Many of these involved, of course, questions of law, and it was not seldom that he applied to me — and thus I can testify with what care and learning and acuteness he wrote upon them. Many of his fugitive pieces were thus occasioned; and should these be, as they ought to be, collected, they will be found to possess even more than temporary interest. I had occasion but lately to refer to his tract on 'Marriage with the Wife's Sister,' and I can only hope that the question will soon be argued in Parliament with the soundness and clearness which are there employed. But even all this does not represent the calls made on his time by private correspondence, by personal visits, or, where it was necessary, by frequent, sometimes by long journeys, taken for the support of religion. I need hardly say that his manner of doing all this concurred in raising up for him that immense personal influence which he possessed; people found in their best adviser the most unpresuming, unwearied, affectionate friend, and they loved as well as venerated him."

The appearance of Dr. Newman's "Apologia" in 1864 was to Keble a great joy. Not that he had ever ceased to love Dr. Newman with his old affection, but the separation of now nearly twenty years, and the cause of it, had been to Keble the sorest trial of his life. If the book contained some things regarding the Church of England which must have pained Keble, there was much more in it to gladden him; not only the entire human-heartedness of its tone, which made its way to the hearts even of strangers, but the deep and tender affection which it breathes to Dr. Newman's early friends, and the proof it gave that Rome had made no change either in his heart or head which could hinder their real sympathy. The result was that in September, 1865, these three, Dr. Newman, Dr. Pusey, and Mr. Keble, met under the roof of Hursley vicarage, and after an interval of twenty years looked on each others' altered faces. One evening they passed together, no more. It happened, however, that at the very time of this meeting, Mrs. Keble had an alarming attack of illness. Keble writes: "He (Dr. Pusey) and J. H. N. met here the very day after my wife's attack. Pusey indeed was present when the attack began. Trying as it all was, I was very glad to have them here, and to sit by them and listen."

Soon after this, in October, Mr. and Mrs. Keble left Hursley for Bournemouth, not to return. Since the close of 1864, symptoms of declining health had shown themselves in him also. The long strain of the duties that accumulated on him in his later years, with the additional anxiety caused by Mrs. Keble's precarious health, had been gradually wearing him. After only a few days' illness he was taken to his rest on the day before Good Friday, 1866. In a few weeks Mrs. Keble followed, and now they are laid side by side in Hursley churchyard.

The picture of this saintly life will of course in time be given to the world. It is much to be hoped that the task will be intrusted to some one able to do justice to it. There are two kinds of biographies, and of each kind we have seen examples in our own time. One is as a golden chalice, held up by some wise hand, to gather the earthly memory ere it is spilt on the ground. The other kind is as a millstone, hung by a partial, yet ill-judging friend, round the hero's neck, to plunge him as deep as possible in oblivion. In looking back on the eminent men of last generation, we have seen one or two lives of the former stamp, many more of the latter. Let us indulge the hope that he who writes of Keble will take for his model the one or two nearly faultless biographies we possess, and above all that he will condense his work within such limits as shall commend it not only to partial friends, but also to all thoughtful readers.

By his character and influence, Keble did more than perhaps any other man to bring about the most widespread quickening of religious life which has taken place within the English Church during the present century. To him, and the party to which his very name was a tower of strength, England owes two great services. First, they, and they preëminently, have turned, and are still turning, a resolute front against the rationalizing spirit, which would pare down revelation to the measure of the human understanding — cut away its foundation in the supernatural, and virtually reduce it to a moral system, encased perhaps in a few historic facts. Secondly, they have introduced into the English Church a higher order of character, and taught it, one might almost say, new virtues. They have diffused widely through the clergy the contagion of their own zeal and resoluteness, their self-devotion and Christian chivalry. These are high services to have rendered to any country in any age. But with these acknowledgments two regrets must mingle: one, that with their defense of Christian truth they should have mixed up positions which are untenable, identifying with the simple faith doctrines which are no part of it, but rather alien accretions gathered by the Church in its progress down the ages. The result of this intermingling with Christianity things that seem superstitious, has been to drive many back into dislike and denial of that which is truly supernatural. The other cause of regret is, that they should have impaired the practical power of their example by the exclusive and unsympathetic side they have turned towards their fellow-Christians in other Reformed communions. This exclusiveness kept back from the Oxford theologians the sympathies of many who, but for this, would have been strongly drawn to them by their unworldliness, fervor, and self-devotion. Both errors have one source, the confounding the Church with the clergy, or rather, perhaps I should say, the attempt to place the essence of the Church in a priestly organization. But though these things must be said, it is not as of a partisan that one would like most to think of Keble. The circumstances of his time forced him to take a side, but his nature was too pure and holy to find fit expression in polemics; and the memory of his rare and saintly character will long survive in the hearts of his countrymen the party strifes in which it was his lot to mingle.

Of his two prose books, his edition of Hooker's works, which has, I believe, superseded every other, and his Life of the good Bishop Wilson of Sodor and Man, the author of the "Sacra Privata," this is not the place to speak. But before turning to "The Christian Year," one word must be said about his later book of poetry, the "Lyra Innocentium." It appeared in 1846, at an interval of nearly twenty years after "The Christian Year." This collection of poems he speaks of in May, 1845, as "a set of things which have been accumulating on me for the last three or four years. It has been a great comfort to me in the desolating anxiety of the last two years, and I wish I could settle at once on some other such work." Children, as we have seen, had always been peculiarly dear to this childless man, and he had at first wished to have made these poems a Christian Year for teachers and nurses, and others much employed about children. In time it took a different shape, and it is perhaps to be regretted that he had not made it what he first intended. Children, their thoughts and ways, and the feelings which they awaken in their elders, are themes of quite exhaustless interest. And yet how seldom has any poet of adequate tenderness and depth approached that mysterious world of childhood! Wordsworth, indeed, has felt it deeply, and expressed it in some of his most exquisite poems: —

> " O dearest, dearest boy, my heart
> For better lore would seldom yearn,
> Could I but teach the hundredth part
> Of what from thee I learn."

This verse from Wordsworth is indeed the motto chosen by Keble for his " Lyra Innocentium."

Of the poems on children which the " Lyra " contains, I am free to confess that they approach their subject too exclusively from the Church side for general interest. " Looking Westward," " The Bird's Nest," " Bereavement," " The Manna Gatherers," are fine lyrics, equal perhaps to most in " The Christian Year." But there is no thought in the " Lyra Innocentium " about childhood that comes near that earlier strain in which the poet, as he looks on children ranged to receive their first lessons in religion, bursts forth —

> " O! say not, dream not, heavenly notes
> To childish ears are vain,
> That the young mind at random floats,
> And cannot reach the strain.
>
> " Dim or unheard, the words may fall,
> And yet the heaven-taught mind
> May learn the sacred air, and all
> The harmony unwind.
>
> " Was not our Lord a little child,
> Taught by degrees to pray,
> By father dear and mother mild
> Instructed day by day? "

Then, after an interval, he goes on —

"Each little voice in turn
Some glorious truth proclaims,
What sages would have died to learn,
Now taught by cottage dames.

"And if some tones be false or low,
What are all prayers beneath
But cries of babes that cannot know
Half the deep thought they breathe?"

Whatever the reason may be, certainly the later book does not strike home to the universal heart as "The Christian Year" did, and it never has attained anything like the same popularity.

The reference to ecclesiastical usages, not known to the many, and the more pronounced High Church feeling which it embodies, will partly account for this. It is certainly much more restricted and less catholic in its range. Partly also it may be that the fountain of inspiration did not flow so fully as in earlier years. It may not have been that time had chilled it; but other duties and cares had come thick upon him since his poetic spring-time. Especially the polemical stir in which his share in the Oxford movement had involved him, and the anxiety in the midst of which the "Lyra Innocentium" was composed, must have left little of that leisure either of time or heart which is necessary for a free-flowing minstrelsy.

It may help to the fuller understanding of "The Christian Year," if we turn for a moment to Keble's theory of poetry. He has set it forth at large in "Prælections on Poetry," more shortly in his review of the "Life of Scott," which, once famous in Oxford, is almost unknown to the present generation. That review, which first appeared in the "British Critic," is well worthy of being republished, both from the insight it gives into Keble's character, and views on poetry, and also as a study of Scott by a reverential admirer, in many things very unlike himself. The theory is that poetry is the natural relief of minds burdened by some engrossing idea, or strong emotion, or ruling taste, or imaginative regret, which from some cause or other they are kept from directly indulging. Rhythm and metrical form serve to regulate and restrain, while they express those strong or deep emotions, "which need relief, but cannot endure publicity." They are at once "vent for eager feelings and a veil to draw over them. For the utterance of high or tender feeling controlled and modified by a certain reserve is the very soul of poetry."

On this principle Keble founds what he regards as an essential distinction between primary and secondary poets. Primary poets are they who are driven by some overmastering enthusiasm, by passionate devotion to some range of objects, or line of thought, or aspect of life or nature, to utter their feelings in song. They sing, because they cannot help it. There is a melody within them which will out, a fire in their blood which cannot be suppressed. This is the true poetic μανία of which Plato speaks. Secondary poets are not urged to poetry by any such overflowing sentiment; but learning, admiration of great masters, choice, and a certain literary turn, have made them poetic artists. They were not born, but being possessed of a certain εὐφυΐα, have made themselves poets. Of the former kind are Homer, Lucretius, Shakespeare, Burns, Scott; of the latter, Euripides, Dryden, Milton. This view, if it be somewhat too narrow a basis on which to found a comprehensive theory of poetry, certainly does lay hold of one side of the truth generally overlooked. In our own day, how many are there! possessed of a large measure of artistic faculty, able to treat poetically anything they take up, wanting only in one thing, — a subject which absorbs their interest. There is nothing in human life, or history, or nature, which they have made peculiarly their own, nothing about which they know more intimately, than the host of educated men. And so, though with a "skill in composition and felicity of language" greater than many poets possess, they are still felt to be literary men rather than poets, because they have no overmastering impulse, no divine enthusiasm, driving them to seek relief in song.

If we apply to himself the author's own canon, "The Christian Year" would place him in the rank of primary poets. Not that it displays anything like the highest artistic faculty, but because it evidently flows from a native spring of inspiration. As far as it goes, it is genuine poetry. The author sings, in a strain of his own, of the things he has known and felt and loved. Beneath all the layers that early education and Oxford training have superimposed, there is felt to be a glow of internal heat not derived from these.

To English Church people without number "The Christian Year" has long been not only a cherished classic, but a sacred book, which they place beside their Bible and their Prayer-Book. On the other hand, a generation of literary young men has grown up, who, having had their tastes formed on a newer, more highly spiced style of poetry, scarcely know "The Christian Year," and, if they knew it, would turn away from what seemed to them its meagre literary merit. It would be impossible to say anything regarding it which would not seem faint praise to the one class, and exaggeration to the other. But without trying to meet the views of either, it is worth while to study the poem for ourselves.

It cannot be too clearly kept in view that Keble is not a hymn writer, and that "The Christian Year" is not a collection of hymns. Those who have come to it expecting to find genuine hymns, will turn away in disappointment. They will seek in vain for anything of the directness, the fervor, the simplicity, the buoyancy of devotion which have delighted them in Charles Wesley. But to demand this is to mistake the nature and form of Keble's poems. There is all the difference between them and Charles Wesley's, that there is between meditation on the one hand, and prayer, or thanksgiving, or praise on the other. Indeed, so little did Keble's genius fit him for hymn writing, that in his two poems which are intended to be hymns — those for the morning and the evening — the opening in either case is a description of natural facts, wholly unsuited to hymn purposes. And so when these two poems are adopted into hymn collections, as they often are, a mere selection of certain stanzas from each is all that has been found possible. Besides these two, there is no other poem in the book, any large part of which can be used as a hymn. For they are all lyrical religious meditations, not hymns at all. Yet true though this is, every here and there, out of the midst of the reflections, there does flash a verse of fervid emotion and direct heart-appeal to God, which is quite hymnal in character. These occasional bursts are among the highest beauties of "The Christian Year." Yet they are neither so frequent nor so long-sustained as to change the prevailingly meditative cast of the whole book. It is owing perhaps to this prevalence of meditation, and that often of a refined and subtle kind, that "The Christian Year" is not, as we have often heard said, so well adapted as some simpler, less poetical collections, to be read by the sick-bed to the faint and weak. Unless long familiarity has made it easy, it requires more thought and mental elasticity to follow it, than the sick for the most part can supply. Yet it contains single verses, many, though not whole poems, which will come home full of consolation to any, even the weakest spirit. On the whole, however, it is not with Charles Wesley, or any of the hymn writers of this or the past century, nor even with Cowper in his hymns or his larger poems, that Keble should be compared. In outward form, and not a little in inward spirit, the religious poets to whom he bears the strongest likeness are Henry Vaughan and George Herbert, both of the seventeenth century. A comparison with these would be interesting, were this the place for it, but at present I must confine myself to the consideration of the special characteristics of "The Christian Year."

These seem to be, *first*, a tone of religious feeling, fresh, deep, and tender, beyond what was common even among religious men in the author's day, perhaps in any day; *secondly*, great intensity and tenderness of home affection; *thirdly*, a shy and delicate reserve, which loved quiet paths and shunned publicity; *fourthly*, a pure love of nature, and a spiritual eye to read nature's symbolism.

> "He sang of love, with quiet blending,
> Slow to begin, and never ending,
> Of serious faith, and inward glee."

1. Its peculiar tone of religious feeling.

It embodies deep and tender religious sentiment in a form which is old, and yet new. Our best critic has lately told us that "the inevitable business for the modern poet, as it was for the Greek poet in the days of Pericles, is to interpret human life afresh, and find a new spiritual basis for it." Keble did not think so.

He was content with the interpretation which Christianity has put on human life, and wished only to read man and nature as far as he might, in this light. Goethe, I suppose, is the great modern instance of a poet who has tried "to give a moral interpretation of man and the world from an independent point of view." Of course it would be simply ridiculous for a moment to place Keble for poetic power in comparison with such an one as Goethe. But, disparate as their powers are, Keble with limited faculty, just by virtue of his having accepted the Christian interpretation, while the other rejected it, has spoken, if one may venture to say so, more words that satisfy man's deepest yearnings, that sink into those simple places of the heart which lie beneath all culture, than Goethe with all his world-width has done. The religion which Keble laid to heart, and lived by, would not seem to have come to him through prolonged spiritual conflicts, as did that of the great Puritans; neither had he reached it by laborious critical processes, as modern philosophers would have us do. He had learned it first at his mother's knee. Then it was confirmed and systematized by the daily teaching of the Church he so devoutly loved. Time brought to it additions from various quarters, but no break. The powerful influences of his University, direct and indirect, chivalry reawakening in Scott's poetry, meditative depth in Wordsworth, these all melted naturally into his primal faith, and combined with the general tendencies of the time to carry him in spirit back to those older ages where his imagination found ampler range, his devotion severer, more self-denying virtues than modern life engenders. Out of that great past he brought some of the sterner stuff of which the martyrs were made, and introduced it like iron into the blood of modern religious feeling. A poet who received all these influences into himself, and vitalized them, could not but make the old new. For not till the authoritative had been inwardly transfused into the moral and spiritual did it for the most part find vent in his poetry. There are exceptions to this, which form what may be set down as the shortcomings of "The Christian Year." But in all its finer, more vital poems, the catholic faith has become personal, rests frankly on intuition and experience, as frankly as the vaguer, more impersonal meditations of greater poets.

> "The eye in smiles may wander round,
> Caught by earth's shadows as they fleet,
> But for the soul no home is found,
> Save Him who made it, meet."

Or again, the well-known —

> "Abide with me from morn till eve,
> For without Thee I cannot live;
> Abide with me when night is nigh,
> For without Thee I dare not die."

Or again —

> "Who loves the Lord aright,
> No soul of man can worthless find;
> All will be precious in his sight,
> Since Christ on all hath shined."

It is the many words, simple yet deep, devoutly Christian yet intensely human, like these, scattered throughout its pages, that have endeared "The Christian Year" to countless hearts within the English Church, and to many a heart beyond it. The new elements in the book are perhaps these — first, it translates religious sentiment out of the ancient and exclusively Hebrew dialect into the language of modern feeling. Hitherto English devotional poets, with the exception perhaps of Cowper, in some passages, had adhered rigorously to the Scriptural imagery and phraseology. This, besides immensely limiting their range, made their words often fall wide of modern experience. Keble took the thoughts and sentiments of which men at the present day are conscious, expressed them in fitting modern words, and transfused into them the Christian spirit. Secondly, there is visible in him, first perhaps of his contemporaries, — that which seems the best characteristic of modern religion, — combined with devout reverence for the person of our Lord, a closer, more personal love to Him as to a living friend. There were no doubt rare exceptions here and there, but, generally speaking, religious men before spoke of our Lord in a more distant way, as one holding the central place rather in a dogmatic system than in the devout affections. The best men of our own time have gone beyond this. The Lord of the Gospels, in his Divine humanity, has come closer to their hearts, and made Himself known in a more intimate and endearing way. In none perhaps was this change of feeling earlier seen, or more strongly marked, than in Keble. Thirdly, there is the close and abundant knowledge of Scripture, with a fine and delicate feeling for the beauty of its language. Without confining himself to the imagery or language of the Bible, he everywhere shows his intimacy with it, and interweaves its words and half sentences, its scenes and imagery naturally and gracefully with his own.

These are some of the more catholic notes of the book which have won for it a place in the affections of Christians of every communion. This depth of catholic religious sentiment, it is, no doubt, which is its chief and most valuable characteristic. From this some may be ready to draw an argument for Christian morality disjoined from Christian doctrine, or for some all-embracing religion which would comprehend whatever the various churches agree in, discarding all in which they differ. What that residuum exactly is, no one has yet stated. But before drawing such an argument from "The Christian Year," it may be as well to ask whether that book would have been so charged with devout Christian sentiment if its author had not held with all his heart those doctrinal truths which were in him the roots out of which that sentiment grew, but which many now wish to get rid of? If we love the consummate flower, it might be as well not to begin by cutting away the root.

There is, however, another side on which "The Christian Year" is less catholic in its character. This, which may be called its ecclesiastical side, is inherent in the very form of the book. A poem for each Sunday in the year would be welcome to very many, but then what is to determine the subject of each Sunday's poem? A chance verse or phrase in the Gospel for the day, as this is given in the Prayer-Book, is hardly a catholic or universal ground for fixing the subject. Again, Christmas, Good Friday, Easter-day, Whitsunday, have of course a catholic meaning, because these days, though not observed by all churches, are yet memorials of the sacred facts by which all Christians live. But the lesser Saints' Days, Circumcision, Purification, as well as the occasional services, have a local and temporary, not a universal import. Accordingly, a perusal of the poems suggests what the preface to them confirms, that they did not all flow off from a free spontaneous inspiration, awakened by the thought natural to each day, but that a good number were either poems previously composed and afterwards adapted to some particular Sunday, or written as it were to order after the thought of rounding "The Christian Year" had arisen. So clear does this seem that it would not be hard to go through the several poems and lay finger here on the spontaneous effusions, there on those of more labored manufacture. The former flow from the first verse to the last lucid in thought, simple and almost faultless in diction; no break in the sense, no obscurity; seldom any harshness or poverty in the diction. The others are imperfect in rhythm and language, defaced by the conventionalities of poetic diction, frequently obscure or artificial, the thread of thought broken or hard to catch. The one set are like mountain streams, that run down the hillside in sunshine, clear and bright from end to end, the other are like streams that find their way through difficult places, often hidden underground or buried in heaps of stones. Yet even the most defective of them come forth to light in some single verse of profound thought or tender feeling, so well expressed as to make the reader willingly forgive for that one gleam the imperfection of the rest.

2. Home-feeling.

The next quality I would notice is the deep tone of home affection which pervades these poems. This, perhaps as much as anything, has endeared them to his home-loving countrymen. Such is that feeling for an ancient home breathed in —

"Since all that is not Heaven must fade,
Light be the hand of Ruin laid
Upon the home I love:
With lulling spell let soft Decay
Steal on, and spare the giant sway
The crash of tower and grove.

"Far opening down some woodland deep
In their own quiet glade should sleep
The relics dear to thought,
And wild-flower wreaths from side to side
Their waving tracery hang, to hide
What ruthless Time has wrought."

Again, the hymn for St. Andrew's Day is so well known and loved as hardly to need quoting. Every line of it is instinct with simple pure affection, yet never, one might think, so deeply felt or so well expressed as here: —

"When brothers part for manhood's race,
What gift may most endearing prove
To keep fond memory in her place,
And certify a brother's love?

. . . .

"No fading frail memorial give
To soothe his soul when thou art gone,
But wreaths of hope for aye to live,
And thoughts of good together done."

Besides the more obvious allusions to the household charities, there are many delicate, more reserved touches on the same chord. Such is the —

"I cannot paint to Memory's eye
The scene, the glance, I dearest love —
Unchanged themselves, in me they die,
Or faint, or false, their shadows prove.

. . . .

"Meanwhile, if over sea or sky
Some tender lights unnoticed fleet,
Or on loved features dawn and die,
Unread, to us, their lesson sweet;

Yet are there saddening sights around,
Which Heaven, in mercy, spares us too."

But there is no need to go on with quotations. Many more such passages will occur to every reader. High education and refined thought in him had not weakened, but only made more pure and intense, natural affection. Yet in all the tenderness there is no trace of effeminacy. True, the woman's heart everywhere shows itself. But as it has been said that in the countenance of most men of genius there is something of a womanly expression not seen in the faces of other men, so it is

17

distinctive of true poetic temper that it ever carries the woman's heart within the man's. And certainly, of no poet's heart does this hold more truly than of Keble's. They, however, must be but blind critics, insensible to the finer pathos of human life, who have on this account called Keble's poetry "effeminate." The woman's heart in him is blended with the martyr's courage. Hardly any modern poetry breathes so firm self-control, so fixed yet calm resolve, so stern self-denial. If these be qualities that can consist with effeminacy, then Keble's poetry may be allowed to pass for effeminate. But those who bring this charge against it, misled, it may be, by the loud bluster that passes with many for manliness, seem to forget that the bravest and most high-souled manhood is also the gentlest and most tender hearted; that, according to the saying, "A man is never so much a man as when he becomes most in heart a child."

3. Reserve.

This naturally leads on to the notice of another characteristic of this poetry — the fine reserve, which does not publish aloud, but only delicately hints, its deeper feelings. It was an intrinsic part of Keble's nature to shrink from obtruding himself, to dislike display, —

"To love the sober shade
More than the laughing light."

And one object he had in publishing "The Christian Year" was the hope that it might supply a sober standard of devotional feeling, in unison with that presented by the Prayer-Book. The time, he thought, was one of unbounded curiosity and morbid craving for excitement, symptoms which have not abated during the forty years since Keble so wrote. He wished, as far as might be, to supply some antidote to these tendencies. Again, modern thought has, as all know, turned in upon itself, and discovered a whole internal world of reflections and sensibilities hardly expressed in the older literature. Keble so far shared this tendency with his contemporaries. But he set himself not to feed and pamper it, but to direct, to sober, and to brace it, by bringing it into the presence of realities higher than itself.

This feeling of delicate reserve, sobered and strengthened by Christian thought, comes out in many of the poems, in none perhaps more than in the one which contains these stanzas: —

"E'en human Love will shrink from sight
Here in the coarse rude earth:
How then should rash intruding glance
Break in upon *her* sacred trance
Who boasts a heavenly birth?

"So still and secret is her growth,
Ever the truest heart,
Where deepest strikes her kindly root
For hope or joy, for flower or fruit,
Least knows its happy part.

"God only, and good angels, look
Behind the blissful screen —
As when, triumphant o'er his woes,
The Son of God by moonlight rose,
By all but Heaven unseen."

I would not pause on verbal criticisms, — only the last line of the second stanza here is one of many instances in which the beauty of the finest thoughts is marred by the admission of some hackneyed conventional phrase. Otherwise, these stanzas, as well as the whole poem in which they occur, are in Keble's finest and most native vein. In keeping with the feeling breathed by these lines is another which should be noted. As he keeps his own deepest feelings under a close veil of reserve, so he loves best the virtues and the characters which are least obtrusive, and generally get least praise. Things which the world least recognizes, for these he reserves his heart's best sympathy. For the loud, the successful, the caressed, he has no word but perhaps one of admonition. It is the poor, the bowed down, the lonely, the forsaken, who draw out his deepest tenderness. And what makes this the nobler in Keble is, that it does not seem to come from the principle of *haud ignarus mali*, but rather from pure strength of Christian sympathy. The traits of character for which he has the keenest eye, the virtues on which he dwells most lovingly, are those which men in general take least note of. Those who belong to "the nameless family of God" kindle in him a deep enthusiasm, such as most poets have reserved for the earth's great heroes. Thus, in one of his finest passages, after contrasting those Christians who live in the "green earth" and under the "open sky" of the country, with those whose lot is cast in the streets and stifling alleys of the crowded city, he bursts forth —

"But Love's a flower that will not die
For lack of leafy screen,
And Christian Hope can cheer the eye
That ne'er saw vernal green;
Then be ye sure that Love can bless
E'en in this crowded loneliness,
Where ever-moving myriads seem to say,
Go — thou art nought to us, nor we to thee — away!

"There are in this loud stunning tide
Of human care and crime,
With whom the melodies abide
Of th' everlasting chime;
Who carry music in their heart
Through dusty lane and wrangling mart,
Plying their daily task with busier feet,
Because their secret souls a holy strain repeat."

And as is the inward tone of feeling, so is its outward expression, chastened and subdued. There is no gorgeousness of coloring, no stunning sound, no highly spiced phrase or metaphor. From what have been the chief attractions of much poetry popular since his day, — scarlet hues and blare of trumpets, staring metaphors and metaphysical enigmas, he turned instinctively. He seemed to say to these, —

"Farewell: for one short life we part:
I rather woo the soothing art,
Which only souls in sufferings tried
Bear to their suffering brethren's side."

Those who have called other parts of Keble effeminate, might perhaps call this ascetic. If it is so, it is an asceticism in harmony with true Christianity, and with the sober wisdom that comes from life's experience.

4. Descriptions of Nature.

Much has been said of Keble's eye for nature. His admirers perhaps exaggerate it, his depreciators as much underrate it. He certainly shared largely in that feeling about the visible world, so identified with Wordsworth that it is now called Wordsworthian, — that feeling which more than any other marks the direction in which modern imagination has enlarged and deepened. The appearances of nature furnish Keble with the framework in which most of his lyrics are set, the mould in which they are cast. Some whole poems, as the one beginning —

"Lessons sweet of spring returning,"

are little more than descriptions of some scene in nature. Many more take some natural appearance and make it the symbol of a spiritual truth. Two small rills, born apart and afterwards blending in one large stream, are likened to two separate prayers uniting to bring about some great result. The autumn clouds, mantling round the sun for love, suggest that love is life's only sign. The robin singing unweariedly in the bleak November wind, suggests a lesson of content —

"Rather in all to be resigned than blest."

These and many more are the natural appearances which, some by resemblance, some by contrast, furnish him with key-notes to religious meditation. In many you feel at once that the poet has struck a true note, one which will be owned by the universal imagination, wherever that faculty is sufficiently cultivated to be alive to it. In some you feel more doubtful, — the analogy appears to be somewhat more faint or far-fetched. In others you seem to see clearly that the resemblance is arbitrary and capricious, a work of the mere fancy, not of the genuine imagination. An instance of the last kind has been severely commented on by a contemporary critic who, on the strength of some doubtful analogies which occur in Keble's poems, has voted him no poet. This critic specially comments on one poem, in which the moon is made a symbol of the Church, the stars are made symbols of saints in heaven, and the trees in Eden of saints on earth. This, if it be not some remote allusion to passages of Scripture, must be allowed to be a mere ecclesiastical reading of nature's symbols, repudiated by the universal heart of man, and therefore by true poetry. But if this and some other instances, pitched on a false key, can be pointed out, how many more are there where the chord struck answers with a genuine tone? Even in the very poem which contains the symbolism condemned, is there not the following: —

"The glorious sky embracing all
Is like the Maker's love,

> Wherewith encompassed great and small
>   In peace and order move."

Here Keble has christianized an analogy, acknowledged not only by the Greek conception of Zeus, but more or less, we believe, by the primeval faith of the whole Aryan race.

Of the many instances that might easily be gathered from these poems, in which that mysterious chord of analogy that binds together human feeling and the outward world is truly touched, one more must be given. It is from the poem on All Saints' Day. As that day falls on the 1st of November, a time so often beautiful with the bright calm of St. Luke's summer, the following lines serve well to harmonize the feeling of the season with the thoughts which the Church Festival is meant to awaken: —

> "How quiet shows the woodland scene!
>   Each flower and tree, its duty done,
> Reposing in decay serene,
>   Like weary men when age is won,
> Such calm old age as conscience pure
> And self-commanding hearts insure,
> Waiting their summons to the sky,
> Content to live, but not afraid to die.

As might be looked for in a real lover of nature, Keble's imagery is that which he had lived in the midst of, and knew. The shady lanes, the more open hursts and downs, such as may be seen near Oxford, and further west and south, "England's primrose meadow paths," the stiles worn by generations, and the gray church-tower embowered in elm-trees, — with these his habitual thoughts and sentiments suit well. Even in this familiar landscape his eye and ear have caught facts and aspects of nature, which, as far as I know, have never before been put down in books. Take that instance from the poem on the Fifth Sunday after Easter —

"Deep is the silence of the summer noon,
When a soft shower
Will trickle soon,
A gracious rain, freshening the weary bower —
O sweetly then far off is heard
The clear note of some lonely bird."

Many an ear before Keble's must have heard a solitary thrush singing in the distant fields amid the deep hush that preludes the thunder-storm; but no poet before Keble, as far as I know, had seized that impressive image and embalmed it in verse. Not a few such images or aspects of the quiet English landscape will be found reclaimed from the fields for the first time in "The Christian Year." With this kind of scenery, which was familiar to him all his life, he is for the most part content, and seldom travels beyond it. Indeed, a very true test of the genuineness of a poet's inspiration would seem to be, whether his imagery is mainly gathered from the scenes amidst which he has lived, or is borrowed from the writings of former poets or other artificial sources. Seldom does Keble visit mountain lands, only once or twice in "The Christian Year." But the poem for the 20th Sunday after Trinity, though good, might have been written by one who had never seen mountains, if only he had read descriptions of them.

Besides the English there is another kind of landscape in which Keble has shown himself at home. Dean Stanley has noted the fidelity with which he has pictured scenes in the Holy Land. This shows not only a close study of the hints that are to be found in the Bible and in the modern books about Palestine, — it proves how quick must have been the insight into nature of one who, though he had never himself beheld that country, could from such materials call up pictures true enough to satisfy the eye of the most graphic of modern travellers even while he gazed on those very scenes.

There are two sides which nature turns towards the imagination. One is that which the poet can read figuratively, in which he can see symbols and analogies of the spiritual world. This side Keble, as we have seen, felt and read, in the main I think truly, though sometimes he may have missed it. What the true reading is, and how it is to be discerned, is a weighty matter to be entered on here. One thing, however, is certain, that the correspondency between the natural object and the spiritual, between nature and the soul, is there existing independently of the individual man. He did not make the correspondency; his part is to see and interpret truly what was there beforehand, not to read into nature his own views or moods waywardly and capriciously. The truest poet is he who reads nature's hieroglyphics most truly and most widely; and the test of the true reading is that it is at once welcomed by the universal imagination of man. This universal or catholic imagination of man is far different from the universal suffrage of men. It means the imagination of those in whom that faculty exists in the highest degree, cultivated to the finest sensibility. The imagination is the faculty which reads truly, the fancy that which reads capriciously, and so falsely. The former seizes true and really existing analogies between nature and spirit; the latter makes arbitrary and fictitious ones. In the school of imagination, as opposed to fancy, Keble was a faithful and devout student. It was the music of his pious spirit to read aright the symbolical side which nature turns towards man.

But nature has another side, of which there is no indication in Keble's poetry. I mean her infinite and unhuman side, which yields no symbols to soothe man's yearnings. Outside of and far beyond man, his hopes and fears, his strivings and aspirations, there lies the vast immensity of nature's forces, which pays him no homage, and yields him no sympathy. This aspect of nature may be seen even amid the tamest landscape, if we look to the clouds or the stars above us, or to the ocean roaring around our shores. But nowhere is it borne in on man as in the midst of the vast deserts of the earth, or in the presence of the mountains, which seem so impressive and unchangeable. Their strength and permanence so contrast with man — of few years and full of trouble; they are so indifferent to his feelings or his destiny. He may smile or weep, he may live or die; they care not. They are the same in all their ongoings, happen what will to him. They respond to the sunrises and the sunsets, but not to his sympathies. All the same they fulfill their mighty functions careless though no human eye should ever look on them. So it is in all the great movements of nature. Man holds his festal days, and nature frowns; he goes forth from the death-chamber, and nature affronts him with sunshine and the song of birds. Evidently, it seems, she marches on, having a purpose of her own inaccessible to man; she keeps her own secret, and drops no hint to him. This mysterious silence, this inhuman indifference, this inexorable deafness, has impressed the imagination of the greatest poets with a vague yet sublime awe. The sense of it lay heavy on Lucretius, Shelley, Wordsworth, and drew out their soul's profoundest music. This side of things, whether philosophically or imaginatively regarded, seems to justify the saying, that "the visible world still remains without its divine interpretation." But it was not on thoughts of this kind that Keble loved to dwell. If they ever occurred to him, he has nowhere expressed them. He was content with that other side of nature, of which I spoke first, the side which allows itself to be humanized, that is, to be interpreted by man's faith and devout aspirations. This was the side that suited his religious purpose, and to this he limited himself. Within this range few have ever interpreted nature more soothingly and beautifully.

These are a few of the qualities that would strike any one on first opening "The Christian Year." They are not, however, enough to account for its unparalleled popularity. Indeed, popularity is no word to express the fact, that this book has been for years the cherished companion of numbers of the best men, in their best moods — men too of the most diverse characters and schools — who have lived in our time. The secret of this power is a compound of many influences hard to state or explain. It has not been hindered by the blemishes obvious on the surface to every one, inharmonious rhythms, frequent obscurity, here and there poverty and conventionality of diction. In spite of these it has won its way to the hearts of the highly educated and refined, as no book of poetry, sacred or secular, in our time has done. Will it continue to do so? Will its own imperfections, and the changing currents of men's feelings not alienate from it a generation rendered fastidious by poetry of more artistic perfection, more highly colored, more richly flavored? Without speaking too confidently, it may be expected to live on, if not in so wonderful esteem, yet widely read and deeply felt; for it makes its appeal to no temporary or accidental feelings, but mainly to that which is permanent in man. It can hardly be that it should lose its hold on the affections of English-speaking men as long as Christianity retains it. For if we may judge from the past, it will be long ere another character of the same rare and saintly beauty shall again concur with a poetic gift and power of poetic expression, which, if not of the highest, are still of a very high order. Broader and bolder imagination, greater artistic faculty, many poets who were his contemporaries possessed. But in none of them did there burn a spiritual light so pure and heavenly, to transfigure these gifts from within. It is because "The Christian Year" has succeeded in conveying to the outer world some effluence of that character which his intimate friends loved and revered in Keble, that, as I believe, it will not cease to hold a quite peculiar place in the affections of posterity.

THE MORAL MOTIVE POWER.

Why is Ethical Science, as pursued in this country, of late years, even to reflecting men, so little attractive and so little edifying? The cognate study of metaphysics has, after long neglect, recently, in a wonderful way, renewed its youth, but to moral science no such revival has as yet come. And yet human character, the subject it deals with, is one, it would seem, of no inconsiderable interest. Physical science has no doubt drained off the current of men's thoughts, and left many subjects which once engaged them high and dry. But man, his spiritual being, and the light which is to enlighten it, his possibilities here, his destiny hereafter, these still remain, amid all the absorption of external things, the one highest marvel, the permanent centre of interest to men. It cannot be said that modern literature — the great exponent of what men are thinking — circles less than of old round the great human problems. Rather with the circuit of the suns, not only have the thoughts of men widened, but also their moral consciousness, I will not say their heart, has deepened. Modern literature, as compared with that of last century, has nothing more distinctive in it than this, — that it has broken into deeper ground of sentiment and reflection, ground which had hitherto lain fallow, non-existent, or unperceived. About the deeper soul secrets, literary men of last century either did not greatly trouble themselves, or they practiced a very strict reserve. But our own and the preceding age has seen an unveiling of the most inward — often of the most sacred feelings — which has sometimes gone beyond the limits of manliness and self-respect. This bringing to light of layers of consciousness hitherto concealed, if at times carried too far, has certainly enriched our literature with new wealth of moral content. In the best modern poetry it has shown itself by greater intensity and spirituality; in the highest modern novels, by delicacy of analysis, discrimination of the finer tints of feeling, variety and fine shading of character hitherto unknown; in the modern essay, by a subtleness and penetrative force which make the most perfect papers of Addison seem almost trivial. It further manifests itself in the growing love and keener appreciation of the few great world poets, who are after all the finest embodiments of moral wisdom. It may be that so much ethical thought has been turned off into these channels that it has left less to be expended in the more systematic form of ethical science. It may be too, that, as the field of moral experience widens, and the meaning of life deepens, and its problems become more complex, it demands proportionably stronger and rarer powers to gather up all this wealth, and illumine it with the light of reason. Certain it is that the modern time produces no such masters of moral wisdom for our day, as Aristotle and Marcus Aurelius were to the old world, or even as Bishop Butler was to his generation. Wide, many-sided, sensitive, deep, complex, as is the moral life in which we now move, if we would seek any philosophic guidance through its intricacies, any thinking which is at once solid, clear, practical, and instinct with life, we must turn, not to any modern treatise, but to the pages of these by-gone worthies. What help ardent spirits, looking for guidance in our day, have found, has been won not from the philosophers, but from some living poet, some giant of literature with no pretension to philosophy, or some inspired preacher. Wordsworth, Coleridge, Carlyle, Newman, Frederick Robertson, these, not the regular philosophers, have been the moral teachers of our generation, and to these young men have turned, to get from them what help they might. And now it seems that in these last days many, wearied out with straining after their impalpable spiritualities, and baffled for lack of a consistent spiritual theory, have betaken themselves to a style of thinking which, *if* it promises less, offers, as they think, something more systematic and more certain. In despair of spiritual truth, they are fain to fill their hunger with the husks of a philosophy which would confine all men's thoughts within the phenomenal world, and deny all knowledge that goes beyond the co-existences and successions of phenomena.

From aberrations like this perhaps no moral philosophy would have delivered men. But it would be well if, warned by such signs, it were to return closer to life and fact, deal more with things which men really feel, if, leaving general sentiments and moral theories, it would attempt some true diagnosis of the very complex facts of human nature, of the moral maladies from which men suffer, the burdens they need to have removed, the aspirations which they can practically live by. Instead of this, — instead of dealing with the actual and the ideal, which co-exist in man, and out of which, if at all, a harmony of life is to be woven, philosophers have been content to repeat a meagre and conventional psychology, taken mostly from books, not fresh from living hearts; or they have lost themselves in the metaphysical problems which no doubt everywhere underlie moral life, but which, pursued too exclusively, distract attention from the vital realities. These two causes have exhausted the strength and the interest of moral study — either a cut-and-dried conventional psychology, or absorbing metaphysical discussion. The former, in which moral truths appeared shriveled up, like plants in a botanist's herbarium, is the style of thing you find in the most approved text-books of the last generation.

"Never before," as one has smartly said, "had human nature been so neatly dissected, so handily sorted, or so ornamentally packed up. The virtues and vices, the appetites, emotions, affections, and sentiments stood each in their appointed corner, and with their appropriate label, to wait in neat expectation for the season of the professorial lectures, and the literary world only delayed their acquiescence in a uniform creed of moral philosophy till they should have arranged to their satisfaction whether the appetites should be secreted in the cupboard or paraded on the chimney-piece; or whether certain of the less creditable packets ought in law and prudence, or ought not in charity, to be ticketed 'Poison.' Everything was as it should be, or was soon to be so — differences were not too different, nor unanimity too unanimous — opinion did not degenerate into certainty, nor interest into earnestness, moral philosophy stood apart, like a literary gentleman of easy circumstances, from religion and politics, and truth itself was grateful for patronage, instead of being clamorous for allegiance. Types were delicate, margins were large, publishers were attentive, the intellectual world said it was intellectual, and the public acquiesced in the assertion. What more could scientific hearts desire?"

This description may contain something of caricature, and yet there are books enough on moral science which justify it — books which have no doubt succeeded in disgusting many with the subject of which they treat. Nor has moral philosophy suffered less from those deeper and more abstract discussions which have often in modern times been substituted for itself. Men of a profounder turn have so busied themselves with investigations of the nature of right, the law of duty, freedom, and necessity, and such like hard matters, that these have absorbed all their interest and energy, and left none for the treatment of those concrete realities which make up the moral life of man. Not that such discussions can be dispensed with. They are always necessary, never more so than now, when the spiritual ground of man's moral being is so often denied by materialistic or by merely phenomenal systems. It would perhaps, however, be well that they should be made a department by themselves, under the title of Metaphysic of Ethics, to be entered on by those who have special gifts for such inquiries. For when substituted for the whole or chief part of moral inquiry, they become "unpractical discussions of a practical subject," and as such alienate many from a study which, rightly treated, would deepen their thought and elevate their character.

For what is the real object with which moral science deals? Every science has some concrete entity, some congeries of facts, which is called in a general way its subject-matter. Botany, we say, deals with plants or herbs, geology with the strata which form the earth's crust, astronomy with the stars and their motions, psychology with all the states of human consciousness. What, then, is the concrete entity with which moral science deals? It is not the active powers of man, nor the emotions, nor the moral faculty — not these, each or all. It is simply human character. This is the one great subject it has ever before it. About this it asks what is character, its nature, its elements; what influences make it, what mar it; in what consists its perfection, what is its destiny? This may seem a very elementary statement, but it is quite needful to recur to it, and even to reiterate it, so much has it been lost sight of in the pursuit of side questions branching out of it. At the outset, before any analysis is begun, the student cannot too deeply take in and ponder the impression of character as a great and substantive reality. Some vague perception of character all men, of course, have. They are aware, whether they dwell on it or not, that men differ not only in face and form and outward appearance, but in something more inward, they cannot exactly tell what. But further than this confused notion most persons do not go. Others there are who see much more than this, who have a keen penetrating glance into every man they meet, apprehend his bias, know what manner of man he is, and deal with him accordingly. This gift, so useful in practice, we call an eye to character; those who possess it, good judges of character. It is the same gift of discerning the quality of men which some persons have of judging of horses and other cattle. Æschylus spoke of a good judge of character as *προβατογνώμων*. But this practical insight, so useful in business, and it may be to a certain extent in speculation, is something distinct from a fine and deep perception of the higher moralities of character. Shrewd observers of human nature are often keen to discern the weaknesses and foibles of men, and even to exaggerate them, but slow to perceive those finer traits of heart which lie deeper. The apprehension of character with which the student should begin, and which his moral studies ought to deepen, is something very different from this. It is an eye open to see, a heart sensitive to feel, the higher excellences of human nature, as they have existed, and still exist in the best of the race. It is a spirit the very opposite of that of the cynic, one which, while it looks steadily at the moral maladies and even basenesses into which men fall, yet, without being sentimental, loves more to contemplate the nobler than the baser side, which, behind the commonplaces and trivialities, can seize life's deeper import, and look up, and aspire towards the heights which have been attained and are still attainable by man. To call out and strengthen in young minds such perceptions is one main end of moral teaching. No doubt there are influences which can do this more powerfully than any teaching. To have seen and known lives which have embodied these fair qualities, to have felt the touch of their human goodness, to have companioned with those —

> " Whose soul the holy forms
> Of young imagination hath kept pure;"

to have fed on high thoughts, and been familiar with the examples of the heroes, the sages, the saints of all time, so as to believe that such lives were once on earth, and are not impossible even now, — these are, beyond all teaching, the "virtue-making" powers. But moral philosophy, though subordinate to these, is useless if it does not supplement them; if it does not at once justify the heart's aspiration on grounds of reason, and strengthen, by enlightening, the will to pursue them. Character, then, in the concrete, truthful, solid, pure, high, as "better than gold, yea than fine gold, its revenue than choice silver," — as the best thing we meet with in all our experience, the one thing needful for a man, which to have got is to get all, to have missed is to miss all, — this cannot be too fully set before the learner at the outset, as the goal to which all his inquiries must tend, which alone gives his inquiries any value. If this is not seen and grasped broadly and deeply at first, and its presence felt throughout all our reasoning, the discussion and analysis that follow become mere words — hair-splitting and logomachy.

To observe moral facts, and retain them steadily, requires a moral perception innate or trained, or both. Every reader of Aristotle's Ethics will remember his saying, that "he should have been well trained in his habits who is to study aright things beautiful and just, and in short all moral subjects. For facts are the starting-point." Quickness and tenacity of moral perception is not so much an intellectual as a moral gift. Nay, it is easy to overdo the intellectual part of the process. Too rigid logic, too exact defining and subdividing of that which often can be but inadequately defined, kills it. It is like trying to hold a sunbeam in an iron vice. The faculty that will best catch the many aspects and finer traits of character must be a nice combination, an even balance between mental keenness and moral emotion. It is the heart within the head which makes up that form of philosophic imagination most needed by the moralist. If moral character, in its higher aspects, were set thus truly and strongly before young minds, it would require little else to counteract materialism. Such elevating views might be left, almost without reasonings, to work their natural effect on all who were susceptible of them.

Character has been defined as "a completely fashioned will." This, as has been said, is to be kept continually before us in all moral inquiry as its practical end, — that which gives it solidity. But when once we have looked at it steadily, whether as it has existed actually in the best men, or in the ideal, the question at once arises, How is this right character to be attained? How is the good that is within to be made ascendant, — the less good to be subordinated, the evil to be cast out? Of the numerous questions which this practically suggests, as to the standard by which character is to be tested, the foundation of moral goodness, and many more, the simplest and most obvious is to ask, What is in man? What are the various elements of man's nature? Thus we are at once landed in psychology. And so it has happened, that almost all great ethical thinkers, whatever their method, even when it depends mainly on certain great *a priori* conceptions, have attempted some enumeration of the various parts or elements which make up human nature. Begun by Plato and Aristotle, carried on by the Stoics, revived in modern times by Hobbes, not neglected even by demonstrative Spinoza, this way of proceeding by observation of living men, and of our own minds, formed the whole staple of Bishop Butler's method. It is strange, as we read the first fetches into human nature of those early thinkers, with how much more living power they come home to us than modern psychologies. This comes probably of their having read their facts straight off their own hearts, or from observation of other men. There is something in the first thoughts of the world which can never recur, something in having been the first utterer of those words, the first noter of those distinctions, which thenceforth were to become the common inheritance of all men. Compared with theirs, the moral psychology of recent times has for the most part become stale and conventional, because, the first main outlines having been already laid down, the moderns have but repeated with slight alterations the old analysis, presenting us with tabulated lists of appetites, desires, passions, affections, and so forth, at which men only yawn. In fairness, however, I must allow, although with an entire dissent from the fundamental principles of Professor Bain's philosophy, that I have found in his elaborate work on the "Emotions and the Will" many facts which are either new, or at least which I have not before seen registered in systematic treatises. Certainly if psychology is to interest and instruct once more, it must leave the stereotyped forms, and enrich itself with new and hitherto unnoted facts, gathered partly from the more subtle and varied shades of feeling, partly from the wider survey of human history, and the deepened human experience which the latest civilization has opened up. The surest method then for ethical science, is to begin with moral psychology; that is, with a close study of the phenomena which make up man's moral nature. This is its beginning, but not its end. From observation of these, it will be led down to fundamental ideas which underlie them; belonging to that border land where morality and religion meet.

Whatever be the method most applicable to systematic moral treatises, there can be little doubt that for the learner and the careful investigator alike, the sure path is from the known to the unknown, starting from the concrete facts of which all may be conscious, to work thence backward towards the hidden principles which these facts embody. To say this is but to say that moral science should adhere to the method which has been found best in all other sciences. This is no new view, but at least as old as Aristotle. The words in which he insists on it, early in his Ethics, are familiar enough. But the old truth has been lately so well stated in an essay by Mr. Wilson of Rugby, on "Teaching Natural Science," that I cannot do better than give in his own words his admirable statement. Substitute the word "moral" for "natural," and every word he says of physical science will apply with still stronger force to ethical, in proportion as the facts which the latter deals with are more dim and hard to grasp, and therefore more liable to pass into mere phrases and formulæ. Mr. Wilson observes, "There are two different methods of teaching science: one the method of investigation, the other the method of authority. The first starts with the concrete and works up to the abstract; starts with facts, and ends with laws; begins with the known, and ends with the unknown. The second starts with what we call the principles of the science; announces laws and includes the facts under them; declares the unknown, and applies it to the known." Of "the two, the latter is the easier, the former is by far the better." Again, why the former is the better he thus shows: "1st, Because knowledge must precede science, which is only systematized experience and knowledge. A certain broad array of facts must preëxist and be known, before scientific methods can be applied. 2d, Whatever new facts you give the learner they must not be purely foreign facts, but must fit on to his already existing stock. It is to this existing knowledge, and to that alone, you must dig down to get a sure foundation, and the facts of your science must reach continuously down, and rest securely thereon. Otherwise you will be building a castle in the air." These observations are as applicable to the learner of moral as of physical science. Nor less worthy of the moralist's attention are Mr. Wilson's further remarks, showing how easily scientific teaching passes from things to words. If strange terms and formulæ are presented to the learner before he has realized the ideas and laws which these express, he is at once landed in "cram." No scientific name should ever be given for a fact or idea, before there is a real need for it; that is, before the fact or idea is clearly grasped, and the want of a name to fix it is really felt. Then, and not till then, the new name may be safely given. No principle of classification should be announced before we have fairly climbed by steps of reasoning up to it. Any one who has observed young students in philosophy knows how readily they catch up technical words, which have a high sound, but are for them almost meaningless. And this danger is much greater in moral than in physical subjects, because from the very nature of the former, unmeaning words so much more easily take the place of thoughts, and the substitution is so much more harder to detect. Many feel this so keenly that they consider it a fatal objection against mental philosophy being made a study for the young. It fills the young head, they say, with windy abstractions merely, which have under them no solid content. When Watt of Harden lifted the cover off the dish which his fair Flower of Yarrow now and then served up to him, he found at least a pair of clean spurs, which told him it was time to rise and ride. But when you lift the cover off these abstractions, they say, you find not even cold hard spurs, but only empty wind. The only way to counterwork this danger, to which, I admit, young philosophers are exposed, is to begin with the facts of consciousness that lie at our feet. We may not be able to climb thence to the upper heights, but we shall at all events make sure of possessing the near, if we do not reach the far.

Let it not be said that, by thus insisting on a broad,

sure basis of fact to begin with, I condemn moral science to pure empiricism, and confound it with mere physical science. This might be true if I confined its aim, as has sometimes been done, to observing and classifying successive "states of mind," and of emotion. But when we remember that the facts it has to take account of are no mere passive states, but such facts as personality, will, conscience, though the method we start with is the same as the physical, our very observations soon transport us into a very different region, in which the thought most forced on us is not the likeness, but the contrast, to physical phenomena. As for staying at home, confined to mere empiricism, we shall soon find that these home-facts, so near us, are close in kin and neighborhood to whatever is highest in being. From the facts of moral consciousness, fully realized, pathways strike off that lead to the remotest distances of history; and down to the profoundest depths of thought. We shall not less surely trace the evolution of moral systems, and the growth of moral ideas, because we have begun with grasping the concrete facts which, in their complex state, have first met us in every-day experience. Nor shall we thus be in a worse position to investigate the fundamental idea of right which lies under all morality, and to inquire whether there is righteousness which pertains not to man only, but in which all rational beings alike are sharers.

There are two ways in which moral psychology may go to work. It may begin at the core of man's being, at the central creative energy, the mysterious conscious "I," the fully formed personal will, and then show how the several powers and feelings stand related to this free centre of spontaneity. But the easier, if less scientific way is, beginning at the outside, to follow what we may conceive to be the historical growth of the individual, as well as of the race, and to show how each of the phases of our being successively rises into prominence. Such a survey would place before us man in his earliest stage as a mass of natural appetencies or instinctive tendencies, each seeking blindly its appropriate end, the reaching of which is necessary to continued existence. Accompanying these primitive desires, we should find certain faculties which are the instruments by which the former read their end, — the executive as it were of the blind impulses. During this stage, the spontaneous action of these appetencies engenders certain secondary passions, such as love of things which help the attainment of their ends, hatred of things which thwart them. Of these primitive outgoings, some we can see have reference to the good of self, some to the good of others, long before self-gratification is set before us as a conscious object. Such is the earliest stage of our existence, — the appetitive, the spontaneous or semi-conscious, as we see it in infants, or in uncivilized tribes. This is the raw material, as it were, out of which character is to be formed. The aggregate amount of all these primitive elements, and the relative proportions in which the higher and the lower are mingled in each man, will go far to determine what he will ultimately become.

But out of the midst of this blind congeries experience develops new powers. Very early in the appetitive life the desires must meet with obstacles, and the faculties that purvey for them are thwarted, driven inward, and forced to concentrate themselves for a more conscious effort to remove the hindrance. Here, then, is the first dawning, the earliest consciousness of will, within us. Again, out of the appetitive life, when experienced long enough, there rises ever more clearly a power of intelligence or reflection which, observing that each desire has its own end, and that the attainment of that end brings pleasure, generalizes from these separate goods the idea of a general good for our whole nature, a satisfaction arising from the permanent gratification of all our desires, or at least of as many of them as may be possible. Reflection soon perceives that desire left to act blindly — our nature swayed now by this, now by that impulse — does not attain to any stable happiness. Some kinds of action, it observes, make towards this happiness, others thwart it; the former it calls useful actions, the latter hurtful. From these observations it generalizes the idea of a total personal good or self-interest as an end to be aimed at, and forms subordinate rules of conduct with a view to attain that end. Self-interest, thus intelligently conceived, may become an end of life, or what is called motive — an ever present motive to guide the will. Governed by this motive, the will can control anarchic passion and introduce order into a man's desires and conduct. In doing this, the will, besides the power of reflection, is fortified by the emotions also; because by a law of our nature, self-interest, when once conceived as an end, is eagerly embraced as a new object for the affections. This is the second or prudential stage of our nature. Some men remain all their lives in the former or appetitive stage, and these we call impulsive men. Others regulate their actions by well-calculated self-interest, and these we call prudent, or it may be, if self-interest is too absorbing, selfish men. But though the two types of character are clear, yet so infinitely diversified are these simple elements in themselves, and in their degrees of strength, that perhaps no two men ever lived in whom they were compounded exactly alike, in no two men was the same physiognomy of character ever reproduced.

But not any or all of the elements yet noticed, however mingled, would make what is called a moral being; they do not yet rise above the life of nature. To do this, there needs to dawn another and higher consciousness. Reflection cannot stop at the idea of merely personal good, for it sees that there are other beings of the same nature and desires as ourselves, who have each a self-interest of their own as well as we. But as the personal good of others often collides with ours, and as one or other must give way, we begin to see that the good of others deserves as much respect, ought to be as sacred in our eyes, as our own. So we rise to feel that, above our sensitive and individual life, there is a higher, more universal order to which we and all individual souls even now belong, that this higher order secures and harmonizes the ultimate good of all rational beings, and that the particular good of each, though in harmony with this order, and an element of it, must be subordinated to it. To realize this spiritual order, and be a fellow-worker with it, is felt to be the absolute, the moral good, an end in itself, higher and more ultimate than all other ends. This idea, this end, this impersonal good, once conceived, comes home to us with a new and peculiar consciousness. In its presence we for the first time become aware of a law which has a right to command us, which is obligatory on us, which to obey is a duty. Seen in the light of this law, the good of others, we feel, has a right to determine our choice equally with our own, and our own good loses its merely temporary and finite, and assumes an impersonal and eternal character. This consciousness it is which makes us moral agents. Only in the idea of such a transcendent law above us, independent of us, universal, and of a will determined by it, does morality begin. All other elements of our nature are called moral, only as they bear on this, the overruling moral principle. The consciousness just described constitutes the third or moral stage of human nature. Not that the second and the third stages occur in every man in the order now laid down. A man may become alive to the moral law, and to its obligation over him, before he has conceived of self-interest as an end of action. But the order here given marks the relative worth of the respective principles, and the culmination of our nature in that one which is its proper end.

It would be easy to show how all the moral systems have taken their character from giving to one or other of these three principles of action, the emotional, the prudential, and the moral, a special prominence, investing some one element or some particular disposition of all the elements, with paramount sovereignty. But I must pass on to notice a defect inherent in this and every attempt to map out human nature into various compartments, — a defect which, when unperceived, as it mostly is, distorts, if it does not falsify, the whole work of the analysts. Even if the most exact enumeration, the most minute analysis could be made, would this give all that makes up character? It is a common mistake with psychologists to suppose that it does. They fancy they can grasp life by victorious analysis. There can be no greater, though there is no more common delusion. What is it that analysis, the most perfect, accomplishes? It gives the various elements which go to make up a moral fact, or it may be said to give the various points of view which a phenomenon or group of phenomena presents. But is this all? Is there nothing more than what is found in the analyst's crucible? The analysis, that is, the unloosing, the taking down into pieces of the bundle, may be complete;

but where is the power of synthesis, the bond which held the bundle together? Where is the life which pervaded the several elements, and made of them one entire power? It is gone, it has escaped your touch. Can the botanist after he has divided a flower into its component parts, pistil, stamen, anther, petals, calyx, put them together once more, and restore the life and beauty that were there? This is the main error of psychologists. They fancy that when they have completed their analysis they have done all, not considering that it is just the most unique and mysterious part of the problem which has eluded them. What the late Professor Ferrier shows so well against the psychologists, that the "ego," the one great mystery, ever escapes them, the same takes place in the analysis of every other living entity. In a human character, when you have done your best to exhaust it, to give its whole contents, that which is its finer breath, has it not escaped you? must not you be content to own that there remains behind a something "which no language may declare?" What end then serves analysis? By bringing out, separately and in detail, each side, aspect, or element in any problem, and fixing the eye on each successively, it helps to give distinctness and exactness to our whole conception of it. But it is only the multiplicity that is thus given; the unity or rather the unifying power still remains ungrasped. And if we are to see character in its truth, we must, after analysis has done its work, by an act of philosophic imagination remake the synthesis, put the elements together again. If we do this rightly, something will reappear in the synthesis which had disappeared in the analysis, and that something will be just the idiosyncratic element — the central creative energy — which individualizes the whole man. To a moral philosophy which shall give the truth, this synthesis is even more essential than the analysis.

Of the many questions which have been, and may still be asked respecting virtuous character, there is one, not the least important, and certainly the most practical of any, which has received less attention from moralists than it deserves. It is this: Supposing that we have settled rightly what the true ideal of character is, how are we to attain to it? what is the dynamic power in the moral life? what is that which shall impel a man to persevere in aiming at this ideal, shall carry him through all that hinders him outwardly and inwardly, and enable him, in some measure at least, to realize it? Other questions, it would seem, more stimulate speculation, none has more immediate bearing on man's moral interests. For confused and imperfect as men's notions of right may be, it is not knowledge that they lack, it is the will and the power to do. Change one word, and all men will make the apostle's confession their own: "To *know* is present with me, but how to perform that which is good I find not."

It is to this subject, then, the dynamic or motive power in moral life, that I would turn attention in the sequel. Under the word *motive* three things are included, which are usually distinguished thus, — the objective truth or reality, which, when apprehended and desired, determines to action; the mental act of apprehending this object; and the desire or affection which is awakened by the object so apprehended. To this last step, which immediately precedes the act of will, and is said to determine it, the term "motive" is often exclusively applied. But in the present inquiry into the dynamic or motive power, I shall use the word in a wider sense, including all the three elements in the process, and applying it more especially to that one which is the starting point, namely, the objective truth or reality which, addressing the understanding, and stirring the affections, ultimately sways the will. And the question I ask is, What is that objective truth, or class of truths, which determines the will in a way which can rightly be called moral? What are those truths which, apprehended and entering into a man, enable him to rise into that state of being which is truly virtuous or moral?

In doing so it will be well to ask first, what answers to this question may be found in the works of some of the great masters of moral wisdom. In his survey of moral systems, Adam Smith remarks that there are two main questions with which moralists have to deal. The first is, What is virtue? or, more concretely, In what consists the virtuous character, — that temper and conduct in a man which deserves to win the esteem of his fellow-men? The second is, What is the faculty in us by which we discern and approve the virtuous character? — in other words, By what power do we distinguish between right actions and praise them, and wrong actions and blame them? Of the question which I propose now to consider, the dynamic power which enables us to do the right, it is remarkable that Smith makes no mention. In discussing this, which I may call the third main question of morals, I shall have occasion to advert to the former two, but shall do so no further than as they bear on the third, which is our more immediate concern.

Smith has classified philosophers mainly by the answers they give to the first of the three questions. Some, he remarks, place virtue in the proper balance and harmony of all the faculties and affections which make up our human nature, some in the judicious pursuit of our own happiness, a third set in benevolence, that is, in the affections which seek the happiness of others. The first of these three answers to the great question, What is the virtuous character? has been sanctioned by the greatest names of past time, — by Plato, by Aristotle, by the Stoics, and by Bishop Butler. Let us glance at their theories, with a view to find what help there is in them as to the dynamic power we are in search of.

With Plato originated the idea that virtue is a proper balance or harmony of the various powers of the soul; and though it has often since been elaborated into detail, it has never been put in a form so beautiful and attractive. It is one of those great though simple thoughts first uttered by that father of philosophy which have taken hold of the world, and which it will never let go. Repeated in our ordinary language, it sounds a commonplace; but in the Greek of "The Republic" it stands fresh with unfading beauty. He divides the soul, as is well known, into three elements, — desire, passion or courage, and intellect; and this division, variously modified, has held its ground in philosophy till now. The δικαιοσύνη, or righteousness of the individual soul, he places in a proper balance or harmony of these three elements, in which each holds that position which rightfully belongs to it. The state is the counterpart of the individual soul, and its δικαιοσύνη, or right condition, is attained when the three orders of guardians, auxiliaries, and producers, answering to reason, passion, appetite respectively, stand in their proper order of precedence. This is the philosophy which Shakespeare makes Ulysses speak. "In the observance of degree, priority, and place," stands —

"The unity and married calm of states."

"How could communities,
Degrees in schools, and brotherhoods in cities,

Peaceful commerce from dividable shores,
The primogenitive and due of birth,
Prerogative of age, crowns, sceptres, laurels,
But by degree, stand in authentic place?
Take but degree away, untune that string,
And, hark, what discord follows! each thing meets
In mere oppugnancy."

The man is righteous in whom each of the three elements holds its proper place, and does its proper work; and this inward harmony expresses itself in an outward life which is every way righteous. The power which discerns the right and orders all the elements of the soul, is intellect or reason, whose right it is to rule. But how is this harmony of soul, once discerned, to be reached, maintained, made energetic? Plato, of philosophers the least mechanical, the most dynamic, the most full of powers of life, cannot have left this question wholly untouched, though he has not dealt with it systematically. His hope was that this may be done in the state by educating the guardians, who are philosophers; in the individual, by educating the reason, which is the sovereign principle, through continual study of real truth, continual contemplation of the ideal good. The highest object of all is the Essential Form or Idea of the Good which imparts to the objects known the truth that is in them, and to the knowing mind the faculty of knowing truth. This idea of the good is the cause of science and of truth. It gives to all objects of knowledge not only the power of being known, but their being and existence. The good is not existence, but is above and beyond existence in dignity and power. "The purpose of education," he says, "is to turn the whole soul round, in order that the eye of the soul, or reason, may be directed to the right quarter. But education does not generate or infuse any new principle; it only guides or directs a principle already in existence." So far in "The Republic."

Again, in the famous myth of the Phædrus where reason is imaged by a charioteer driving a chariot drawn by two horses, one high-spirited and aspiring, the other earthward groveling, Plato makes the charioteer able just to raise his head, and look out for a moment on that super-celestial place, which is above heaven's vault, and to catch a glimpse of the realities that are there, — the colorless, formless, intangible substance on which the gods gaze without let or hindrance. The glimpse, which the better human souls thus get, fills them with love of the reality. They see and feast on it, and are nourished by it. It is this idea or essence of the good, the cause of existence and knowledge, the vital centre in the world of thought, as the sun is in the world of sight, which is the object of contemplation to the reason. "And reason," Plato says, "looking upwards, and carried to the true Above, realizes a delight in wisdom, unknown to the other parts of our nature." This idea of good is the centre at once of morals and politics, the rightful, influencing power in human action. It should be ever present to the mind; a full philosophic consciousness of it should be the ruling power in everything. Nor is it an object merely for the pure reason, but for the imagination also, and an attractive power for the higher affections which side with reason. This glimpse, then, vouchsafed to none but the purest in their purest hour, may be supposed to be to them an inspiration that will not desert them all their lives after. It will make them hunger and thirst after truth and righteousness, and despise, in comparison of these, all lower goods. So far this intuition of the good will be a dynamic power. But this master-vision, if it be possible at rare intervals, for the select souls of earth, and if it were adequate to sustain them in the pursuit of goodness, is at best a privilege for the few, not an inheritance for mankind. And Plato did not dream of it as more. From the mass of men he turns in despair, and leaves them to their swine-troughs. He did not conceive that for all men there was an ideal, or any power sufficient to raise them towards it. In Plato, then, the moral dynamic force we are seeking is in small measure, if at all to be found.

Shall we find it in Aristotle? Although the "Ethics" contains more than one division of human nature, which helped forward psychological analysis, yet the whole system is not determined by any such division, but by certain leading objective ideas. Foremost among these is that of an end of action. There is an absolute end of all action, an end in itself, and man's constitution is framed conformably to this end, and in realizing it lies the total satisfaction of his nature, his well-being. Everything in nature has its end, and fulfills it unconsciously, but a moral being must fulfill his end not blindly, but with conscious purpose. The end in itself consciously chosen and pursued, this is Aristotle's fundamental ethical idea.

The end or the good for man is a vivid consciousness of life, according to its highest excellence, or in the exercise of its highest powers. Sir Alexander Grant, in his very able dissertation on ἐνέργεια, shows, with great felicity, how Aristotle regarded man's chief good as "nothing external to him, but as existing in man and for man; existing in the evocation, the vividness, and the fruition of his powers. It is the conscious vitality of the life and the mind in the exercise of its highest faculties. This, however, not as a permanent condition, but one that arises in us, oftenest like a thrill of joy, a momentary intuition. Were it abiding, we should be as God." In order to find in which part of man this highest excellence is to be found, Aristotle has recourse to a psychological division, not of his own making, but apparently well known at the time. He divides the internal principle (ψυχή) into the physical or vegetative part, the semi-rational or appetitive, and the purely rational. The first has no share in human excellence, in the second lies moral excellence or virtue, in the third lies intellectual excellence. Aristotle here founds the distinction between moral and intellectual, beyond which we have not yet got. Practical moral excellence has its seat in the second division of our nature, in the passions which, though not purely rational, have communion with reason. And though Aristotle, in the end, gives to the purely intellectual excellence, which consists in philosophical contemplation, a higher place than he assigns to the exercise of the moral virtues, yet it is of these he chiefly treats, and with these we have now to do. Moral virtue, then, he defines as consisting in a developed state of the moral purpose, in a balance relative to ourselves, which is determined by reason. This is Aristotle's famous doctrine, that virtue is a mean, an even balance, a harmony of man's powers. It is a mean as exhibited in particular actions, and also a mean or balance struck between opposite excesses of feeling. Feelings, passions, actions, are the raw materials out of which character is to be wrought by aiming at a balance. Right reason is the power which determines what the mean or balance is. It reviews the whole circumstances of the case, strikes the balance, apprehends the rule by which the irregular feelings may be reduced to that regularity in which virtue consists, virtue as well in particular acts as in habits, and in the whole character. The mean is not a "hard and fast line," but a balance struck anew in each particular case, from a consideration of all the circumstances. The virtuous character is slowly elaborated by a repetition of virtuous acts; acts, that is, midway between extremes. And then as to knowing what the real mean is, man must begin and act from his own perceptions, such as they are. His own individual reason must be the guide he starts with, but he is not therefore shut up in subjectivity. He has a surer standard than individual judgment to appeal to, even the universal moral sentiment of men. Or rather in the wise man, the ideally perfect man, he has a kind of objective conscience, an embodiment of moral law; and he judges according as he knows that this ideally wise man would judge. Here, then, we have a theory of virtue and the virtuous character, but no answer to the question, What is the motive power which shall propel men towards this ideal? Indeed, full though his treatise is of wise and penetrating practical remarks on character, this subject is nowhere discussed by Aristotle; but if one were to gather from him an answer for one's self, it might perhaps be something like this: —

Reason of itself cannot reach the will and mould the choice. Yet reason and those emotions which are most obedient to it, act and react on each other. In time, by the law of habit, they blend together and make up a moral habit of soul, which restrains and directs all the lower impulses. When intellect and the more generous emotions combine in seeking one end, and by repeated acts form a habit, the result is the perfected moral judgment or practical wisdom, which itself is both a guide and a sufficient motive power to impel the soul steadily to good. *Φρόνησις* is with Aristotle the perfection of the moral intellect. He does not say that it is an interpenetration of the moral with the intellectual side of human nature, but that there is an inseparable connection between this practical wisdom (φρόνησις) and moral virtue. In his view, these two sides, if not blended in one habit, are brought much closer together than in Plato, and that, both in the discerning and in the ruling moral faculty.

The elaboration of the virtuous character by the formation of good habits is a long and slow process. Does Aristotle point to any spring of inspiration which may carry a man through it? Plato after his own fashion does. Far off and inaccessible as his idea of the good may be, there is something in it, and in his enthusiasm for it, which must kindle, as by contagion, all but the dullest. But in Aristotle, though at every turn you meet insights into human nature which you feel to be penetratingly true, you are, after all, left to evolve the virtuous habit out of your own inward resources. There is in him no hint of anything which may come home to a man inwardly, and supplement his moral weakness by a strength beyond his own. All that he suggests is of a merely external kind. Besides moral teaching, such as himself and other moralists give, he bids men look for help to such institutions, either domestic or political, as may assist them in the cultivation of virtue.

Amongst moderns, Bishop Butler, as is well known, has been the chief expounder of the idea which originated with Plato, that the virtuous character consists in a harmony of the different powers of man. This, the leading idea of his sermons, has so worked itself through his teaching into modern thought, that it need not now be dwelt on. A system, a constitution, an economy, in which the various parts — appetites, passions, particular affections — are all ranged in due gradation under the supreme conscience ; this is his doctrine of man. In working out this idea, while the great Bishop has contributed much of his own, especially the masterly analysis by which he proves the existence in man of originally unselfish, as well as of self-regarding affections, he recalls here the teaching of Plato, there that of Aristotle. Though he deals entirely with individual man, he illustrates his idea of gradation and moral harmony by Plato's image of a civil constitution, with its various ranks subordinated under one supreme authority. On the other hand, his idea of conscience comes much nearer to that of Aristotle's φρόνησις than that of Plato's reason. But in Butler's "conscience," there is a much more distinct presence of the emotional or moral element, while the notion of an obligatory power or right to command, so characteristic of modern as distinguished from ancient thought, comes strongly out. But paramount as is this idea with Butler, it is strange that whenever we go beyond it, and ask for a reason why conscience should be supreme, he fails us. Entrenched within his psychological facts, he refuses to go beyond them. Ask what is the rule of right, the canon by which conscience decides, he replies, Man is a law to himself; every plain honest man who wishes it, will find the rule of right within himself, and will decide agreeably to truth and virtue. This is like saying that conscience decides by the rule of conscience. If asked, Why should I obey conscience? Butler can but assume that conscience "carries its own authority with it, that it is our natural guide," that it belongs to our condition of being, and therefore it is our duty to obey it. If a further sanction is sought, he seems to find it in the fact of experience, that the path of duty and that of interest coincide, "meaning by interest happiness and satisfaction." If there be exceptions, these will be set right in the final distribution of things. "Duty and interest are perfectly coincident, for the most part here, entirely hereafter; this being implied in the very notion of a good and perfect administration of things." In this coincidence of duty and interest, so far fulfilled in our present experience, and ultimately made sure by the existence of a Moral Governor of the world, seems to lie a great part of the dynamic power in Butler's system. To this may be added his remark, in the spirit of Aristotle, that obedience to conscience, when it has grown into a habitual temper, becomes a choice and a delight.

But in the sermons on the Love of God he strikes another strain. He there demonstrates to an unbelieving age that the affection he speaks of is no dream, but a most sober certainty. For as we have certain lower affections which find sufficing objects in the world around us, so we have higher faculties and moral emotions, which find but inadequate objects in the scattered rays of created wisdom, power, and goodness which this world contains. To these faculties and affections God himself is the only adequate supply. They can find their full satisfaction only in the contemplation of that righteousness which is an everlasting righteousness, of that goodness in the sovereign mind which gave birth to the universe. This is Butler's highest doctrine, which he sets forth with a calm suppressed enthusiasm almost too deep for words. This contemplation can create the highest form of happiness, but it is not for this that it is sought. It would cease to be the ultimate end that it is, if sought for the sake of happiness, or for any end but itself. There can be no doubt that if once realized, this would be, as we shall see, in the highest measure, the dynamic of the soul.

Butler's search for virtue is wholly through psychology. Plato and Aristotle, though they do not begin with it, very soon have recourse to it. Kant, on the other hand, when seeking for principles of morality, disdains to fumble after them among the *débris* of observation and experience, but searches for them wholly *a priori* among the pure ideas of the reason. We find nothing in him about the virtuous character consisting in a harmony of the mental elements, although it might be said that his idea of virtue is a will in harmony with the moral universe. Laying his hand at once on the individual will, and intensifying to its highest power the idea of responsibility, he starts with the assertion that the only real and absolute good in the whole world is a good will. And a good will is one purely and entirely determined by the moral law. This law is not a law generalized out of human experience, binding therefore only within the range of that experience, but a law which transcends it; is wide as the universe, and extends in its essential principle to all beings who can think it. Man, according to Kant, shut in on every side of his being to a merely relative knowledge, in the moral law for the first time escapes out into absolute truth, truth valid not only for all men, but for all intelligents. Human conscience is nothing but the entering into the individual of this objective law — the witness, as it has been called, that the will or self has come into subjection to, and harmony with, the universal reason, which is the will of God.

From the reality of this law Kant deduces three great moral ideas. First, since it commands imperatively, unconditionally, we must be able to obey it. Freedom, therefore, as a necessary consequence, follows from the consciousness of an imperative law of duty. Again, in this phenomenal life, we see the will that would obey duty hindered by many obstacles, crushed by many miseries, unrewarded with that happiness which rightfully belongs to it. There must, therefore, be a life beyond this phenomenal one, where the hindrances shall be removed, where duty and the will to obey it shall have full play, where virtue and happiness, here often sundered, shall at last meet. That is, there must be an immortality. Lastly, reason represents to us the moral will as worthy of happiness. But we see that here they do coincide. Nature does not effect such a meeting; man cannot constrain it. There must be somewhere a power above nature, stronger than man, who will uphold the moral order, will bring about the union between virtue and happiness, between guilt and misery. And this being is God. Such is Kant's practical proof of the great triad of moral truths in which the morally-minded man believes, — Freedom, Immortality, and God. The necessity for the belief in these arises out of the reality of the moral law.

To Kant's ideal of duty it matters nothing, though it is contradicted by experience, though not one instance could be shown of a character which acted on, or even of a single action which emanated from, the pure unmingled moral law. The question is not what experience shows, but what reason ordains. And though this ideal of moral excellence may never yet have been actualized, yet none the less it remains a true ideal — the one standard which the moral judgment of man approves, however in practice he may fall beneath it. On this pure idea of the moral law Kant would build a science of ethics, valid not for man only, but for all intelligent beings. Applied to man, it would need to be supplemented by an anthropology, and would then stand to pure ethics, as mixed stand to pure mathematics.

As to the relation in which, according to Kant, the objective moral law stands to the human conscience, there is a very ingenious speculation of the late Professor Ferrier, which may illustrate it. He asks the question whether it is the existence of our minds which generates knowledge, or the entering of knowledge into us which constitutes our minds? Is the radical and stable element Mind, and is Intelligence the secondary and derivative one? Professor Ferrier's reply is, that "It is not man's mind which puts him in possession of ideas, but it is ideas, that is knowledge, which first puts him in possession of a mind." The mind does not make ideas, but ideas make mind. In like manner, applying the same principle to poetic inspiration, he shows that it is not the poetic mind which creates the ideas of beauty and sublimity which it utters, but those ideas which, entering into a man, create the poetic mind. And so in moral truth, it is not our moral nature which makes the distinction between right and wrong, but the existence of right and wrong, apprehension of them by us, which create our moral nature. "I have no moral nature," he says, "before the distinction between right and wrong is revealed to me. My moral nature exists subsequently to this revelation. At any rate, I acquire a moral nature, if not after, yet in the very act which brings me the distinction. The distinction exists as an immutable institution of God prior to the existence of our minds. And it is the knowledge of this distinction which forms the prime constituent, not of our *moral* acquisitions, but of our *moral* existence." This very ingenious speculation, which is in the very spirit of the Platonic philosophy, may serve to illustrate Kant's view of the priority and independence of the moral law to our apprehension of it.

Where, then, is the motive power in the Kantian

ethics? Kant's answer is plain. It is the naked representation of duty, the pure moral law. And this, according to Kant, exerts so strong a motive power over the will, that it is only when a man has acknowledged its obligatory force, and obeyed it, that he learns for the first time his own free causal power, his independence of all merely sensitive determinators. The naked moral law, defecated, as he speaks, of all emotions of the sensory, is the one only dynamic which he admits as truly moral. This acting on the will, with no emotion interposed, will alone, he insists, place morality on a true foundation, will create a higher speculative ethics, and a higher practical morality, and will awaken deeper moral sentiments, than any system of ethics compounded now of ideal, now of actual elements, can do.

In the rigidity with which he holds that in pure moral action the law shall alone sway the will, that all emotion, love the purest, pity the tenderest, shall have no place, Kant is ultra-stoical. The representation of duty, when embraced, will awaken reverence for the law, and this is a pure moral emotion. But in determining the act, the stern imperative must stand alone, and refuse all aid from emotion or affection. For these there is no room in a pure morality, except as the submissive slaves of duty.

In making this high demand it should be remembered that Kant is setting forth, not an actual state which he expects to find in human nature, but an ideal, which nevertheless, because it is an ideal, affects human nature more powerfully than any maxim merely generalized from experience. And perhaps if the moral idea is to be set forth in its native strength and dignity, it is well that it should be exhibited thus nakedly. It does come shorn of much of its power, when so largely mingled, as it is in Butler, with considerations of mere prudence.

As has been remarked, however, even Kant, much as he desired to get rid of experience in constructing his morality, was not able to do so. He was obliged to come to experience before he could give content to his moral law — "So act, that thou couldst consistently will the principle of thy action to become law universal for all intelligents." So Kant shaped his imperative. This is not very unlike Austin's utilitarian question, "What would be the probable effect on the general happiness or good, if similar acts were general or frequent?" Again, as we saw, he is obliged to supplement his moral life here with the belief of a future life, where virtue and happiness shall be one, where the ideal shall become actual; thus proving that human feelings cannot to the end be banished from a moral system, that of happiness some account must be taken. And yet Kant is right in giving to such considerations a subordinate, not a primary, place.

From this brief survey of the motive power as it appears in the systems of some of the most famous "Intuitive Moralists," it would have been interesting, had space allowed, to have turned to the Utilitarian theorists, and examined at length the answers they give to the same question. As it is, however, a few remarks must suffice. This school of philosophers, as is well known, maintains that utility, or the tendency to promote pleasure or to cause pain, is the only quality in actions which makes them good or bad. They hold, moreover, that pleasure and pain are the only possible objects of choice, the only motives which can determine the will. These are the fundamental tenets of that school of philosophers represented by Epicurus in the ancient world, and by Bentham and his followers, Mr. Mill and Professor Bain, in our own day. If by the happiness which is said to be the end of action is meant merely the happiness of one's self, the system is one of the plainest and most intelligible, the dynamic force is the most obvious, and the most surely operating, that can well be imagined. But then the course of action dictated by the desire of exclusive self-interest is not, according to the view of most men, a moral one at all, and the motive is not moral, but selfish. The aim of all morality, truly conceived, is to furnish men with a standard of action, and a motive to work by, which shall not intensify each man's selfishness, but raise him ever more and more above it. If, on the other hand, it is said that it is not my own private interest, but the general interest, which I am to aim at, this may be said in two distinct senses: Either I am to seek the greatest happiness of all men, the sum total of human interests, because an enlightened experience tells me that my happiness is in many ways bound up with theirs. But the good of others thus pursued is only a means to my own private good, and I am still acting on a selfish motive — a strong but not a moral one. Or I am to aim at the general happiness for its own sake, and not merely as a means to my own. But then I am carried beyond the range of self-interest, and acknowledge as binding other motives which lie outside of the utilitarian theory. To the question, Why am I to act with a view to the happiness of others? the utilitarian can, on his own principles, give no other answer than this, Because it is your own interest to do so. If we are to find another, we must leave the region of personal pleasure and pain, and acknowledge the power of some other motive which is impersonal. With Bentham it is a fundamental principle that the desire of personal good is the only motive which governs the will. This is the one exclusive mode of volition which he recognizes. He denies the other two, unselfish regard for others, and the moral law or the abstract sense of right, and yet these two exist as really as self-love. It is just as certain a fact that men do sometimes act from generous impulses, or from respect to what they feel to be right in itself, apart from all consequences, as that they do often act merely with an eye to their own happiness. In the naked form, therefore, in which Bentham puts it, utilitarianism is founded on a psychological mistake. But the utilitarian system takes many forms. Yet, as Jouffroy, who has discriminated between the varieties with great acuteness, observes, "Whether a man pursues the gratification of impulse, or the accompanying pleasure, or the different objects fitted to produce it; whether he prefers, as most fitted to promote his highest good, the satisfaction of certain tendencies and pleasures; or finally, whether for the attainment of his end he adopts the circuitous means of general interest, or the direct pursuit of his own, is of little consequence to determine: he is impelled to act, in every instance, by calculations of what is best for himself. Self-love remains essentially the same under all its forms, and impresses a similar character upon the various schemes of conduct to which it leads."

In Mr. Mill's treatise on "Utilitarianism" there is in words no departure from the fundamentals of the utilitarian creed, though ingenuity is strained to the utmost to make that creed include principles and sentiments which are really alien to it. Indeed, in this treatise one prominent characteristic of all the author's writings is more than usually conspicuous. On the one hand, with an amiable obstinacy he adheres to the sensational and utilitarian tenets which formed his original philosophic outfit. On the other hand, he employs a redundance of argument, sometimes verging on special pleading, to reconcile to his favorite hypothesis views and feelings gathered in alien regions, with which his widened experience has made him familiar. The effort continued throughout his "Utilitarianism" has occasioned, if one may venture to hint it, a want of clear statement and of precise thought, with sometimes a straining of the meaning of terms, which one hardly expects to meet with in so trained a logician. This comes no doubt from the fact, that in order to adapt the utilitarian theory to the primary moral perceptions of men, it is necessary to go counter to the natural current of thought, and to give a twist to forms of speech, which have interwoven themselves into the very texture of language. One of these strange contortions is the following opinion: that it is the idea of the penal sanction which makes men feel certain acts to be wrong; not that they are wrong in themselves, and therefore visited with punishment. Or, as Mr. Mill otherwise expresses it, "the deserving or not deserving punishment lies at the bottom of the notions of right and wrong." This doctrine, which Mr. Mill seems to hesitate to state in all its breadth, else instead of "deserving" he would probably have written "imposition of punishment," has been stated more explicitly by Professor Bain, who maintains that "the imposition of punishment is the distinctive property of acts held to be morally wrong;" and again, that "the primary germ and commencement of conscience is the dread of punishment." Another equally startling position maintained by Mr. Mill, is that virtue is pursued primarily only as a means to an end, namely happiness, just as money is; but that in time it comes to be regarded as part of the end, happiness, and as such is pursued for its own sake, just as misers come to love money for itself, and not for its uses. He holds that in man originally there is no desire of virtue, or motive to it, save as a means to gain pleasure or avoid pain. But even when desired for its own sake, which he grants it comes to be, its worth arises, not from its own intrinsic excellence, but from its being the most important of all means to the general happiness.

But what it more concerns us to remark at present is the answer which Mr. Mill gives to the question, What is the sanction of the utilitarian ethics, what the motive to conform to this standard? It is of two kinds, the external and the internal. The external motive is the hope of favor or the fear of punishment from our fellow-men or from the Supreme Ruler. The internal motive is primarily the desire of our own happiness, which, however, when enlarged by intelligence, expands into a desire for the good of others. It does so because the more we are enlightened the more clearly we perceive that our own good is inextricably bound up with theirs; because there is in us a natural desire to be in unity with others; lastly, because an unselfish regard for our neighbors springs, by the principle of association, out of intercourse begun at first merely from self-regard. It is observable, however, that Mr. Mill, though he stretches to the utmost the motive of self-regard, combining with it as much as possible of what is otherwise admirable in human nature, and though he seems to allow the existence, in a certain subordinate degree, of purely unselfish sympathies, yet in the last resort makes self-regard the centre to which all the other feelings, as accretions, cling, and around which they are woven into "a complete web of corroborative association." In this ground-plan of human nature, the unselfish sympathies and the moral principle are not made to occupy — what I believe they in reality do occupy — as substantial and independent a place as the feeling of self-interest. Hence neither the standard of action, nor the motive power he sets forth, however much transformed by the magic touch of association, ever gets clear of the original taint of self-reference. Mr. Mill's utilitarianism does not, any more than other forms of the same doctrine, give either a really moral standard, or a self-forgetting and moral motive. As water cannot rise above the level from which it springs, no more can moral theories. Self-love may be, and as a fact often is, the first impulse that drives a man to seek to become morally and religiously better. And there is a measure of self-regard which is right, wherein the individual self is identified with the universal self. But before a man can become either truly moral or religious, private self-regard must have been wholly subordinated to, if not entirely cast out by a higher principle of action and a purer affection.

In the opening chapter of his work on "Jurisprudence," Austin sets forth the utilitarian doctrine with a distinctness of outline which far surpasses Mr. Mill's exhibition of it. He does not, like the latter, assert that conduciveness to general happiness is the essence, but only that it is the index of right action. The rightness and wrongness of all acts Austin grounds primarily on the Divine will or command. God designs the happiness of all his creatures; and as He has given us faculties to perceive what actions tend to produce this, and what actions tend to thwart it, He has given us therein a criterion by which to know what his will is, that is, what actions we ought to do, what to avoid. This representation of the theory furnishes a lever above and independent of utility, namely, the will of God — and therefore, in one point of view, a motive which, if once realized, is every way adequate to engender moral action. But still it does not rise above the utilitarian subjection to pleasure and pain. For Austin sums up the Divine will in pure benevolence, and grounds obedience to it solely on the fact that God can reward and punish to the uttermost. But to obey God chiefly or entirely for such a reason, does not amount to moral obedience, nor is such a motive a moral motive.

There may perhaps be held a view which, differing in other respects from the utilitarian theory, agrees with it in regarding pleasure as the universal motive power in moral as well as in all other action. It may be said that in all cases where a choice is made, pleasure, or, as it is sometimes phrased, interest, is the determinator of the choice; that in all conscious actions, thoughts, feelings, where a preference is made, it is because the pleasure of the one preferred is felt by the agent to be greater than the pleasure of those not preferred. The maintainer of such a theory would say that the commonly received distinction between pleasure and duty is a misleading one. For whenever any act is preferred, this itself proves that act, however painful it seems, to be not only pleasurable, but the most pleasurable. Let there be two acts, it would be said, one a gratification of sense, and as such pleasurable, the other a denial of this gratification, and so far painful, yet if the latter is done from what is called a sense of duty, the fact that it has been preferred proves that it was not only pleasant, but the most pleasant to him who preferred it. For that which in the event is chosen to be done is thereby proved to be the most pleasurable. To this it may be replied that to make the pleasurable synonymous with that which is actually preferred, is to give the term a quite new meaning. So to stretch the idea of pleasure is to change it entirely, and to render it wholly vague and empty of meaning.

It may be true that in most, perhaps in all, moral acts, there is present more or less a conscious pleasure, but it is present as a consequence, not as an antecedent of the choice. It is also true that virtue and pleasure are so far from being incompatible, that the higher a man advances in virtue the greater is his delight in it; indeed, that the measure of his delight is in some sort a gauge of his moral progress. But, on the other hand, it is no less true that while man remains in the present state of moral struggle, in some of his acts of purest duty the ingredient of pleasure must be so faintly present as to be inappreciable. To all theories of virtue which give pleasure or self-love a foremost place in it, whether as entering into its nature, or operating as its moving spring, it is enough to answer that they withdraw from moral action that which is a main constituent of it, namely, its unselfish character, and so reduce it to the level of at least mere prudence. They fail to recognize what Dr. Newman has so well described as "a remarkable law of ethics, which is well known to all who have given their minds to the subject. All virtue and goodness tend to make men powerful in this world; but they who aim at the power have not the virtue. Again, virtue is its own reward, and brings with it the truest and highest pleasures; but they who cultivate it for the pleasure-sake are selfish, not religious, and will never have the pleasure, because they never can have the virtue." There is no truth of ethics more certain than this. And it is not merely an abstract principle, but one which embodies itself in practice every day before our eyes. How continually do we see that the pleasure-seeker is not the pleasure-finder; that those are the happiest men who think least about happiness! Because, in order to attain to that serene and harmonious energy, that inward peace, which is the only true happiness, a man must cease to seek pleasure, and apprehend some higher object to live for. So true is it that, as has been said, the abandoning of some lower end in obedience to a higher aim, is often made the very condition of securing the lower one. Or, as the author of "Ecce Homo" writes, "It is far from universally true that to get a thing you must aim at it. There are some things which can only be gained by renouncing them." And such a thing moral pleasure is. Does not this characteristic, that when you make the pleasure your conscious aim, it is gone, — at least the purer essence, the finer bloom of it, — prove that it is merely a subsidiary accompaniment of moral action, the attendant shadow, not the substance, and cannot therefore be its propelling power?

The foregoing survey of systems, ancient and modern, has been long, perhaps even to weariness, and yet it has not given us the thing we seek. In what have been called the intuitive theories, the motive presented, if high, has been remote and impalpable, not such as would naturally come home to the hearts of ordinary men. The narrower forms of utilitarianism offer a motive near and strong enough — self-love; but then it is one which men of moral aspiration most long to rise above. When the endeavor is made to combine with it benevolence, and to take in the whole human race, the motive is no doubt elevated, but at the expense of its power; it is emptied of the strength which self-love peculiarly possesses. On the whole, then, from this want of practical help in many ways, and especially from their lack of a moral dynamic, it is no wonder that most men turn from ethical theories with weariness and even disgust. Young students, and older men professionally interested in these subjects, can hardly imagine how widely this is the case, not only with those so immersed in transitory interests as to have no time or heart for higher matters, but also with the devoutly religious, with men of ideal longings, with those who have been much exercised with earnest questionings. Men who are simply religious turn from theories of virtue, as not only useless, but as cold, hard, unloving — obstructions that come between them and that their heart most loves to commune with. Morality seems to draw all its help from man's own internal resources, and they feel too keenly that not in these is help to be found, but in a strength out from and above themselves. The inmost breathing of the devout heart is, "Lead me to the rock that is higher than I." And the deep-hearted poet, weary of abstractions, and longing for life, more life, and fuller, turns from moral theories with a passionate —

"Away, haunt not thou me,
Thou vain Philosophy!
Little hast thou bestead,
Save to perplex the head
And leave the spirit dead.
Unto thy broken cisterns wherefore go,
While from the secret treasure depths below,
Fed by the skyey shower,
And clouds that sink and rest on hill-tops high,
Wisdom at once, and Power
Are welling, bubbling forth, unseen, incessantly?
. . . .
Why labor at the dull mechanic oar,
When the fresh breeze is blowing,
And the strong current flowing
Right onward to the eternal shore?"

Broken cisterns! this was all one of the deepest-minded men and most thoughtful poets of our time found in our moral systems after long enough study of them.

Again, when we read the lives of those men who have had the deepest spiritual experience, to whom, on the one hand, the infinity of duty, the commandment exceeding broad, and, on the other, the depth of their own spiritual poverty, has been most laid bare — we find them confessing that the seventh chapter of Romans describes their condition more truly than any philosopher has done. With their whole hearts they have felt St. Paul's "O wretched man that I am! who shall deliver me?" Such are the men who, having themselves come out of great deeps, become the spirit-quickeners of their fellow-men, the revivers of a deeper morality. To all such there is a grim irony in the philosophic ideas when confronted with their own actuals. So hopelessly wide seems the gap between their own condition and the "Thou shalt" of the commandment. Not dead diagrams of virtue such men want, but living powers of righteousness. They do not quarrel with the moralist's ideal, though it is neither the saint's nor the poet's. They find no fault with his account of the faculty which discerns that ideal, though it is not exactly theirs. But what they ask is not the faculty to know the right, but the power to be righteous. It is because this they find not, because what reason commands, the will cannot be or do, that they are filled with despair. As well, they say, bid us lay our hand upon the stars because we see them, as realize your ideal of virtue because we discern it.

But is there no outlet by which, from the mere forms of moral thought, a man may climb upward to the treasure-house of its power? Let us turn and look once more at the moral law, as exhibited in its purest form by Kant. In this view the moral law is not a higher self, but an independent reality, which, entering into a man, evokes the higher self within him. To the truth, as well as the sublimity of Kant's conception, all hearts bear witness, by the reverence they must feel in its presence. And yet we know that, when we lay this bare law to heart, it engenders not strength, but despair. A few there may have been who have been able to dispense with all tender feelings, and to live high lives by dint of the law of duty alone. All honor to such hardy spirits! no word shall be said in their disparagement. However imperfect their principle may be, their face is set in the right direction; they are on the way, who but must believe it? to all good. Yet their lives, upright though they may be, will be stern and unrejoicing, wanting in much that hearts set free should have. But for most men, and among these for many even in the nobler sort, such a life would be impossible. Under such an iron rule, a large, and that the finer part of man's being, would have no place; the soul's gentler but more animating forces would be starved for lack of nutriment. Still, as this law contains so much of highest truth, let us keep fast hold of it, and see whence it comes, and whither it leads.

On reflection we find that there are many facts of human nature and of the world, many separate lines of thought, all leading upward and converging on one spiritual centre. These are like so many mountain paths, striking upward in diverse directions, but leading all at last to one great summit. Of these the moral law is the loftiest, the directest, the most inward, the most awe-inspiring.

But to begin with the outward world, there is, I shall not say so much the mark of design on all outward things, as an experience forced in upon the mind of the thoughtful naturalist, that, penetrate into nature wherever he may, thought has been there before him; that, to quote the words of one of the most distinguished, "there is really a plan, a thoughtful plan, a plan which may be read in the relations which you and I, and all living beings scattered over the surface of our earth, hold to one another." The work of the naturalist, as he goes on to say, "consists only in an attempt to read more and more accurately a work in which he has had no part, — a work which displays the thought of a mind more comprehensive than his own ; his task is to read the thoughts of that mind as expressed in the living realities that surround us ; and the more we give up our own conceit in this work, the less selfish we become, the more shall we discern, the deeper we shall read, and the nearer we shall come to nature ; " and, it may be added, to Him whose thought nature is.

Again, when we look within, there is " the causal instinct of the intellect," as it has been called, — the mental demand for a cause of every event, or rather the ineradicable craving for a Power behind all phenomena, of which they are but the manifestations, — a craving which no form of Comtean philosophy will ever exercise.

Again, there is the passionate longing of the imagination, aspiring after an ideal perfection for ourselves and others, apprehending a beauty more than eye has seen or ear heard.

Again, there is " the unsufficingness of self for self," the dependency of the affections, feeling the need of an object like themselves ; yet higher, more enduring, all-perfect, on which they can lean, in which they may find refuge.

Again, another avenue upward is a feeling of the derivative nature, not of our affections merely, but of our whole being. We are here a little while, — each a small rill of life, — containing many qualities. We feel, think, fear, love ; no facts are more certain to me than these. Yet it is just as certain that I am here not by my own will. I did not place myself here ; cannot keep myself here. My life is in the grasp of powers which I cannot, except in the smallest measure, and for only a little while, control. There must be a source whence this life, and all the other similar lives around me, come. And that source cannot be anything lower, or possessed of lower qualities, than myself, but rather something containing, in infinite abundance, all the qualities which I and all other beings like to me, in finite measure, have. There must be some exhaustless reservoir of being from which my small rill, and these numberless like rills of being, come, — a fountain that contains in itself the all of soul that has been diffused through the whole human race, and infinitely more. This is no elaborate argument, but almost an instinctive perception. Call it anthropomorphic, if you please; it is none the less a natural and true way of thinking, and as old as the Stoics. Cicero puts it in the mouth of his Stoic Balbus, and has supplied him with no better argument.

Lastly, and chief of all, there is the law of duty, coming home to the morally awakened man more intimately, affecting him more profoundly, than anything else he knows. What is it — whence comes it — this law, which lies close to all his thoughts, an ever-present, though often latent consciousness, haunting him like his very being? Mr. Mill speaks slightingly, as it seems, of "the sort of mystical character which is apt to be attributed to the idea of moral obligation," but he has not as yet been able in any measure to remove the mystery. If instead of trying to resolve it unsatisfactorily into lower elements, as the analyst is apt to do, or to shrink from it as the sensual nature always will do, or to act out merely the letter of it, as the legalist will try to do, we can but get ourselves to look at it steadily, and with open heart, the mystery of its nature and origin will not grow less to us, but more. What is it; is it mere abstraction? That which reason apprehends, and the personal will bows to, as an authority superior to themselves, cannot be a mere abstraction, but something which is congenerous with themselves. The moral law must be either a self-existing entity, like to our highest nature, or must inhere in one who possesses all that we have of reason and will, only in an infinitely greater degree. That which our inner self, our personality, feels to have rightful supremacy over it, must be either in personality, or something more excellent than personality, if that is possible. Lower than a personality it cannot be, and lower all mere laws and abstractions undoubtedly are. To some such conviction as this we are led up, by asking what is this moral law which we apprehend, and whence does it come? Here, if anywhere, we find the golden link which connects the human nature with the Divine.

Putting then all these converging lines of thought together, we see that they meet in the conviction that there is behind ourselves, and all the things we see and know, a Mind, a Reason, a Will, like to our own, only incomprehensibly greater, of which will and reason the moral law is the truest and most adequate exponent we have. Not that these lines, any or all of them, are to be taken as proofs demonstrating the existence of God. That is a truth, I believe, incapable of scientific demonstration. The notion of God seems to be, as Coleridge has well expressed it, essential to the human mind, not derived from reasonings, but as a matter of fact actually called forth into distinct consciousness mainly by the conscience. When, however, we come to reflect on that belief afterwards, we find hints and confirmations of it, mainly in the existence of our moral nature and of the law of duty, and secondarily in those other lines of thought which, as we have seen, converge towards the same centre. But these are dim tracts of thought hard to tread with firm step. Yet though the lines as here traced are imperfect and broken, they may be taken for what they are meant to be, — hints for thought on an exhaustless subject.

In this discussion I have taken for granted that the morality of man is in its essence identical with the morality of God — that when we use the word *righteous* of man and of God, we do not use it in two different senses, but in the same sense. This position, implicitly held before by all, both philosophers and ordinary men, has been more explicitly brought out and established by the polemic which the late Dean Mansel's denial of it called forth. The result of a real faith not merely in an abstract moral law, but in a Personal Being, — in whom dwells the moral law and whatever of highest is in ourselves, of whose moral Being our moral nature is a faint but true image, — will be to let in on the soul a new motive power, a new centre of existence. This is the first condition of a living morality as well as of vital religion, that the soul shall find a true centre out from and above itself, round which it shall revolve. The essence of all immorality, of sin, is the making self the centre to which we subordinate all other beings and interests. To be delivered from this, the condition of the natural man is the turning-point of moral progress, and of spiritual renewal. The new and rightful centre which shall draw us out of our self-centre, and by its attraction make us revolve round itself, must be that which contains the moral law, and whatever is best in ourselves, and in all other created selves. He only in whose image we are made can be such a centre to our creaturely wills. But further, neither the God whom mere science hints of, nor the God whom the bare unrelenting moral law sets forth, is capable of being a real resting-place for the heart of man. There are warm emotions within it, which, before representations of a God of mere law, whether natural or moral, die down like herbs beneath an arctic winter. To call forth these, it requires the unveiling of a Living and a Personal Will, in sympathy not only with whatever moral principle is in us, but also with whatever is most pure and tender in our affections. When we come to conceive thus of God, then there becomes possible a going forth towards Him of the tenderer and devouter emotions, as well as of the more purely moral sentiments. Such a Being becomes to man the centre and the end for his reason, affections, and conscience alike — a foundation on which his whole being can permanently repose.

But few, and these only the most favored of the sons of men, have, apart from revelation, ever attained so to conceive of God. A pure-minded sage here and there — Plato, when he drops his dialectics and gives vent to his devouter mind, as in the well-known passage of the "Theætetus," Marcus Aurelius here and there in his meditations — may have in some measure, though far off, so caught a glimpse of Him. To most men who have sought Him at all, outside of Christianity, it has been at best but a dim feeling after Him, if haply they might find Him. It required the appearance of Christ on earth to bring close to the hearts of any number of men the power of moral inspiration which is laid up in the very thought of God. Till then He seemed too high, too remote for this. But when Christ in human form came near to them, his presence touched the moral springs in men, hitherto dormant, and made new forces of spiritual life stir within them. Christ henceforth, both by his own personal teaching and example, and also by the new light of God's character which He let in on men's hearts, — Himself the channel through which that light was let in, — became a new dynamic power of virtue, an inspirer of goodness. The virtue-making power which He used was different from that which had been employed by the philosophers. They addressed the reason; He touched the whole man by his words, by his deeds, above all by contact with Himself. The two methods are well contrasted in the following passage of "Ecce Homo": —

"Who is the philosophic good man? He is one who has considered all the objects and consequences of human action; he has, in the first place, perceived that there is in him a principle of sympathy, the due development of which demands that he should habitually consider the advantage of others; he has been led by reflection to perceive that the advantage of one individual may often involve the injury of several; he has therefore concluded that it is necessary to lay down systematic rules for his actions, lest he should be led into such miscalculations, and he has in this reasonable and gradual manner arrived at a system of morality. This is the philosophic good man. Do we find the result satisfactory? Do we not find in him a languid, melancholic, dull, and hard temperament of virtue? He does right, perhaps, but without warmth or promptitude. And no wonder! The principle of sympathy was feeble in him at the beginning for want of contact with those who might have called it into play, and it has been made feebler still by hard brain-work and solitude. On the other hand, who is the good man that we admire and love? How do men become for the most part pure, generous, and humane? By personal, not by logical influences. They have been reared by parents who had these qualities, they have lived in society which had a high tone, they have been accustomed to see just acts done, to hear gentle words spoken, and the justness and the gentleness have passed into their hearts and slowly moulded their habits, and made their moral discernment clear; they remember commands and prohibitions which it is a pleasure to obey for the sake of those who gave them; they think of those who may be dead, and say, How would this action appear to him? Would he approve that word, or disapprove it? . . . . They are never alone, because the absent Examples, the Authorities they still revere, rule not their actions only, but their inmost hearts; because their conscience is indeed awake and alive, representing all the nobleness with which they stand in sympathy, and reporting their most hidden indecorum before a public opinion of the absent and the dead."

It was this last mode of appeal, one not wholly unknown before his day, that Christ adopted. But though the channel was familiar, the use He made of it was not; for the influence He poured through it was not only the purest human, but the Divine. The philosophers had addressed the reason, and failed. Christ laid hold of a passion which was latent in every man, and prevailed. What was this passion? It was the love, not of man, "not of all men, nor yet of every man, but of *the man* in the man." But this in all men is naturally a weak principle; how did He make it a powerful one, make it "a law-making power, a root of morality in human nature?" He gave a command to love all men without exception, even our enemies. Now a command cannot create love; but with the commandment He gave Himself to love, and to awake the love that lies dormant in every man. This, which is the central teaching of "Ecce Homo," must be given in the author's own words, so full of beauty and power:—

"Did the command to love go forth to those who had never seen a human being they could revere? Could his followers turn upon him and say, How can we love a creature so degraded? . . . . Of this race Christ Himself was a member, and to this day is it not the best answer to all blasphemers of the species, the best consolation when our sense of its degradation is keenest, that a human brain was behind his forehead, and a human heart beating in his breast, and that within the whole creation of God nothing more elevated or more attractive has yet been found than He? . . . . It was because the edict of universal love went forth to men whose hearts were in no cynical mood, but possessed with a spirit of devotion to a man, that words which, at any other time, however grandly they might sound, would have been but words, penetrated so deeply, and along with the law of love the power of love was given. Therefore, also, the first Christians were enabled to dispense with philosophical phrases, and instead of saying that they loved the ideal of man, could simply say and feel that they loved Christ in every man. . . . . Christ believed it possible to bind men to their kind" (and to all goodness), "but on one condition, that they were first bound fast to Himself."

To his followers who walked with Him on earth, his presence, and to many in every age since, his image has been the strongest of all levers to lift them out of selfishness, and to new-create into goodness. They have found in his life and character an objective conscience better than all other ideals of perfection; in their sympathy with Him they have had the most unerring test by which to discern what was right and what was wrong to do; and in their love and veneration for Him, a motive power beyond all powers, enabling them to do what was right from the love of it, — a power of loving God and of loving man, because they loved both in Him. To such the law of love absorbed into itself and transfigured the law of duty, and became, in a new and preëminent way, the fulfilling of the law. Morality to them was no longer subjection and obedience to a dead abstract law, which they might revere but could not love, but an inspiration caught by contagion with Him who contained the moral law and all the springs of morality in Himself. This is that central truth, long tacitly recognized, but enforced with such power in "Ecce Homo" as almost to appear new.

If we were to go no further, we have enough to prove that Christ introduced into the moral heart of man that which all philosophers have been unable to find, — a new dynamic force, which not only told them what was good, but inspired them with the love and the power of being good. In short, He was the living centre of a new moral and spiritual creation. But if we go thus far, we cannot stop here, it would seem — we must go further than the author of "Ecce Homo" does. For Christ claimed for Himself, and all who had followed Him most closely have acknowledged, that there are other powers and truths in Him, which in that able survey are either left in the background or altogether passed by. Those more transcendent doctrines, Christ's atonement, his resurrection, the indwelling of his Spirit, are as much part of the testimony about Christ and of the agencies by which He has changed the world, as anything that we know of his character. Indeed they are part, and a large part, of what makes his character. You cannot cut off the one without shaking the foundations of the other; and these doctrines are, if true at all, not merely in conformity with the purest moral and spiritual principles, but must be their very essence, must lie at their very root. Those who have most laid to heart and lived by these doctrines, have found in the Atonement the obliterating of all past sin, the lifting off the whole load of guilt. This is not the place to enlarge on these things. But no fact in man's moral history is more certain than this, that the simple statement of Scripture, "Christ has appeared to put away sin by the sacrifice of Himself," has been found efficacious to reach down to the lowest depths of men's souls beyond any other truth ever uttered on this earth. In the Resurrection, they have found the assurance that what conscience prophesies will in the end come true, that, though experience often seems against it, "right is stronger than wrong, truth is better than falsehood, purity shall prevail over sensual indulgence, meekness shall inherit the earth; for right, truth, and purity are summed up in their champion Christ, and He has conquered death, the one unconquerable champion of the enemy." In the promise of the indwelling Spirit, and its fulfillment, they have found a surety that the impulse which Christ first gave will not fail nor grow old, but will overcome all obstacles and outlast time. One great practical result of these truths is the animating confidence they give that "God is for us." There is nothing so crushing to moral effort as the suspicion that however we may strive to live rightly, the great forces of the universe may be after all against us. But here the Atonement and the Resurrection come in. They tell us that this suspicion is groundless, that God is not against us, but on our side, that the faintest desire to be better He sympathizes with, and will help; that even on the heart where no such desire is yet stirring, He still looks tenderly, that He wills its salvation, and has proved that He really and deeply wills it by a self-sacrificing love greater than we can conceive. Can any strength for moral improvement go beyond this?

Nor is it merely a one-sided view of the love of God which thus comes to our aid. His righteousness too — since we must speak of these two things separately, though in reality they are one — his righteousness, if it turns on our selfish and sinful nature a side that is fearful, turns also on all our better longings a side that is full of hope. A righteousness that is perfect, that is, a Divine righteousness, cannot be fully satisfied with merely apportioning reward and punishment according to desert. This, though one aspect of righteousness, is its lower and incomplete work. The righteousness which is perfect, or rather the perfectly Righteous One, must long to bring all his intelligent creatures in sympathy with his own righteousness, to make them partakers of it, and cannot be fully satisfied with any other result. As it has been expressed, "Righteousness in God is craving for righteousness in man, with a craving which the realization of righteousness in man alone can satisfy." So also of holiness. In one view it repels the sinner, and would banish him to outer darkness, because of its repugnance to sin. In another it is pained by the continued existence of sin and unholiness, and must desire that the sinner should cease to be sinful. So that the sinner, awakening to his own evil state, and saying to himself, "By sin I have destroyed myself; is there yet hope for me in God?" may hear an encouraging answer, not only from the love and mercy of God, but also from his very righteousness and holiness. When he meditates on the character of the Lord his consolation will be, "Surely the Divine righteousness desires to see me righteous — the Divine holiness desires to see me holy; my continuing unrighteous and unholy is as grieving to God's righteousness and holiness as my misery through sin is to his pity and love?" It is in such faiths as these, such glances upward to God, that the soul finds the only true restorative.

The result of all that has been said is this, that only in vital Christianity, or rather, to speak plainly, in God revealed in Christ, lies the adequate and all-sufficient moral motive power for man. For in Him thus revealed all the principles of man's composite nature find their object. The natural desire for happiness, the yearning of the affections, the moral needs of conscience, the aspiration to be perfect, all are satisfied. And these diverse principles so centered are turned into motive powers, or rather into one composite motive power, in which the lower, more self-regarding elements, are gradually subordinated and absorbed by the higher.

But you say, perhaps, that these things, if true, are things of faith, and morality stands on grounds of reason. Is it so? Is it, then, certain that morality is independent of faith? To prefer an unseen duty because it is right, to a seen pleasure because it is pleasant, — what is this but an act of faith? It requires faith to do the simplest moral act, if it is to be done morally. And the highest religious truths, if once they are apprehended vitally and spiritually from within, and not merely taken passively on authority from without, will be found to require but an expansion of that same principle of faith by which, in its more elementary form, we realize the simplest moral truths.

There can be no manner of doubt that the promise,

"I will put my laws into their hearts, and in their minds will I write them," is the one great work which philosophy could not do, which the gospel has to some extent done. It has brought in that which moralists in vain sought after, and without which their schemes were vain — a living "virtue-making power." This was held forth as a hope in the Old Testament, "All my fresh springs are in thee;" "In thy light shall we see light;" "Then shall I run in the way of thy commandments, when thou shalt enlarge my heart." When Christianity was first preached, it was in large measure fulfilled. To St. Paul and the first Christians the law became no longer a stern commandment, standing outside of them, threatening them from above; but a warm law of love within them — not only a higher discernment of the good, but a new and marvelous power to do it, cheerfully, and with joy. And down all the ages, whatever obscurations Christianity has undergone, this, the true apostolic succession, coming straight from the Divine Source to each individual recipient anew, has never failed. In such as Augustine, À Kempis, Luther, Pascal, Leighton, Fénélon, Henry Martyn, the pure and sacred fire has been relit from age to age. They, by what they were, and what they did, became, each to their generation, the renewers of a deeper, more substantive morality. For the Christian light in them was not a tradition or an orthodoxy, but a living flame, enlightening and warming themselves, and passing from them to others. And so to this day their works are storehouses of moral and spiritual quickening, more than all the books of all the moralists. When you read Leighton, for instance, you feel yourself breathing a spiritual air, compared with which the atmosphere of the moral systems is dull and depressing. For in Leighton, and such as he, morality is, as Mr. Arnold finely expresses it, "lighted up with the emotion and inspiration needful for carrying the sage along the narrow way perfectly, for carrying the ordinary man along it at all." The saintly Archbishop was speaking of what few have a right to speak of, but what he had seen and known when he said, "One glance of God, a touch of his love, will free and enlarge the heart, so that it can deny all, and part with all, and make an entire renouncing of all to follow Him." Again, "It is in his power to do it for thee. He can stretch and expand thy straitened heart, can hoist and spread the sails within thee, and then carry thee on swiftly; filling them, not with the vain air of men's applause, but with the sweet breathings and soft gales of his own Spirit, which carry it straight to the desired haven."

This is the language of those who, like Leighton, have known most immediately, to use again his own words, "the sensible presence of God, and shining of his clear-discovered face on them." Perhaps ordinary men had better speak little of these things, they are so far beyond their experience. But language like this, because it has been often repeated as a mere hearsay by those who had no experience of it, has come to be regarded by many as merely a decorous tradition among religious people, which other men nauseate. Still, however overlaid it has been with words, and however remote from it most men must confess themselves to be, the thing here spoken of remains none the less a reality — towards which end not only the religious, but even the uprightly moral heart, must look and aspire.

In the light of these thoughts regarding the spiritual springs of morality, how vain appears that cry so often heard in this day, "Give us Christian morality without the dogmas!" In as far as any dogmas may be the mere creations of churches, or may be truths crusted over with human accretions, by all means let them be either swept away or purified. There is much need that all doctrines taught should be adjusted fittingly to the moral nature of men, so as, by manifestation of the truth, to commend themselves to every man's conscience in the sight of God. It is also true that as men advance in spiritual insight, their view of doctrine becomes more simple, more natural, more transparent with moral light. But still it is no less true that love to a transcendent object, to a living person, is the one root of Christian virtue, and that to expect Christian well-doing without a soul based on Christian faith, is to expect fruit from a tree which has no root. As was often said by one whose long life of Christian wisdom and love gave weight to his words: "Renan and others admire the morality of the Sermon on the Mount, but reject altogether the doctrines or transcendent truths of Christianity. They would divide the one from the other as with a knife, preserving this, throwing away that. Now only think of it in this way. Take that one precept, "Love your enemies, do good to them that hate you." How am I really to fulfill this? If the law of my country gives me a command, bids me do this or not do that overt act, I can give it an outward mechanical obedience, and with this human law is satisfied. But the divine precept commands not an outward act, but an inward spiritual condition of being. How am I to attain to this? By my force of will? My will can rule my outward acts, but cannot change my inward dispositions. What shall avail to turn the whole tide of feeling, and change the natural hatred of enemies into love for them? Nothing short of the forgiveness and the love of God in Christ to me and to all men felt to be a reality. This has power to change the natural hatred into a forgiving love. Nothing else can." This seems clear as demonstration. And in like manner it might be shown that there is not one Christian precept which has not its root, its motive spring, directly in some transcendent truth of God's nature, and of the soul's relation to Him. Deny these and the precepts fall. Vain, therefore, is the dream of a Christian morality without a true Christian theology supporting and inspiring it from beneath.

But this tendency to seek the fruits of Christianity while rejecting its root, is as nothing compared with the extravagance of that modern system, which teaches that "the service of humanity" may be raised to the level of a practical and all-powerful moral motive, while all belief in a personal immortality and in the existence of God is denied, and a vague something, called the "spirit of humanity," is made the only object of worship. This strange persuasion has at this time its devotees, some of them men of great parts, and, I believe, of benevolent lives. That there should be some such — men possessed by fanaticism for a creed which parodies Christianity while it rejects it — is not more to be wondered at than any other form of fanaticism. The causes that have produced this strange phenomenon might not be difficult to find. But it is a thing to be wondered at that a cool-headed philosopher like Mr. Mill, who has never showed much tendency to fanaticism for this or any form of religion, should have thrown over it the shield of his patronage. Yet so it is. While professing that he entertains the strongest objections to M. Comte's system of politics and morals, he still thinks that that system has "superabundantly shown the possibility of giving to the service of humanity, even without the aid of a belief in Providence, both the psychological power and the social efficacy of a religion; making it take hold of human life, and color all thought, feeling, and action, in a manner of which the greatest ascendancy ever exercised by any religion may be but a type and foretaste." Mr. Mill may have thrown all the more strength into this statement of opinion, that he was advocating a mode of thought which he knew to be unpopular. For certainly it is one of his characteristics, that whether from the desire to help the weaker party, or from the love of paradox, he loves to cut prejudice against the grain. Can it be that to the same reason is to be attributed that other strange statement of his, that the ideal of Christian morality is negative rather than positive, passive rather than active, abstinence from evil rather than energetic pursuit of good? If this is not to be put down to the love of paradox, it is an instance of ignorance in a writer of high repute, to which it would be hard to find a parallel. To refute it there is no need to turn to the New Testament, though, if one did so, one should have to quote nearly the half of it; neither need one point to the lives of the most eminent Christians, and the extent to which philanthropy purely Christian has changed the world. For a sufficient refutation I need only refer to a modern authoress, who plainly enough shows that she is as free as Mr. Mill is from any weakness for orthodoxy. In her essay on Christian Ethics, Miss Cobbe sets forth with great force how Christ changed the negative law of the Jews into a positive, and thereby transformed the whole spirit of morality, giving to men the being good, and doing good for their aim. And then she contrasts with this what she thinks the unmanly ethics of the modern churches, — the mere refraining from evil and leading harmless lives. But to return to Mr. Mill's assertion, that "the service of humanity" may probably be found to be a motive force as powerful, or even more powerful, than any hitherto known. Is it not a fact of history that it was Christ, who by his character, his teaching, his whole revelation, for the first time so enlarged men's narrow hearts as to make some of them at least conceive an universal love for their kind? How He did this we have partly seen already, and cannot dwell more on it now. Is it not also a fact of history, that since his sojourn on earth a new virtue, philanthropy, has come into being, and that of the great benefactors of mankind by far the largest number, and those the noblest and most self-denying, have been men who have confessed that they drew their inspirations to well-doing directly from Him? Have these not declared that the power which enabled them to overcome natural shrinking, and to seek out their fallen fellow-creatures, even under the most unlovely and revolting circumstances, was the simple faith that God and Christ have had pity on themselves, and on all men, even the most degraded? This worth of human nature, the most degraded, in the eyes of Christ, has for his true followers invested it, even when most marred, with a new sacredness. In saying this it is no mere feeling or fancy I speak of, but one of the soberest, best attested facts. If for eighteen centuries this has been proved to be the strongest motive power in the breasts of great philanthropists, will men's devotion to the good of their kind become wider or more intense if you remove those beliefs which have hitherto fed it? Permanent devotion to any object is exactly in proportion to the belief in the worth of that object. Will men's sense of the worth of the race be greater when you have removed from their minds all thought of an eternal destiny, and convinced them that their yearnings towards God are a delusion? Would human life seem more lovely or more sublime, if you could take Christ out of the heart of the race, and obliterate all sense of the relation in which we stand to God? Would the music of humanity sound more grand and deep if you could silence these, its tenderest, profoundest tones? Nothing that we know of the past or of the nature of things makes it in the least probable that by withdrawing what has hitherto proved the chief creative power of philanthropy, you will increase its volume. And if we are to wait till trial can be made of the new panacea, the suspense will be long, and the result disastrous to the best interests of mankind. It will, I suspect, require something more than the mere assertion of any philosopher to make sober-minded men hazard the experiment.

Not to Christian morality, without the faith which underlies it, still less to the Comtean "service of humanity," can we look with hope for the moving force which shall make man fulfill his moral end. There is still another agency, which is so ably recommended that it must not be passed without a word. There are some at this day who look to Culture, taken in its largest sense, as the remedy for all our ills, the solvent to break the horny crust that hardens round men's hearts, the leavening power which shall transform all that is coarse, and low, and selfish into purity and light. Culture, in this large sense, is made to include not only the usual intellectual and æsthetic elements, but also moral, and even religious ones. The aim, it is said, which the widest culture sets before itself, is to train man not only to an æsthetic but to a spiritual perfection. And since man has religious needs, true culture will take account of these and set itself to supply them. Thus religion becomes a large ingredient in culture, — a means, perhaps the highest means, toward perfection, yet still a means. For culture, in its ideal of "a harmonious expansion of all the human powers," goes beyond religion and subordinates religion to itself. So conceived, culture, it is said, "adding to itself the religious idea of a devout energy, is destined to transform and govern" religion. According to this view, culture is the end, religion but the means.

There are, however, things which, because they are ultimate ends in themselves, refuse to be employed as means, and if attempted to be so employed, lose their essential character. Religion is one, and the foremost of these things. Obedience, conformity of the finite and the imperfect will of man to the infinite and perfect will of God, this, which is the essence of religion, is an end in itself, the highest end which we can conceive. It cannot be sought as a means to an ulterior end without being at once destroyed. This is an end, or rather the end in itself, which culture and all other ends by right subserve. And here in culture, as we saw in pleasure, the great ethic law will be found to hold, that the abandoning of it as an end, in obedience to a higher, more supreme aim, is the very condition of securing it. Stretch the idea of culture and of the perfection it aims at wide as you will, you cannot, while you make it your last end, rise clear of the original self-reference that lies at its root; this you cannot get rid of, unless you go out of culture, and beyond it, abandoning it as the end, and sinking it into what it really is, a means towards the perfection of human nature. No one ever really became beautiful by aiming at beauty. Beauty comes, we scarce know how, as an emanation from sources deeper than itself. If culture, or rather the ends of culture, are to be healthy and natural growths, they must come unconsciously, as results of conformity to the will of God, sought not for any end but itself. On the other hand, culture, making its own idea of perfection the end and religion the means, would degenerate into an unhealthy artificial plant, open to the charges urged against it by its enemies.

It cannot indeed be denied that these two, culture or the love of beauty, religion or the love of godliness, appear in individuals, in races, in ages, as rival, often as conflicting forces. In themselves, and essentially, it cannot be that they are opposed; but when either enters the human spirit, so absorbing is the attraction, that it for the most part casts out the other. The votary of beauty shrinks from religion as something stern and ungenial, the devout Puritan discards beauty as a seductive snare, and even those who have hearts susceptible of both, find that a practical crisis will come when a choice must be made whether of the two they will serve. The consciousness of this disunion has of late years been felt deeply in the most gifted minds. Painful often has the conflict been, when the natural love of beauty was leading one way, loyalty to that which is higher than beauty called another, and no practical escape was possible, except by the sacrifice of feelings which in themselves were innocent and beautiful. This discord has doubtless been intensified by the fact that ever since the Reformation men have taken the one or the other definite road, not dreaming that the two might be reconciled, or that it was desirable to reconcile them. Only in recent times have we begun to feel strongly that both are good, that each without the other is so far imperfect, and that some reconciliation, if it were possible, is a thing to be desired. Violent has been the reaction which this new consciousness has created. In the recoil from what they call Puritanism, or religion without culture, many have given themselves up to culture without religion, or, at best, with a very diluted form of religion. They have set up for worship the golden calf of art, and danced round it to the pipe which the great Goethe played. They have promulgated what they call the gospel of art, — as Carlyle says, the windiest gospel ever yet preached, which never has saved and never will save any man from moral corruption. Not that way lies the true solution. It is but a vain attempt to build up culture on the denial of man's first and deepest need. That need is still what it ever has been, that his will be brought into contact with a Will higher, purer, stronger, than itself, on which it can hang, from which, as an ever-present " Personal Inspirer," it can draw all it needs of purifying strength. Set right by allegiance to the All-righteous Will, in dependence not in self-centered perfection, — in service not in culture, — in a higher self than itself, — the soul finds its true well-being. This centre once found — Christ as the life of individual hearts, as the cementing bond of all humanity — culture may be added without stint. In subservience to Him, used as an instrumentality in building up his kingdom, culture has a beneficent work to do. Apart from this, setting up for itself, it can never clear itself of the original taint of self-reference. But if it will understand its true calling to be the means not the end, the servant not the master, large service lies ready before it. To adjust the claims, and determine the place of culture in reference to religion, is, I know, a hard problem; and it were a useful work, for those who can, to help to adjust it. But the first condition of success is, that we recognize the true centre, and look for harmony by seeing the other elements held in their places by the force of the central attraction.

I have attempted to show how a new and more vital force is imported into morality, when we regard the abstract moral law of ethical science as absorbed into the

All-righteous, All-loving Personal Will which Christianity reveals. In doing so I have touched, and that very imperfectly, I am well aware, but one side of a many-sided, indeed of an exhaustless problem. When man's natural moral sentiments are confronted with the Christian revelation, many other questions arise, some of them more fundamental, though none perhaps more practical, than the one here discussed. Of these fundamental inquiries one of the foremost is, how far man naturally possesses within himself certain moral sentiments which serve as criteria by which the truth of a revelation may be judged. On this grave question I cannot even enter at the close of this discussion. Only I would remark, that the moral nature in man must be that to which any objective religion, which claims to be universal, must mainly make its appeal. Else man has no internal standard at all by which to try any religion which claims to be received; and on purely external grounds, it is conceivable that a religion, teaching immorality, might have much to say for itself. Christianity, at first, though it came with external signs and wonders, yet rested its claim mainly on its adaptation to man's moral nature, and must do so more and more, as the moral perceptions it has itself quickened become deeper and purer. It must be so, if revelation be indeed the appeal which God makes through facts of history to the witness of Himself which He has left in conscience. In this view, Christian faith receiving revealed truth is the leaping up of like to like, the exile recognizing once more a voice from his home.

The appeal to a power of judging in man is made in many different forms by our Lord Himself: "Why even of yourselves judge ye not what is right?" St. Paul, too, says that he strove in all he taught, to commend himself to every man's conscience. And the more either individuals or the race advance in spiritual intelligence, the more readily will they respond to this appeal in preference to all others. Morality and Christianity have for eighteen centuries acted and reacted on each other, the outward truth quickening the inward perceptions, and these, when quickened, purifying men's apprehensions of the outward truth. And these two have become so interwoven that it is now impossible to separate them, and to say, this was drawn from the one source, and that from the other. Christianity, from the first, appealing partly to men's natural desire to escape from the dreaded consequences of sin, partly to the moral longings for righteousness, never wholly dead in the race, has, through this mingling of prudential and moral motives, elevated the best of mankind, and made their moral perceptions what they now are. And these moral perceptions, thus refined, react on the objective religion, and require ever more stringently that the truths presented by it shall be not moral only, that is, conformable to all that is best in man, but that they shall complement this, strengthen, elevate it. They require not only that nothing which is un-moral shall be taught as true of God and his dealings with man, but that all which is taught concerning Him shall be in the highest conceivable degree righteous, shall be such as to lay hold of and to cherish whatever susceptibility of righteousness there is in man, and carry it on to perfection. This is so obvious that it seems a truism. It is so readily assented to that no one would think of denying it when stated in this general way. Yet it is painful to think how much and how persistently it has often been lost sight of in popular religious teaching, and with how disastrous consequences. I am quite aware of the difficulties which this principle has to meet when turned to certain points in the elder and more rudimentary forms of revelation. To solve these fairly would require a combination of moral and historical insight, with various kinds of knowledge, such as few possess. But when this principle is applied to the latest and completed revelation, Christianity can meet its requirements in their most exacting form. If precept or truth can elevate, what height of morality can be conceived which shall go beyond such precepts as this: "Be ye perfect, even as your Father in heaven is perfect"? or such announcements as these: "God is love;" "God is light, and in Him is no darkness at all"? Indeed, it is only when the inner moral eye has been clarified that the meaning of these statements comes out at all, and evermore as the moral nature rises these great truths rise above it infinitely. And if it be said that after all these are but general announcements, void of content, and we still need to know what perfection, light, love, are, then there remains our Lord's own life, with his teaching, actions, character, to fill these general words with living substance.

It were well that those who have to teach religion should consider these matters more closely, — make a study more searching than is commonly made of what there is in moral man, — what this longs for, with what alone it will be satisfied. The most thoughtful teachers know this, know that for want of thus meeting the moral needs of men, — thus grappling with the higher moral side of questions, — there is danger lest the purest morality of modern time part company with the received religion. Men who are to teach cannot see too clearly or seize too firmly the distinction between that which is really moral and that which is merely prudential in man; and though they may not altogether pass by motives drawn from the latter region, on the former mainly they must throw themselves, to it must be their chief appeal. They must cease to be content if they can raise men merely to the prudential level of a desire for safety, they must feel that their work is hardly begun till those they teach have come to desire righteousness for the love of itself. They must refuse to meet moral yearnings by un-moral doctrines or expedients, — for bread giving men a stone. They must keep steadily before them that nothing can permanently satisfy the moral being in man, but something not less, but more moral, more spiritual than itself. They must feel themselves, and make others feel, that in the Divine economy, though there is much which is now dark and mysterious, there is nothing which is not supremely moral, and which will not at last be clearly seen to be so. In ceasing to use so exclusively the weapons of merely earthly, and wielding more confidently those of pure spiritual temper, they need not fear that the old armory of Christianity will fail them. In the old words, the old truths, the old facts, more vitally and spiritually apprehended, because brought closer to the moral heart of man, they will find all they need. This close contact between Christian truths and the highest moral thought of the time, while it vitalizes and makes real the former, will react no less powerfully on the latter. There is no moral truth which is not deepened when seen in the light of God. That which, regarded from the side of man, is felt merely as a yielding to his own sensual nature, when seen from the side of God becomes disobedience to a loving and righteous will to which he owes everything, and is deepened into a sense of sin. Character, which when regarded from a merely moral point of view almost inevitably becomes a building up from our own internal resources, takes altogether another aspect when it is seen that true character is in the last resort determined by the attitude in which the spirit stands to God. Then it comes to be felt that the rightness men search for cannot be self-evolved from within, that they must cease from attempting this, must go beyond self, must fall back on a simple receptivity, receiving the rightness and the right-making power, which they have not in themselves, from out of the great reservoir of righteousness which is in God. Only on thus falling back on God, and feeling himself to be, as of everything else, so of righteousness, a recipient, is a man truly rightened. Thus the last moral experience and the first upward look of religion agree in one, "A man can receive nothing except it be given him from above."

www.ingramcontent.com/pod-product-compliance
Lightning Source LLC
LaVergne TN
LVHW010149110826
845151LV00002B/466

* 9 7 8 1 4 2 5 5 3 7 8 2 1 *